ADA
HANDBOOK

Employment & Construction Issues Affecting Your Business

Martha R. Williams
Marcia L. Russell

Real Estate Education Company
a division of Dearborn Financial Publishing, Inc.

While a great deal of care has been taken to provide accurate and current information, the ideas, suggestions, general principles and conclusions presented in this text are subject to local, state and federal laws and regulations, court cases and any revisions of same. The reader is thus urged to consult legal counsel regarding any points of law—this publication should not be used as a substitute for competent legal advice.

Publisher: Carol L. Luitjens
Acquisitions Editor: Margaret M. Maloney
Production Coordinator: Janet C. Webster

Contents

FOR OUR PARENTS

Preface

Learning about the ramifications of the Americans with Disabilities Act of 1990 (ADA) has been a revelation for both business and real estate owners and users. As each part of the law comes into effect, it is as if another veil is lifted from the eyes of those who are lucky enough to be considered "abled." We are truly undergoing a national consciousness-raising.

The good news, of course, is that as we become more sensitized to the needs of the disabled, we tend to improve the work and marketplace environments for all of us. The statistics cited in the Act, which is included in Appendix A of this book, serve to remind us that the difficulties faced by the disabled are ultimately faced by us all.

The many research studies and publications financed by the Department of Justice provide a wealth of useful information for employers and businesses that come under the ADA requirements. Most often, the information is available at no or low cost. In compiling the information that lead to the writing of this *ADA Handbook*, the authors were pleasantly surprised time and again at the numerous resources available for the asking, including private consultations regarding particular compliance problems. As many of these resources as space permits are listed in this book.

What has not been as readily available is a well-indexed copy of the Act printed in readable type. The authors have attempted to solve that difficulty with the reset version of the Act that appears in Appendix A.

Another problem has been the lack of quick and easy access to a copy of the ADA Accessibility Guidelines drafted by the Architectural and Transportation Barriers Compliance Board at the request of Congress. While there are publications that discuss various specifications set out in the Accessibility Guidelines, the guidelines themselves are the best reference for structural compliance questions. To help answer these questions, the Accessibility Guidelines are reprinted here exactly as they appear in the Federal Register.

The *ADA Handbook* begins with an introduction to the background of the Act and a summary of its contents. The next two sections of the book discuss the most important employment and building accessibility issues raised by ADA. In this way, the authors hope to familiarize the reader with the rationale behind the Act as well as to highlight the areas that should be dealt with as part of an ongoing compliance effort. References to the Act and the Accessibility Guidelines are made throughout the discussion to help introduce the reader to the law as naturally as possible.

Some of the case situations presented in the discussion summarize past court decisions dealing with similar matters. Other case situations suggest areas that may be the subject of future litigation.

The review quizzes that conclude the discussion of key employment and construction issues will check the reader's comprehension of the points raised.

ACKNOWLEDGMENTS

The authors have been very fortunate in having at their disposal the publications and willing input of many enthusiastic and dedicated professionals.

A special note of appreciation must go to Margaret E. Davidson and Robert C. Conklin, attorneys with the firm of Kelleher and McLeod, Albuquerque, New Mexico.

The staff of Real Estate Education Company, and in particular Acquisitions Editor Margaret M. Maloney and Production Coordinator Janet C. Webster, was a pleasure to work with. Susan Potter of Novato, California, proofread the text with her usual cheerfulness. Thanks to all of them for their help.

Finally, our spouses and children bore the brunt of our creative labors with heroic patience and understanding. We will try to make it up to them—at least until next time.

Martha R. Williams
Novato, California

Marcia L. Russell
Albuquerque, New Mexico

Part I: Introduction

> We hold these truths to be self-evident, that all men are created equal, that they are endowed by their Creator with certain unalienable rights, that among these are life, liberty and the pursuit of happiness. That to secure these rights, governments are instituted among men, deriving their just powers from the consent of the governed. . . .
>
> *From the Declaration of Independence*
> *Adopted in Congress July 4, 1776*

From its inception, the government of the United States has strived to attain the goal of providing its citizens with the freedom to exercise the rights that will allow them to lead lives that are not only productive but fulfilling. At times, movement toward that goal has seemed to occur at an agonizingly slow pace. Overall, however, progress has been made. One of the most recent examples of that progress, the Americans with Disabilities Act of 1990, is the focus of this book.

THE BLESSINGS OF LIBERTY

Early on, the individual governments composing the United States realized the need to identify by law the rights that had been so hard won by the Revolutionary War. The Constitution of the United States, adopted in 1787, was followed in 1791 by ratification of the first ten amendments to the Constitution—what we refer to collectively as the *Bill of Rights*. They include recognition of the rights of free exercise of religion, freedom of speech and of the press, protection against unreasonable searches and seizures, the right to due process of law and the right to receive just compensation for the taking of private property, among others.

Over the years, other constitutional amendments have expanded the range of rights enjoyed by citizens of the United States. In 1865, the Thirteenth Amendment prohibited slavery. In 1868, the Fourteenth Amendment extended the rights of equal protection and due process to include laws imposed by the individual states. In 1870, the right of former slaves to vote was affirmed by the Fifteenth Amendment. In 1920, the Nineteenth Amendment extended the right of suffrage to women, and in 1971 that right was accorded to all citizens eighteen years of age and older by the Twenty-Sixth Amendment.

Congressional legislation also has served to expand the concept of liberty. The Civil Rights Act of 1866 recognized the rights and needs of the newly freed slaves by prohibiting all racial discrimination, both private as well as public, in the sale or rental of property. Almost a century later, the Civil Rights Act of 1964 prohibited racial discrimination in employment as well as in provision of federally funded housing.

While the impetus for fair housing and employment legislation began as an outgrowth of the civil rights movement for racial equality, it quickly drew advocates for other groups experiencing discrimination. The Equal Pay Act of 1963, as amended, prohibits discrimination on the basis of sex in payment of wages to women and men performing substantially equal work in the same establishment.

Title VII of the Civil Rights Act of 1964, as amended, prohibits discrimination on the basis of race, color, religion, sex or national origin in hiring, promotion, discharge, pay, fringe benefits and other aspects of employment. The Federal Fair Housing Act (Title VIII of the Civil Rights Act of 1968) prohibited discrimination in housing based on race, color, religion or national origin. The Housing and Community Development Act of 1974 added sex as another basis on which discrimination was prohibited. With the Fair Housing Amendments Act of 1988, protection against discrimination was extended to persons with handicaps and families with children.

The Age Discrimination in Employment Act of 1967, as amended, prohibits discrimination on the basis of age in the hiring, promotion, discharge, compensation, terms, conditions or privileges of employment of applicants and employees 40 years of age or older.

In addition to federal law, the states have taken action to ensure equality of rights for all, particularly in regard to housing. There are many other protections as well, such as federal and state laws that prohibit discrimination in the granting of credit. Considerable strength has been added to the enforcement of all of these laws by numerous judicial decisions, perhaps the most notable being the landmark 1968 ruling in *Jones v. Mayer* (392 U.S. 409), in which the U.S. Supreme Court upheld the Civil Rights Act of 1866.

RECOGNIZING THE NEEDS OF THE DISABLED

When the needs of the disabled were explored, it became apparent that change would be required in many areas in addition to employment and housing to bring the blessings of liberty to all.

The Rehabilitation Act of 1973 (29 U.S.C. §794 [1973]) provided an important first step toward full recognition of the rights of the disabled. In fact, many definitions and other features of the Rehabilitation Act of 1973 have been incorporated in the Americans with Disabilities Act of 1990.

The 1973 Act prohibits discrimination against the disabled in federally funded programs and activities. Those affected include colleges and universities receiving federal grants, as well as political subdivisions and their agents (libraries, parks, fire/police departments, and so on) that receive federal grants. The Rehabilitation Act of 1973 also requires federal contractors to use affirmative action in hiring and promoting qualified disabled persons. As emphasized by the Civil Rights Restoration Act of 1987 (20 U.S.C. §1687 [1987]), the 1973 Act applies to *all* endeavors of federal fund recipients, not just the specific projects to which government money is allotted.

NOTE: The Rehabilitation Act of 1973 is still good law and must be followed where applicable. The many references to the Rehabilitation Act of 1973 that are found within the Americans with Disabilities Act point out the ongoing significance of this legislation.

Equal Employment Opportunity Is the LAW

Private Employment, State and Local Governments, Educational Institutions

The Americans with Disabilities Act of 1990 prohibits discrimination on the basis of disability and protects qualified applicants and employees with disabilities from discrimination in hiring, promotion, discharge, pay training, fringe benefits and other aspects of employment. The law also requires that covered entities provide qualified applicants and employees with disabilities with reasonable accommodations that do not impose undue hardship. The law covers applicants to and employees of most private employers, state and local governments, educational institutions, employment agencies and labor organizations.

If you believe that you have been discriminated against, you immediately should contact:

The U.S. Equal Employment Opportunity Commission (EEOC), 1808 L Street, NW, Washington, DC 20507, or an EEOC field office by calling toll free 800-669-EEOC. For individuals with hearing impairments, EEOC's toll-free TDD number is 800-800-3302.

Employers Holding Federal Contracts or Subcontracts

Section 503 of the Rehabilitation Act of 1973 prohibits job discrimination because of handicap and requires affirmative action to employ and advance in employment qualified individuals with handicaps who, with reasonable accommodation, can perform the essential functions of a job.

38 U.S.C. 4212 of the Vietnam Era Veterans Readjustment Assistance Act of 1974 prohibits job discrimination and requires affirmative action to employ and advance in employment qualified Vietnam era veterans and qualified special disabled veterans.

Any person who believes a contractor has violated its nondiscrimination or affirmative action obligations under Section 503 of the Rehabilitation Act or 38 U.S.C. 4212 of the Vietnam Era Veterans Readjustment Assistance Act should contact immediately:

The Office of Federal Contract Compliance Programs (OFCCP) Employment Standards Administration, U.S. Department of Labor, 200 Constitution Avenue, NW, Washington, DC 20210, (202) 523-9368, or an OFCCP regional or district office, listed in most telephone directories under U.S. Government, Department of Labor.

Programs or Activities Receiving Federal Financial Assistance

Section 504 of the Rehabilitation Act of 1973 prohibits employment discrimination on the basis of handicap in any program or activity that receives federal financial assistance. Discrimination is prohibited in all aspects of employment against handicapped persons who, with reasonable accommodation, can perform the essential functions of a job.

Adapted from "Equal Employment Opportunity Is the Law," a poster available from EEOC.

AMERICANS WITH DISABILITIES ACT OF 1990 (ADA)

In 1986, the National Council on Disability released a study entitled "Toward Independence." The Council, which reviews and makes recommendations on federal laws affecting the disabled, pointed out the inability of existing laws to fully protect the disabled. Its recommendation was that comprehensive civil rights legislation be enacted to define and protect the rights of the disabled throughout American society.

The work of the National Council on Disability provided the basis for the first version of ADA, which was submitted to Congress in 1988. A modified version, submitted in 1989, was amended by the Senate and passed on September 7, 1989, by a vote of 76-8. An amended version of the Senate bill was passed by the House of Representatives on May 20, 1990, by a vote of 403-20. A joint Senate-House conference produced a final draft that was approved by the House on July 12, 1990, with a vote of 377-28, and by the Senate the next day, with a vote of 91-6. The President signed the Act into law on July 26, 1990. The final version of the law appears in Appendix A of this book.

Both the Department of Justice (DOJ) and Equal Employment Opportunity Commission (EEOC) have issued administrative rules on application of the various provisions of ADA. The discussion that appears in this book is based, in large part, on those rules. The resource lists that appear at the end of the second and third parts of this book indicate how copies of the final rules of the DOJ and EEOC may be obtained.

NOTE: Many states, such as California, have laws similar to ADA in place. When state and federal requirements conflict, the more demanding of the two must be followed.

The Americans with Disabilities Act prohibits discrimination by employers and businesses on the basis of physical and/or mental disability. A disabled individual is defined as (1) anyone with a physical or mental impairment that substantially limits a *major life activity*, (2) anyone who has had such an impairment, or (3) anyone *perceived* as having such an impairment. Major life activities include caring for one's self, performing manual tasks, walking, seeing, hearing, speaking, breathing, learning and working.

ADA covers *all* impairments, including vision, hearing, learning, speech, neuromuscular, emotional, mental retardation, drug and alcohol and mobility, as well as such chronic conditions as AIDS, HIV infection, cancers, heart disease, diabetes and mental illness. ADA does *not* cover homosexuality or bisexuality; transvestism, transsexualism, pedophilia, exhibitionism, voyeurism, gender identity disorders not resulting from physical impairments, or other sexual behavior disorders; compulsive gambling, kleptomania, or pyromania; or psychoactive substance use disorders resulting from current illegal use of drugs (controlled substances as defined in the Controlled Substances Act, 21 U.S.C. 812).

ADA is divided into five major sections, called titles.

Title I—Employment

Title I prohibits an employer from discriminating against a disabled job applicant or employee who, with or without a reasonable accommodation, is qualified to perform the essential duties of a job. The employer is expected to make reasonable accommodation for an otherwise qualified employee with a disability, unless the employer can demonstrate that the accomodation would impose an *undue hardship* on the operation of the business.

An employer is obligated to make reasonable accommodation only to the *known* physical and/or mental limitations resulting from the disability of a qualified applicant or employee. The applicant or employee has the duty to inform the employer of the disability and request an accommodation. An employer is not allowed to ask a job applicant if he or she has a disability. What the employer can ask is, "Can you perform the duties of the job as they have been described to you?"

As of July 26, 1992, Title I applies to public and private employers with 25 or more employees. As of July 26, 1994, Title I will apply to employers with 15 or more employees. Employers of fewer than 15 employees are not covered by Title I.

Title II—Public Services

Title II requires that *all* state and local government services, as well as Amtrak services, be available without discrimination to individuals with disabilities.

Operational, non-structural methods of compliance were to be in place as of January 26, 1992. Required structural changes must be identified in a transition plan due by July 26, 1992, and actually completed by January 26, 1995.

All new facilities on which construction is begun after January 26, 1992, must be made readily accessible to, and usable by, disabled individuals.

Title III—Public Accommodations and Services Operated by Private Entities

Public facilities, goods and services must be accessible to customers who have disabilities. The obligation not to discriminate is imposed on any person who owns, leases, leases to, or operates a place of public accommodation.

Public accommodations include 12 categories of private entity if their operation affects *commerce* among states, between any foreign country or territory or possession and a state, or between points in the same state but through another state or foreign country.

Part III of this book details the types of establishments that come under Title III. The range is impressive, from restaurants and inns to bakeries, lawyers' offices, hospitals, zoos, amusements parks, homeless shelters and golf courses.

Public accommodations must:

- remove architectural barriers whenever readily achievable; that is, when removing a barrier can be done without undue expense or difficulty. If barrier removal is not readily achievable, an alternative way to provide goods and services to customers who have disabilities must be explored.

- make reasonable changes in company policies, practices or standards that deny people with disabilities equal access to a business, unless such changes would impose an undue burden, result in a fundamental change in the goods and services of the business or cause a direct threat to the health or safety of others.

The United States Architectural and Transportation Barriers Compliance Board has issued *ADA Accessibility Guidelines for Buildings and Facilities* (ADAAG). The guidelines are heavily illustrated and give required specifications for such areas as parking and passenger loading zones and such features as curb ramps, stairs, elevators, windows, doors, drinking fountains and water coolers, restroom fixtures, handrails, alarms, signage and telephones. The complete text of the guidelines is included in Appendix B of this book.

The only exceptions from Title III requirements apply to religious organizations and exclusive, private membership clubs.

Title III became effective January 26, 1992, for the most part. It is effective as of January 26, 1993, for new construction designed for occupancy after January 1993.

Title IV—Telecommunications

Effective July 26, 1993, all telephone systems must have telecommunications relay provisions in place to make public accommodations more accessible to hearing-impaired and speech-impaired persons.

If a public accommodation offers nondisabled guests the opportunity to make outgoing telephone calls on more than an incidental basis, then it must provide a telecommunication device for the deaf (TDD) on request. Owners of public accommodations should make themselves aware of, and use, any existing private telephone relay services in their community until the Title IV mandates are implemented by their local telephone company.

The Communications Act of 1934 is amended to provide that any television public service announcement produced or funded in whole or in part by any agency or instrumentality of the federal government must include closed captioning of the verbal content of the announcement.

Title V—Miscellaneous Provisions

Title V covers a variety of topics, including prohibition of retaliation or coercion against any individual seeking to enjoy any right granted or protected by the Americans with Disabilities Act.

ADA is not intended to apply a lesser standard than any imposed under the Rehabilitation Act of 1973. Nothing in ADA shall be construed to invalidate or limit the remedies, rights and procedures of any federal law, or law of any state or political subdivision of any state or jurisdiction, that provides greater or equal protection for the rights of individuals with disabilities than are afforded by ADA.

ADA is not intended to prohibit or restrict an insurer, hospital or medical service company, health maintenance organization, entity that administers benefit plans or similar organization from underwriting risks, classifying risks or administering such risks, as provided by state law.

ADA does *not* require an individual with a disability to accept an accommodation, aid, service, opportunity or benefit that the individual chooses not to accept.

An action may be brought against a state for a violation of the requirements of ADA.

The U.S. Architectural and Transportation Barriers Compliance Board is authorized by ADA to issue minimum guidelines to ensure that buildings, facilities, rail passenger cars and vehicles are accessible in terms of architecture and design, transportation and communication to individuals with disabilities. Special procedures applicable to qualified historic buildings and facilities also shall be established.

Technical assistance, including the publication of technical assistance manuals, is to be provided by the U.S. Attorney General in cooperation with other federal officials to assist federal agencies as well as entities covered under the Act.

ADA encourages the use of mediation, arbitration or some other method of dispute resolution as an alternative to legal action, when appropriate. If a legal action is brought, the court or agency may allow the prevailing party payment of reasonable attorney's fees, including litigation expenses and costs.

Compliance with Federal and State Disability Laws

Marin County, California

The California Attorney General's office has warned Marin County that it may be sued for violating state law requiring that public facilities be accessible to all. Marin County's Civic Center (an imposing structure renowned as the only government facility designed by Frank Lloyd Wright that was ever built) fails to comply with 15 of 20 key areas. They include:

Parking. Not enough accessible spaces and no van-designated spaces. Curb ramp is not marked to discourage blocking by a parked vehicle.

Entry doors. Too narrow and close too fast.

Corridors. Floors are too slippery.

Interior doors. Too narrow.

Stairs. Lack handrail extensions at top and bottom.

Elevators. Rotary dials on some emergency phones cannot be used by some disabled people; doors close too fast; controls are mounted too high and are without braille signage; there are no audible floor signals.

Drinking fountains. Some project more than four inches into corridors; less than half meet height and knee-space requirements.

Toilets. Not all floors of the building have accessible toilets; clearance, door hardware and grab-bar heights do not comply with requirements; some toilets are too low, and urinals and mirrors are too high.

Alarms. There are no visual alarms.

Signs. No raised-letter or braille signs are provided.

Phones. Inaccessible in wall recesses and mounted too high or project too far into corridors; no text telephones or volume controls.

Counters. Too high.

The County Administrator has voiced concerns about conflicting state and federal requirements: "For example, state law says the county can get an exception from the requirement that fire alarms be low enough to be activated by people in wheelchairs while federal law says no exception is allowed. Fire officials worry that lower alarms are vulnerable to vandalism by children." But a local advocate of accessibility for the disabled remarked about a recent Civic Center remodeling, "They spent money on things like elevators and bathrooms and did not do it right. This is an issue of civil rights for people with disabilities [and] the county is not protecting these rights." (Excerpted from "Advocates for Disabled Blast County," by Paul Peterzell, *Marin Independent Journal*, April 6, 1992.)

Congress and the "instrumentalities of Congress" are committed to the practice of nondiscrimination in employment. Other aspects of ADA also are to be observed, with Senate and Congressional oversight. Instrumentalities of Congress include the:

- Architect of the Capitol;

- Congressional Budget Office;

- General Accounting Office (although the General Accounting Office Personnel Act of 1980 and regulations are still in effect);

- Government Printing Office;

- Library of Congress;

- Office of Technology Assessment; and

- United States Botanic Garden.

TAX BREAKS TO EASE COMPLIANCE WITH ADA

The Internal Revenue Code has been amended to provide some tax relief to businesses that must comply with ADA.

There is a tax *deduction* of up to $15,000 per year for expenses associated with the removal of qualified architectural and transportation barriers.

A tax *credit* is available to eligible small businesses. A small business is defined as one with a work force of no more than 30 full-time employees *or* gross receipts of no more than $1 million a year. For a business that qualifies, a credit of 50% of eligible expenditures that exceed $250 but are no more than $10,250 may be taken. Allowable expenditures include the necessary and reasonable cost of removing barriers, providing auxiliary aids and acquiring or modifying equipment or devices.

A WORD TO THE WISE . . .

Employers and business owners should make a good faith effort to comply with ADA.

A logical first step is to read the law. Then, consult with an attorney or other qualified expert to determine what you are expected to do to bring your building or business into compliance.

Finally, keep a detailed record of your good faith efforts to comply with the law. Include memoranda of your discussions, investigations and other efforts of compliance. Try to get specific advice, whether from a government agency or other source, in writing. If you cannot, make a memorandum of the conversation and follow up with a letter to the source confirming your understanding of what was said.

NOTE: The American Institute of Architects, the Council of Better Business Bureaus and other groups have warned of bogus consultants who are trying to profit from the fears of small business owners who think they need special help to comply with ADA. There is no such thing as a "certified ADA consultant." Companies should be wary of high-priced consultants and instead should use disabled people in their communities as advisers on complying with the law. A good resource would be one of the 300 federally funded Center for Independent Living offices. These provide limited free counseling, as well as additional low-cost consulting.

Part II: Employment

Congress recognized, in its Preamble to the Americans with Disabilities Act, that individuals with disabilities have historically occupied an inferior status in our society. As a group they have been subjected to purposefully unequal treatment and thus have been denied the opportunity to compete on an equal basis with others. The result is that, of the estimated 43 million disabled persons residing in the United States at the time of the creation of the Americans with Disabilities Act, 67 percent were unemployed.*

ADA will open many new doors for the disabled, including doors to the workplace. The nondiscrimination mandate of ADA requires that individuals with disabilities be given the same consideration for employment as individuals without disabilities. Employers are prohibited from restricting the employment opportunities of qualified individuals with disabilities on the basis of stereotypes and myths. Instead, employers must focus on the capability of every individual on a case-by-case basis. Attitudinal barriers, such as fear of non-acceptance of the disabled worker by others, *must* be overcome.

As pointed out in the Final Rule of the Equal Employment Opportunity Commission (EEOC) regarding Equal Employment Opportunity for Individuals with Disabilities (29 CFR 1630), the requirements of the Americans with Disabilities Act differ from those provided by earlier civil rights legislation for the protection of other groups. The Civil Rights Act of 1964 prohibits consideration of such personal characteristics as race or national origin; the characteristic must simply be ignored. If an otherwise qualified individual's disability creates a barrier to employment, however, ADA requires the employer to go further by providing a *reasonable accommodation* to allow the disabled individual equal opportunity to all aspects of employment.

The required reasonable accommodation is best understood as a means by which barriers to the equal employment opportunity of an individual with a disability are removed or alleviated. An accommodation may allow a disabled individual to attain the same level of job performance, or enjoy the same level of benefits and privileges of employment, available to the average employee without a disability. An employer is not required to provide an accommodation if it can demonstrate that to do so would be an *undue hardship*. The employment regulations of ADA are contained in Title I.

---

*For other equally dismaying statistics, see the Introduction to *What Business Must Know About the Americans with Disabilities Act,* listed in the Resources section on page 22.

ADA TITLE I

Title I of the Americans with Disabilities Act applies to job applicants as well as to those presently employed. It applies to all persons with disabilities—not just United States citizens. Under Title I of ADA, an employer shall not discriminate against a qualified individual with a disability because of the disability. This mandate applies to the following:

- Job application procedures
- Hiring, advancement and discharge
- Employee compensation
- Job training
- Other terms, conditions and privileges of employment

ADA's employment provisions became effective July 26, 1992, for employers with 25 or more employees who work 20 or more weeks per calendar year. They will take effect July 26, 1994, for employers with 15 to 24 employees who work 20 or more weeks per year. In addition to employees, Title I covers agents of employers and others, such as employment agencies, labor organizations and joint labor-management committees. All covered employers must post notices, in an accessible format, of applicable provisions of the Act.

It is not clear whether ADA applies to independent contractors, such as real estate agents who work on an independent contractor basis for a brokerage office.

The only exemptions to Title I apply to the United States government, corporations wholly owned by the federal government, Indian tribes and private membership clubs exempt from taxation under Section 501(c) of the Internal Revenue Code of 1986. Religious organizations are *not* exempt from the employment provisions of ADA. A religious corporation, association, educational institution or society may give preference in employment to individuals of the religion but may not discriminate against an applicant of the same religion with a disability.

UNDERSTANDING TITLE I

The following definitions are based on those found in Section 3 and Title I of ADA and in the Final Rule of the EEOC (29 CFR 1630).

A *disability* means, with respect to an individual, (1) a physical or mental impairment that substantially limits one or more of the individual's major life activities, (2) a record of such an impairment, or (3) being regarded as having such an impairment.

A *physical or mental impairment* is:

- any physiological disorder or condition, cosmetic disfigurement or anatomical loss affecting one or more of the following body systems—neurological, musculoskeletal, special sense organs, respiratory (including speech organs), cardiovascular, reproductive, digestive, genito-urinary, hemic and lymphatic, skin and endocrine; or

- any mental or psychological disorder, such as mental retardation, organic brain syndrome, emotional or mental illness and specific learning disabilities.

Major life activities include caring for oneself, performing manual tasks, walking, seeing, hearing, speaking, breathing, learning, working and other functions that the average person in the general population can perform. An impairment that *substantially limits* a major life activity is one that significantly restricts the condition, manner or duration of the activity's performance. With respect to work responsibilities, such a limitation means that an individual is significantly restricted in the ability to perform either a class of jobs or a broad range of jobs in comparison to the average person having comparable training, skills and abilities.

A *qualified individual with a disability* is someone with a disability who satisfies the requisite skill, experience, education and other job-related requirements of the employment position the individual holds or desires. The individual, with or without reasonable accommodation, can perform the essential functions of the position.

NOTE: The terms *disability* and *qualified individual with a disability* do not include individuals currently engaging in the illegal use of drugs. However, the terms do include an individual who has successfully completed or who is participating in a supervised drug rehabilitation program and is no longer engaging in the illegal use of drugs, as well as an individual erroneously regarded as engaging in such use.

The *essential functions* of a position are the fundamental job duties required to hold it. Marginal functions are not considered fundamental job duties.

Qualification standards are the eligibility standards established by an employer for a position and may encompass personal and professional attributes, including skill, experience, education, physical, medical, safety and other requirements.

A *reasonable accommodation* is a modification to an employer's policies, practices, equipment or facilities that enables an employee with a disability to enjoy equal benefits and privileges of employment. An accommodation can be either of the following:

- A change in the *job application process* that enables a qualified applicant with a disability to be considered for the position the applicant desires

- An alteration made to the *work environment* to enable a qualified individual with a disability to perform the essential functions of the position

Examples of reasonable accommodations include job restructuring, such as implementation of a part-time or modified work schedule; acquisition or modification of equipment or devices; modification or adjustment of examinations, training materials or policies; provision of qualified readers or interpreters; and alteration of existing facilities to make them accessible to individuals with disabilities.

An *undue hardship* imposed upon an employer in providing an accommodation means that the accommodation can be made only with significant difficulty or expense. Factors to be considered in deciding whether an accommodation would impose an undue hardship include the following:

1. The nature and net cost of the accommodation, taking into consideration the availability of tax credits and deductions and/or outside funding

2. The overall financial resources of the facility involved, the number of persons employed at the facility and the effect of the accommodation on expenses and resources

3. The overall financial resources of the employer, as well as the overall size of the business in terms of number of employees and number, type and location of facilities

4. The type of business operation, including the composition, structure and functions of the work force, as well as the geographic separateness and administrative or fiscal relationship of the facility in question to the entire business

5. The impact of the accommodation upon the operation of the facility, including the impact on both the ability of other employees to perform their jobs and the ability of the facility to conduct business

A *direct threat* to health or safety means a significant risk, which cannot be eliminated or reduced by reasonable accommodation, of substantial harm to the health or safety of an individual with a disability or others. ADA requires that a direct threat determination be made of the individual's *present* ability to perform safely the essential functions of the job. The assessment must be based on sound medical judgment that relies on the most current medical knowledge and is supported by the best available objective evidence. Factors to be considered include: (1) the duration of the risk, (2) the nature and severity of the potential harm, (3) the likelihood that the potential harm will occur, and (4) the imminence of the potential harm.

DETERMINING ESSENTIAL JOB FUNCTIONS

The determination of which functions of a job are essential may be critical in determining whether or not an individual with a disability is qualified. Essential functions are best described as the fundamental job duties of the position in question; in other words, those duties that the individual must perform unaided or with the assistance of a reasonable accommodation. A job function may be considered essential for a number of reasons. The reason the position exists may be to perform the function. The function may be considered essential due to the limited number of employees available to perform it. The function may be highly specialized and require a certain level of expertise or skill.

Whether a particular function is essential is a factual determination that must be made on a case-by-case basis. Evidence of whether or not a particular function is essential could include one or more of these factors:

- Employer's business judgment
- Written job description prepared before advertising or interviewing job applicants
- Amount of work time spent in performing the function
- Consequences of not requiring the individual to perform the function
- Terms of a collective bargaining agreement
- Work experience of persons who have held the job
- Current work experience of persons in similar jobs

INQUIRIES UNDER ADA TITLE I

An employer must show the utmost discretion in determining whether a job applicant or employee has a disability. ADA prohibits an employer at the pre-offer stage of the selection process from asking directly if an individual has a disability or what the nature or severity of a disability is.

An employer may ask questions that relate to an applicant's ability to perform job-related functions, with or without an accommodation, if the questions are not phrased in terms of disability. The employer can ask, "Can you perform the duties of the job as they have been described to you?" The question can refer to both essential and marginal job functions; however, an employer may not exclude an applicant with a disability because of the applicant's inability to perform marginal functions.

The employer also may ask an applicant to describe or demonstrate how, with or without reasonable accommodation, the applicant will be able to perform job-related functions.

Medical Examinations

A medical examination may be required after an offer of employment has been made and before the employee actually starts work. The employer may condition the offer of employment on the results of the examination, provided that all entering employees in the same job category are subject to the exam regardless of disability. Results obtained from medical examinations must be collected and maintained on separate forms and in separate medical files that are subject to strict confidentiality requirements, with the following three exceptions: (1) supervisors and managers may be informed of necessary restrictions on the work or duties of the employee and any necessary accommodations; (2) first aid and safety personnel may be informed if the disability might require emergency treatment; and (3) government officials investigating compliance may be provided relevant information.

Drug and Alcohol Testing

A test to determine the illegal use of drugs is not considered to be a medical examination. ADA does not encourage, authorize or prohibit drug testing; however, the results of such tests may be used as the basis for disciplinary action. An employer may:

- prohibit the illegal use of drugs and the use of alcohol at the workplace by all employees;

- require that employees not be under the influence of alcohol or be engaging in the illegal use of drugs at the workplace;

- require that all employees behave in conformance with the requirements established under the Drug-Free Workplace Act of 1988;

- hold an employee who engages in the illegal use of drugs or who is an alcoholic to the same qualification standards for employment or job performance and behavior as other employees, even if the unsatisfactory performance or behavior is related to the employee's drug use or alcoholism; and

- require employees subject to the regulations of the Department of Defense, Department of Transportation or Nuclear Regulatory Commission to comply with such rules.

NOTE: An employer's group insurance policy may exclude coverage for preexisting conditions or may limit or exclude coverage for certain conditions as long as the insurance policy exclusions are applied equally to all employees. Nothing in ADA prohibits an insurer, hospital or other health benefit organization from underwriting or classifying risks; however, a person with a disability may not be denied insurance or be subjected to different terms or conditions of insurance based on disability alone, unless the disability poses increased risks.

DETERMINING THE APPROPRIATE REASONABLE ACCOMMODATION

Once a qualified individual with a disability has made a request for an accommodation, the employer must make a reasonable effort to determine the appropriate accommodation. This should be a flexible, interactive process involving both the employer and the qualified individual. The process involves assessment of the particular job at issue as well as the specific physical or mental limitations of the individual needing the accommodation. An employer could utilize a problem-solving approach, such as that listed below:

1. Analyze the particular job in terms of its purpose and essential functions.

2. Consult with the person with the disability to determine the exact job-related limitations imposed by the individual's disability.

3. Together with the individual needing the accommodation, identify the potential accommodations and assess the effectiveness of each in enabling the individual to perform the essential functions of the position.

4. Taking into consideration the preference of the individual to be accommodated, select and implement the accommodation most appropriate for both employer and employee.

UNDER ADA TITLE I, IT IS UNLAWFUL FOR AN EMPLOYER TO . . .

. . . use *qualification standards*, *tests* or other *selection criteria* that tend to screen out an individual with a disability, unless the employer can demonstrate that the standard, test or criterion is job related and consistent with business necessity. If an employment test is used, the employer must select and administer the test in a manner that accurately reflects the skills and aptitudes of the individual rather than the individual's impaired sensory, manual or speaking skills.

. . . use *standards*, *criteria*, or *methods of administration* that are not job related and not consistent with business necessity and have the effect of discriminating on the basis of disability or that perpetuate discrimination.

. . . *limit*, *segregate*, or *classify* a job applicant or employee in a manner that adversely affects his or her employment opportunities or status on the basis of disability. For example, covered entities would be prohibited from segregating qualified employees with disabilities into separate work areas or into separate lines of advancement. Employers must also accord equal access to health insurance coverage to disabled employees.

. . . *limit* or *deny* equal opportunities or benefits to a qualified individual because that individual has a relationship with or is associated with someone who has a disability. Thus, an employer could not deny employment based on the speculation that an individual with a disabled spouse would have to miss work frequently in order to care for the spouse. This prohibition also applies to other benefits and privileges of employment, even if the provision of such benefits would result in increased health insurance costs for the employer. On the other hand, an employee would not be entitled to a modified work schedule to enable the employee to care for a spouse with a disability.

. . . *fail* to make reasonable accommodation to the known physical or mental limitations of an otherwise qualified applicant or employee with a disability, unless it can be shown that the accommodation would impose an undue hardship on the business operation of the employer. In addition, an employer may not deny employment opportunities to an otherwise qualified job applicant or employee with a disability based on the need to make a reasonable accommodation to the individual's physical or mental impairment.

. . . *coerce*, *intimidate*, *threaten*, *harass* or *interfere with* any individual in the exercise or enjoyment of any right protected by Title I of ADA or because that individual aided or encouraged any other individual in the exercise of any protected right.

. . . *participate* in a contractual or other arrangement that has the effect of subjecting the employer's qualified applicant or employee with a disability to the discrimination prohibited by Title I. In other words, an employer would not be allowed to do through a contractual or other relationship what it is prohibited from doing directly. The term "contractual or other relationship" includes, but is not limited to, a relationship with an employment or referral agency, a labor union (including collective bargaining agreements), an organization providing fringe benefits and an organization providing training and apprenticeship programs.

EXAMPLES OF REASONABLE ACCOMMODATIONS IN EMPLOYMENT:

- Providing a rubber pencil sleeve (cost: $2) to enable a worker with a disability to write

- Lowering a shelf to enable an employee with a disability to reach it

- Modifying employment qualification tests so that they may be taken by individuals with disabilities

- Providing materials in large print by using a photocopier to enlarge pages (cost: $.05/page)

- Putting a belt (cost: $3) on the head of a computer printer to convert the print to braille, enabling a blind employee to perform the duties of a computer programming analyst

- Abandoning the policy of asking all new employees to provide a driver's license for identification

- Rearranging furniture to widen access aisles

- Allowing flexible work hours

- Moving the desk of a blind person closer to an exit

- Placing telephone books or blocks under a desk to raise its height and provide knee clearance for an individual in a wheelchair

- Moving the personnel office to a street-level location

- Placing stick-on braille symbols next to elevator call buttons

- Allowing an individual with multiple sclerosis to take occasional rest breaks

- Making paper cups available at water fountains to assist individuals who can reach the water tap but cannot drink directly from the fountain

- In all employment advertising in which a telephone number is listed, also providing a TDD (telecommunications device for the deaf) number

- Allowing access to a refrigerator for an individual requiring frequent snack breaks for medical reasons

EMPLOYER DEFENSES

An individual with a disability may claim to have been subjected to different treatment on the basis of the disability. An employer may defend such a charge of *disparate treatment* by claiming that the challenged action is justified for a legitimate, nondiscriminatory reason, such as poor performance unrelated to the person's disability. This defense may be rebutted by the person claiming discrimination if the alleged nondiscriminatory reason can be shown to be an attempt to conceal the true reason for the action.

A uniformly applied criterion may have an adverse impact on an individual with a disability or a disproportionately negative impact on a class of individuals with disabilities. An employer may have a defense to a charge of such *disparate impact* if the employer can demonstrate that the qualification standard, test or selection criterion applied was job related and consistent with business necessity. The employer has the burden of proving that the job performance could not be accomplished with the provision of a reasonable accommodation.

A defense to a charge of discrimination under ADA Title I may be that a requested or necessary accommodation would impose an undue hardship on the operation of the business. Whether or not a particular accommodation would impose an undue hardship must be determined on a case-by-case basis. If the undue hardship is based on *cost*, the employer may still be required to make the accommodation if the individual with a disability can arrange to cover the portion of the cost that rises to the undue hardship level or can otherwise arrange to provide the accommodation. Factors other than excessive cost which *might* provide an employer with a defense to making a reasonable accommodation could be that the accommodation would be unduly disruptive to the other employees or to the functioning of the business or that the decision against making the accommodation is based on the terms of a collective bargaining agreement.

An employer also might offer as a defense the obligation to comply with a conflicting federal law or regulation involving medical standards or safety requirements.

ENFORCEMENT

An individual claiming employment discrimination under the Americans with Disabilities Act may file a complaint with the Equal Employment Opportunity Commission within 180 days of the violation. If the case is not resolved by the EEOC, the complainant may bring a civil action in federal district court, or the Attorney General may bring suit if a "pattern or practice" of discrimination is believed to exist or if the case involves a matter of general public importance.

Available remedies include hiring, promotion, reinstatement, back pay or other remuneration or reasonable accommodation (including reassignment). In addition, compensatory damages and punitive damages are possible and attorney's fees and costs of litigation may be awarded.

PUTTING IT ALL TOGETHER

There are some basic steps that any employer can take to help insure compliance with the Americans with Disabilities Act. The Compliance Checklist on the next page shows how the law affects the employment process. At each step of the process, the employer should be careful to take into account any disparate treatment that may be felt by a disabled individual, as well as any reasonable accommodation that may be necessary to assist that person.

Above all, every employer should exercise *good faith* in making ADA compliance efforts. Good faith involves ongoing review of employment policies and practices as well as equipment and facilities. New testing methods, equipment and other devices appear regularly. As a result, an accommodation that was unreasonable yesterday may be reasonable tomorrow.

COMPLIANCE CHECKLIST—EMPLOYMENT

___ 1. Determine the essential job duties required.

___ 2. Can the job applicant or employee perform the essential duties of the job with or without an accommodation?

___ 3. If no, no further action is required.

   or

   If yes, is an accommodation necessary?

___ 4. If no, no further action is required.

   or

   If yes, is the accommodation reasonable?

___ 5. If reasonable, make the accommodation.

   or

   If not reasonable, does the disabled person wish to make the accommodation at his or her own expense?

___ 6. If no, no further action is required.

   or

   If yes, make the accommodation.

As pointed out in Part I of this book, an employer should contact an attorney or other person qualified to discuss the Americans with Disabilities Act. The choice of advisor should itself be an informed one. There is no such thing as an ADA-certified consultant.

The agencies listed on page 22 can help employers stay well informed. The best consultants on a question dealing with a particular disability may be found by contacting one of the agencies that focuses on individuals with that disability. Often the consultant will have the same disability.

Industry and trade groups, through their publications and programs, can help their members keep up-to-date on important issues. With the many available sources of information, it will be extremely difficult for any employer to justifiably claim ignorance of how an individual could have been accommodated if an accommodation was readily available.

CASE SITUATIONS

Many questions regarding the Americans with Disabilities Act will be answered by the courts. Some decisions can be predicted, based on cases interpreting prior laws. Other questions will be answered only by litigation brought under ADA. This section summarizes some past legal decisions, then points out issues that may be resolved in future cases.

PRIOR CASE LAW

Impairment

Evans v. City of Dallas, 861 F.2d 846 (5th Cir. 1988). An employee with a knee injury requiring surgery need not be treated as an individual with a handicap. Even though the injury may have limited the individual's life activities during recuperation, the injury was not of a continuing nature. This decision under the Rehabilitation Act of 1973 would probably be the same under ADA.

Tudyman v. United Airlines, 608 F.Supp. 739 (C.D. Cal. 1984). Weight exceeding an airline's maximum allowance for an applicant for a flight attendant position was not considered a handicap. The weight resulted from a voluntary body building program, and the individual was not substantially limited in any major life activity. The court noted:

> For good or evil, private employers are generally free to be arbitrary and even capricious in determining whom to hire, unless the employer somehow discriminates on the basis of race, national origin, alienage, age, sex, or handicap status, considerations which Congress has determined to be prohibited. But it is only after the employment qualification or policy has been found to have some impact upon a member of a protected group that the defendant is required to justify that requirement or policy. [pp. 746, 747]

This decision under the Rehabilitation Act of 1973 is likely to be the same under ADA.

Torres v. Bolger, 610 F.Supp. 593 (N.D. Tex. 1985). A left-handed postal worker who could not follow mail delivery procedure using his right hand was terminated and brought suit. The court held that left-handedness is not an impairment as defined by the Rehabilitation Act of 1973 because it does not "substantially limit" Torres from working, only from holding a particular job. This decision is likely to be the same under ADA.

School Board of Nassau County v. Arline, 480 U.S. 273 (1987). An individual with the contagious disease tuberculosis may be a "handicapped individual" within the meaning of the Rehabilitation Act of 1973. The next determination is whether or not the individual is "otherwise qualified" to perform the job in question. Because the factual findings before the U.S. Supreme Court failed to indicate the duration and severity of Arline's condition or the probability that she would transmit the disease, the case was remanded to the district court for consideration of whether or not she was qualified for the position.

Testing

Stutts v. Freeman, 694 F.2d 666 (11th Cir. 1983). Stutts, a dyslexic, was denied a job as heavy equipment operator for the Tennessee Valley Authority because he could not pass a written test used to qualify those entering the training program. The issues presented were whether or not the reading required for the test and training program was a necessary criterion for the job of heavy equipment operator and whether or not a reasonable accommodation could enable the applicant to meet the criterion. The court noted that everyone conceded that Stutts could perform the job and that he should not be eliminated from consideration without implementation of an alternative test (oral) or adjustment of the entry requirements to accommodate him. Applicable law was the Rehabilitation Act of 1973; the same result is likely under ADA.

Employment Qualifications

Lucero v. Hart, 915 F.2d 1367 (9th Cir. 1990). An emotionally handicapped typist who typed 44 words per minute was found to be unqualified for a job that required the ability to type 45 wpm. On a retest, she had experienced an extreme stress reaction and scored only 19 wpm. The employer had made reasonable efforts to accommodate her by providing another opportunity to pass the typing test or to obtain alternative employment, but she had not responded. This result under the Rehabilitation Act of 1973 would probably be the same under ADA.

Dexler v. Tisch, 660 F.Supp. 1418 (D. Conn. 1987). An employee suffering from achondroplastic dwarfism was found to be unqualified for a position as postal distribution clerk. Possible accommodations, such as a portable step stool from which the handicapped employee could fall and that would be an obstacle to others, would impose undue hardships on the employer in the form of health and safety risks and loss of productivity. The court speculated that job restructuring, by assigning certain portions of the work to other employees, might have provided an accommodation but was not proposed by the handicapped individual. Applicable law was the Rehabilitation Act of 1973, although the same result is likely under ADA.

Reasonable Accommodation

Fuller v. Frank, 916 F.2d 558 (9th Cir. 1990). An employer, to reasonably accommodate an alcoholic employee, must inform him of available counseling services, provide a "firm choice" between treatment and discipline, afford opportunity for outpatient treatment or inpatient treatment if outpatient treatment fails, assist the employee in locating a suitable treatment program and give the employee time off to participate in it. In this case, the Postal Service was found to have fulfilled its duty to reasonably accommodate the employee's alcoholism. This result under the Rehabilitation Act of 1973 would probably be the same under ADA.

Langon v. U.S. Dept. of Health and Human Services, 749 F.Supp. 1 (D.D.C. 1990). An employer reasonably accommodated an employee who suffers from multiple sclerosis by offering work station relocation, flexible work scheduling and frequent rest periods, even though the employer did not grant the employee's request to work at home. Although the employee claimed that the only appropriate accommodation was elimination of her commute to work, she failed to provide medical evidence of this claim or of her claims that her illness had worsened and the only reasonable accommodation in her case was permission to work at home. This case was decided under the Rehabilitation Act of 1973. Under ADA, the same evidentiary problems would exist, although currently available technology might produce a different result.

Undue Hardship

Southeastern Community College v. Davis, 442 U.S. 397 (1979). A person with a serious hearing disability sought and was denied admission to a nursing program. The court held that alterations needed to accommodate the handicapped person's needs were far more than the "modification" required by regulations interpreting the Rehabilitation Act of 1973. An accommodation is not reasonable if it either imposes "undue financial and administrative burdens" or requires "a fundamental alteration in the nature of the program." The same ruling would be expected under ADA.

Treadwell v. Alexander, 707 F.2d 473 (11th Cir. 1983). The Army Corps of Engineers was not required to accommodate an employee whose heart and nervous conditions made him unable to perform alone the patrol duties of a seasonal park technician. It would be an undue hardship to expect the employer to double up the number of employees assigned to duty, because only two to four other workers were available to patrol 150,000 acres and the agency had limited resources. The Corps presented evidence that another park technician, who had undergone heart bypass surgery, had decided to retire because the position was too arduous. Treadwell presented no evidence of his capabilities despite his medical condition. This decision under the Rehabilitation Act of 1973 is likely to be the same under ADA.

WHAT DOES THE FUTURE HOLD? YOU BE THE JUDGE

The next two pages describe a variety of employment situations that present issues that may be decided in future court cases involving the Americans with Disabilities Act of 1990. Use what you have learned in reading the law and the discussion in this book to decide what you would do if you were the judge handling the case. In each situation you will be required to consider one or more of the following questions:

- Is the job applicant or employee an individual protected by ADA? In other words, does the individual have a disability as defined by the law?

- Must the employer meet the requirements of ADA? Is the employer a covered entity?

- Is the job applicant or employee qualified for the position sought?

- Is an accommodation necessary?

- Is any necessary accommodation also a reasonable one? In other words, should the employer be expected to make the accommodation?

- If an accommodation is not reasonable, is there any other way in which the applicant's or employee's rights should be protected, such as by making an accommodation that could be paid by the disabled individual?

The Case of the Computer Programmer

Acme Software, which already has 150 full-time employees, has advertised for a computer programmer capable of creating programs in MS-DOS. Applicant Jim, who suffers from cerebral palsy, does not yet know MS-DOS but offers to learn it on his own time and at his own expense. Jim will need no special computer equipment to do so. Acme refuses Jim's offer and hires someone else. Jim files a complaint with EEOC, alleging a violation of the Americans with Disabilities Act. What is your decision, based on these facts?

The Case of the Accounting Clerk

Melanie was seriously injured in an automobile accident five years ago, which resulted in permanent and complete hearing loss in one ear and severe scarring to that side of her face. Since the accident, Melanie has worked as an accounting clerk for Premiere Products Corporation, a major manufacturer and distributor of office supplies, based in Chicago. Melanie's work record has been excellent and she is a well regarded member of the organization's staff.

Premiere needs another sales representative for its New England territory and has advertised in newspapers in both Chicago and Boston. To attract applicants to this entry-level position, Premiere offers a thorough training program in sales techniques. The job requires a good deal of travel, most of which would be done by automobile. Melanie submits an application for the position, indicating that she has a valid driver's license and pointing out her knowledge of the company's business practices and client base. She also mentions that she was a prizewinning debater in high school and would thus be an effective salesperson.

Sharon, Premiere's sales manager, is responsible for reviewing the 85 applications received for the sales rep position. Melanie, who is the only company employee seeking the position, is one of the top five candidates. Sharon's final decision is to hire someone from outside the company who has no previous employment experience. Sharon informs Melanie that she has not been chosen for the position because of her hearing impairment and its effect on her depth perception and ability to drive an automobile safely. Privately, Sharon is also concerned that Melanie's facial scars may be upsetting to clients.

Melanie files a complaint against Premiere with the EEOC, alleging a violation of the Americans with Disabilities Act.

The Case of the Temporary Teacher

For three years, Kevin has taught a course in real estate finance on a temporary basis at Education Unlimited, a small private school near his home. The class meets once a week for three hours. Kevin suffers from chronic back pain, a stress-induced condition that sometimes requires him to take medication and avoid standing or otherwise straining his back. By having his wife drive him to the school and sitting during class lectures, Kevin has never missed a session because of his back problem. His students have always rated him highly in their evaluations of his course.

There is an opening for a permanent, full-time real estate instructor at E.U. to augment the staff of ten part-time instructors, one secretary and one administrator. Kevin applies for the position, pointing out his many years of experience as a bank officer, real estate broker and teacher. Kevin is considered the leading contender for the position but is ultimately rejected because of his occasional immobility in the classroom. The school administrator believes that effective teaching demands a dynamic presentation requiring full use of all classroom facilities.

Kevin seeks to file a complaint against Education Unlimited, alleging a violation of the Americans with Disabilities Act.

The Case of the Warehouse Supervisor

Jason has been a supervisor at the International Widgets warehouse for nine years. Jason had polio as a child and, as a result, does not have full strength in his left leg. This has not been an impediment to his work performance, as he can lift the 50-pound loads required for the job. Jason has great hopes of future advancement at IW, one of the largest manufacturers of widgets in the world.

Charles, the manager of the IW distribution center, which includes the warehouse, would like to promote someone from the warehouse to the job of chief of inventory, a position on the administrative staff. The most obvious choice for the job is one of the two warehouse supervisors—Louise, who has been a supervisor for five years, and Jason. Charles instead chooses Sam, his nephew, who has worked as a loader in the warehouse for six months.

Jason files a complaint with the EEOC, alleging that International Widgets has violated the Americans with Disabilities Act.

The Case of the Night Nurse

Annette, a veteran who suffers post-traumatic stress disorder, is a nurse at Memorial Hospital, a large private facility. Because of an unexpected drop in hospital income, some of the members of the nursing staff must be reassigned. Annette, who has worked only the day shift, is told that she will have to work the night shift because of her low seniority. She protests, stating that she is unable to drive to work at night because of her disability, and no public transportation is available. Annette asks for assistance in getting to work, but is told that the hospital budget won't allow any special privileges for any employees. Annette is notified that, as a result of tight finances, she will be laid off unless she works the night shift.

Annette manages to get to work on the first night of her new assignment by taking a taxi, which is very expensive. She tells her supervisor that she will be unable to do so the next night because of the expense. The next day, after Annette fails to show up for work, the hospital terminates her employment. Annette immediately contacts EEOC to file a complaint against Memorial Hospital, alleging a violation of the Americans with Disabilities Act.

RESOURCES

The following are some of the many resources available to help in complying with the Americans with Disabilities Act of 1990. The Equal Employment Opportunity Commission is a good place to start. For questions regarding a particular disability, one of the specialized agencies probably has the most useful information. Page 38 lists additional resources for information on making buildings accessible.

General information and enforcement:
Equal Employment Opportunity Commission
1801 L Street, NW
Washington, DC 20507
800-669-EEOC, voice; 800-800-3302, TDD

Office on Americans with Disabilities Act
Civil Rights Division
U.S. Department of Justice
P.O. Box 66118
Washington, DC 20035-6118
202-514-0301, voice; 202-514-0381, TDD; 202-514-6193, modem

The National Institute on Disability and Rehabilitation Research of the U.S. Department of Education has established 10 regional disability and business technical assistance centers. A Technical Assistance Manual for each title of ADA is now or soon will be available at no charge from each center. To reach your local center to order these and other publications, call 800-949-4232, voice and TDD.

Foundation on Employment & Disability, Inc., Torrance, California. Within California, call 800-499-4232, voice or 800-499-0559, TDD; from out of state, call 310-214-8661, voice or 310-214-8663, TDD, for free publications prepared under grant from the Department of Justice. Calls are accepted in Cambodian, Cantonese, Korean, Mandarin, Spanish and Vietnamese, as well as English. Publications include *Understanding the Americans with Disabilities Act* (20 pages), *The ADA: Removing Barriers in Places of Public Accommodation* (27 pages) and *Accessible Building Design* (40 pages), which includes specifications for doorways, elevators and so on.

Disability Rights Education Defense Fund: 800-466-4232, voice and TDD

National Council on Disability: 202-267-3846, voice; 202-267-3232, TDD

Issues of vision and hearing impairment:
American Federation for the Blind and Gallaudet University: 202-223-0101, voice and TDD

Mental retardation: Association for Retarded Citizens of the United States: 800-433-5255, voice only

Tax deductions and credits: Internal Revenue Service: 202-566-3292, voice only

The Job Accommodation Network: 800-DIALJAN, modem only

The President's Committee on the Employment of People with Disabilities:
202-376-6200, voice; 202-376-6205, TDD

United States Chamber of Commerce. Call local office for free brochure, *How to Comply with the Americans with Disabilities Act.* The U.S. Chamber also publishes a lawyer-prepared handbook, *What Business Must Know About the Americans with Disabilities Act,* available at a cost of $14 for U.S. Chamber members and $21 for nonmembers by calling 800-638-6582.

EMPLOYMENT REVIEW QUIZ

1. Under Title I of the Americans with Disabilities Act, an employer may

   a. ask if an individual has a disability.
   b. inquire into the nature or severity of a perceived disability.
   c. require that a disabled individual pay for the cost of any necessary accommodation.
   d. inquire as to a job applicant's ability to perform job-related functions.

2. The definition of a *person with a disability* includes all of the following *except*

   a. a person suffering from emotional illness.
   b. an individual with a specific learning disability.
   c. a current illegal drug user.
   d. an individual who tests HIV positive.

3. An employer's defense to the provision of a reasonable accommodation could include all of the following *except* the fact that the

   a. appearance of the individual might have an adverse impact on the business operation.
   b. decision was job related and consistent with business necessity.
   c. accommodation would pose an undue hardship on the employer.
   d. decision was based on a significant risk to the health and safety of others that could not be reduced or eliminated by the accommodation.

4. An individual claiming employment discrimination under the Americans with Disabilities Act may file a complaint with the EEOC within

   a. 90 days.   c. 180 days.
   b. 120 days.   d. one year.

5. Which of the following statements is *true* regarding medical examinations?

   a. A medical examination may be required before an offer of employment is made.
   b. Medical examination results must be kept in separate, confidential files.
   c. An employer is never permitted to exclude an individual based on the outcome of a medical examination.
   d. An employer may selectively require medical examinations of individuals in the same job category.

6. Which of the following entities is *not* exempt from Title I of ADA?

   a. The United States Government
   b. Indian tribes
   c. Employers of from 15 to 24 employees
   d. Private membership clubs

7. In determining the essential functions of a job, which of the following would *not* be considered a factor?

   a. The employer's business judgment
   b. The work experience of past incumbents of the job
   c. A written job description
   d. The applicant's business judgment

8.   Employers with 25 or more employees must comply with Title I of ADA as of

      a.   January 26, 1992.   c.   January 26, 1993.
      b.   July 26, 1992.   d.   July 26, 1994.

9.   The reasonableness of an accommodation is determined

      a.   by cost alone.
      b.   primarily by the impact on the operation of the employer.
      c.   on a case-by-case basis.
      d.   by the impact of the accommodation on the ability of other employees to do
            their jobs.

10.   Under Title I, which of the following is a *true* statement?

      a.   Employers must give preference to individuals with disabilities.
      b.   An employer must provide a reasonable accommodation to every applicant who
            requests one.
      c.   An employer may not refuse to hire a qualified individual because of the
            impact of the new hire on the business's health insurance premiums.
      d.   Employers must create new positions for persons with disabilities.

11.   Which of the following would *not* be excluded from the definition of disability?

      a.   Illegal use of drugs   c.   Alcoholism
      b.   Transvestism   d.   Homosexuality

12.   Which of the following statements is *true* regarding Title I of ADA?

      a.   The Act decreases the risks for employers in employment discrimination suits.
      b.   The Act prohibits both intentional and unintentional discrimination.
      c.   The Act requires a plaintiff to prove that alleged employment discrimination
            was based solely on disability.
      d.   The Act exempts labor organizations from coverage.

13.   Title I precludes employers from doing all of the following *except*

      a.   utilizing contractual relationships that have a disparate impact on persons with
            disabilities.
      b.   discriminating against an individual based on that individual's relationship or
            association with a disabled person.
      c.   denying employment opportunities based on the need to provide an accommoda-
            tion.
      d.   hiring a more qualified individual who does not have a disability.

14.   Which of the following entities is *not* covered by ADA Title I?

      a.   An employment agency
      b.   A labor organization
      c.   An employer with fewer than 15 employees
      d.   A joint labor-management committee

Part III: Building Accessibility

The Americans with Disabilities Act makes clear that businesses or other facilities open to the public must consider the needs of the disabled. Whenever practical, or *readily achievable*, architectural barriers must be removed, and business policies, practices and standards must be changed to make commercial enterprises accessible to all members of society. The rules that apply to publicly available accommodations, goods and services operated by private entities are contained in Title III of ADA.

The Department of Justice was charged by Congress with preparing the regulations to help clarify and assist in enforcement of the building accessibility requirements of both Title II and Title III of ADA. In March 1991, public hearings were held in major cities across the country. The hearings, at which 392 persons testified, produced 1,567 pages of testimony. In addition, thousands of organizations and individuals made their opinions known by submitting written statements to the Department of Justice. Based on those comments, the legislative history of ADA and its own research, the Department of Justice issued its *Final Rule on Nondiscrimination on the Basis of Disability by Public Accommodations and in Commercial Facilities* (28 CFR 36), which was published in the Federal Register, July 26, 1991.

The Final Rule of the Department of Justice contains background information, a section-by-section commentary on Title III of ADA, and the Americans with Disabilities Act Accessibility Guidelines prepared by the U.S. Architectural and Transportation Barriers Compliance Board. The commentary in the Final Rule clarifies ADA and establishes procedures for compliance and enforcement. The ADA Accessibility Guidelines (ADAAG) detail the construction specifications that meet minimum ADA requirements.

The discussion in this part of the *ADA Handbook* is based on both the Americans with Disabilities Act and the commentary provided in the Final Rule. The complete text of ADAAG, with its many useful illustrations, is reproduced in Appendix B of this book. It is the best resource for construction professionals and others who must comply with the Act.

NOTE: Businesses are required to follow both federal and state law regarding accessibility for the disabled. If there is any conflict, the more demanding law generally will prevail. In other words, a facility that complies with federal guidelines may require additional improvements in order to comply with state guidelines and vice versa.

ADA TITLE III

Title III of the Americans with Disabilities Act provides another in a series of legal protections enacted to insure access for the disabled to all the benefits of society. One of the earliest, the Rehabilitation Act of 1973, requires that federally funded programs and activities be accessible to and usable by the handicapped, even when major structural alterations to buildings are necessary. ADA Title II requires that all state and local government services, including Amtrak, be available to individuals with disabilities.

ADA Title III provides that no individual shall be discriminated against on the basis of disability in the full and equal enjoyment of the goods, services, facilities, privileges, advantages or accommodations of any place of *public accommodation.*

Title III applies to all private entities (non-governmental businesses, organizations or other groups) with facilities open to the public, whether to provide goods or services or for some other purpose, as long as operation of the facility affects commerce. Title III provides that:

- when readily achievable, architectural barriers and communication barriers that are structural in nature must be removed to make goods and services accessible to individuals with disabilities;

- auxiliary aids and services must be provided to insure that no individual with a disability is excluded, denied services, segregated or otherwise treated differently than other individuals, unless to do so would fundamentally alter the nature of the good, service or accommodation or result in an undue burden; and

- all new commercial construction must be accessible to the disabled, unless structurally impractical.

If a structure contains a facility that comes under Title III, the law applies to any person who owns, leases, leases to or operates the facility.

In general Title III became effective January 26, 1992, 18 months after enactment of ADA. All commercial structures designed and constructed for first occupancy after January 26, 1993, *whether or not they are open to the public,* must comply fully with the law unless to do so would be structurally impractical.

The requirements of Title III overlap and in some cases go beyond the requirements of Title I, which protects employees and job applicants. Some employers who are not covered by Title I will be required to make structural and other changes to comply with Title III. Thus, employers of fewer than 15 employees, who are not required to comply with Title I, must nevertheless take whatever steps are necessary to comply with Title III.

The only exemptions from Title III's accessibility requirements apply to religious organizations and exclusive, private membership clubs.

UNDERSTANDING TITLE III

The following definitions, except where otherwise noted, are based on those found in Section 3 and Title III of ADA, the Final Rule of the EEOC (29 CFR 1630) and the Final Rule of the DOJ (28 CFR 36). The terms *disability, physical or mental impairment,* and *major life activities* are defined just as they are for Title I.

A *disability* means, with respect to an individual, (1) a physical or mental impairment that substantially limits one or more of the individual's major life activities, (2) a record of such an impairment, or (3) being regarded as having such an impairment.

A *physical or mental impairment* is:

- any physiological disorder or condition, cosmetic disfigurement or anatomical loss affecting one or more of the following body systems—neurological, musculoskeletal, special sense organs, respiratory (including speech organs), cardiovascular, reproductive, digestive, genito-urinary, hemic and lymphatic, skin and endocrine; or

- any mental or psychological disorder, such as mental retardation, organic brain syndrome, emotional or mental illness and specific learning disabilities.

Major life activities include caring for oneself, performing manual tasks, walking, seeing, hearing, speaking, breathing, learning, working and other functions that the average person in the general population can perform. An impairment that *substantially limits* a major life activity is one that significantly restricts the condition, manner, or duration of an activity's performance.

A *public accommodation* is a facility operated by a private entity when the operation affects commerce. Public accommodations include the following:

- Places of lodging, such as an inn, hotel or motel

- Establishments serving food or drink, such as a restaurant or bar

- Places of exhibition or entertainment, such as a motion picture house, theater, concert hall or stadium

- Places of public gathering, such as an auditorium, convention center or lecture hall

- Sales or rental establishments, such as a bakery, grocery store, clothing store, hardware store or shopping center

- Service establishments, such as a laundromat, dry cleaner, bank, barber shop, beauty shop, travel service, shoe repair service, funeral parlor, gas station, office of an accountant or lawyer, pharmacy, insurance office, real estate office, professional office of a health care provider or other secure establishment

- Stations used for specified public transportation, such as a terminal or depot

- Places of public display or collection, such as a museum, library or gallery

- Places of recreation, such as a park, zoo or amusement park

- Places of education, including a private nursery, elementary, secondary, undergraduate or postgraduate school

- Social service center establishments, such as a day-care center, senior citizen center, homeless shelter, food bank or adoption agency

- Places of exercise or recreation, such as a gymnasium, health spa, bowling alley or golf course

Also included in the definition of a public accommodation is any portion of a private residence that is used as a place of business. If a business is conducted out of a home office, for instance, the front sidewalk (if any), door or entryway, hallway, restroom or other part of the home that may be used by customers or clients must conform to ADA requirements.

The *private entity* referred to in Title III is any entity other than a *public entity,* which is defined in Title II as a state or local government; any department, agency, special purpose district or other instrumentality of a state or local government; and the National Railroad Passenger Corporation and any commuter authority (as defined in the Rail Passenger Service Act). Even though Title III is limited to non-governmental organizations, state and local governments must comply with the accessibility requirements of Title II.

The term *commerce* includes travel, trade, traffic, commerce, transportation or communication among the states, between any foreign country or any territory or possession and a state, or between points in the same state but through another state or foreign country.

A *commercial facility* is a facility intended for nonresidential use, when its operation will affect commerce. The requirement that new construction and alterations comply with Title III applies to all commercial facilities, whether or not they are places of public accommodation.

An action required by Title III is considered *readily achievable* when it can be easily accomplished and carried out without much difficulty or expense. The five factors that will be considered in determining whether or not an action is readily achievable are:

1. the nature and cost of the action needed to comply with the Act;

2. the overall financial resources of the facility or facilities involved in the action, taking into account the number of persons employed, the effect of the accommodation on expenses and resources, or the impact of the accommodation in any other way on the operation of the facility;

3. the overall financial resources of the covered entity, taking into account the overall size of the business or entity with respect to the number of its employees and the number, type and location of its facilities;

4. the type of operation or operations of the covered entity, including the composition, structure and functions of the work force; and

5. the geographic separateness and administrative or fiscal relationship of the facility or facilities in question to the covered entity.

Any action that would otherwise be required by Title III need not be undertaken if to do so would pose a *direct threat* to the health or safety of others. A direct threat exists if the action would present a significant risk that could not be eliminated by a modification of policies, practices or procedures or by the provision of auxiliary aids or services.

ADAAG

The U.S. Architectural and Transportation Barriers Compliance Board has prepared the *Americans with Disabilities Act Accessibility Guidelines for Buildings and Facilities,* referred to as ADAAG. The accessibility guidelines (reproduced in full in Appendix B of this book) give required specifications for such areas, structural components and facilities as:

- Parking and passenger loading zones
- Curb ramps
- Stairs, elevators and doors
- Drinking fountains and water coolers
- Alarms and detectable warnings
- Water closets, toilet stalls, urinals
- Signage and telephones
- Medical care facilities
- Business and retail establishments, including grocery checkout aisles
- Libraries
- Transient lodgings (hotels, motels)

DETERMINING WHO MUST COMPLY

ADA Title III applies to any person who owns, leases, leases to or operates a public accommodation or commercial facility. The parties to a lease or other agreement may decide between themselves who will bear the cost or other burden of compliance; nevertheless, the Act does not relieve a party to such an agreement from the responsibilities imposed by the law.

Leases should stipulate the party responsible for ADA compliance. What about the many existing leases drawn up before the requirements of ADA were known? Apportionment of the burden of compliance is strictly a matter for negotiation between the parties.

Sometimes the ADA Accessibility Guidelines specify different requirements for different covered entities. In general, for instance, new construction of less than three stories or less than 3,000 square feet per floor need not include installation of elevators. Certain multistory facilities must comply with the law regardless of size, however. *Every* new building that houses a multistory shopping center or shopping mall, a professional office of a health care provider or a terminal, depot or other public transportation station must have an elevator.

Alterations Affecting the Path of Travel

The construction of a new facility or alteration to an existing one must be made free of architectural barriers. If an alteration involves the primary function of the structure, then the *path of travel* to the altered area and the restrooms, telephones and drinking fountains serving that area must be made readily accessible and usable to the maximum extent feasible, *unless* the cost of such changes exceeds 20 percent of the cost of the alteration.

Agents of Persons Who Must Comply

In general, agents of a covered entity take on the same responsibilities as the person by whom they are employed. Title III makes clear that an individual or organization covered by Title III cannot evade responsibility by assigning the task of compliance to someone else.

Property management firms, as operators of a public accommodation or commercial facility, are independently bound by ADA's rules if they are in a position to make decisions affecting building accessibility or any other provision of ADA.

The liability of real estate sales or leasing agents is less clear. Real estate agents will need to have some knowledge of the Americans with Disabilities Act, if only to determine requirements applicable to the agent's own office and services. In dealing with the property of others, a prudent course appears to be for the agent to make commercial clients and customers aware of the existence of ADA without taking the role of ADA advisor. That function is better left to an attorney or architect familiar with the law. The California Association of REALTORS® has prepared a one-page form that can be appended to a commercial property sale or lease agreement. A copy of the form appears on page 30.

Real estate appraisers must be careful to define the limits within which the appraisal is prepared. When appraising commercial property, the appraiser could indicate in the appraisal report that the property may or may not be in compliance with ADA requirements, but that the appraiser has made no such determination. Unfortunately, this approach may still not relieve the appraiser of liability for failure to identify and estimate the effect on value of conspicuous property features that present barriers to the disabled.

The National Council for Interior Design Qualification administers a test for residential and commercial interior designers who wish to be state licensed to design for disabled people. The test covers barrier-free design, energy conservation and other topics. Information on the testing procedure can be obtained from the council at 212-473-1188.

AMERICANS WITH DISABILITIES ACT SUPPLEMENT/ADDENDUM
CALIFORNIA ASSOCIATION OF REALTORS® (CAR) STANDARD FORM

The following terms and conditions are hereby incorporated in and made a part of the ☐ Commercial Real Estate Purchase Contract and Receipt for Deposit ☐ Investment Real Estate Purchase Contract ☐ Counter Offer ☐ Exclusive Authorization and Right to Sell, Lease, Exchange or Option ☐ Property Management Agreement
☐ Other _____ dated _____ 19___
on property known as: _____
in which _____
is referred to as: (circle one)   Buyer / Seller / Landlord / Tenant / Broker
and _____
is referred to as: (circle one)   Buyer / Seller / Landlord / Tenant / Broker.

On July 26, 1990 the Americans With Disabilities Act of 1990 (ADA) was signed into law. This federal civil rights legislation prohibits discrimination against individuals with disabilities. The ADA affects almost all commercial facilities and public accommodations. Residential properties are not typically covered by the ADA but may be governed by its provisions if used for certain purposes. The ADA can require, among other things, buildings to be made readily accessible to the disabled. Different requirements apply to new construction, alterations to existing buildings, and removal of barriers in existing buildings. Compliance with the ADA may require significant costs. Monetary and injunctive remedies may be incurred if the property is not in compliance.

A real estate broker does not have the technical expertise to either determine whether a building is in compliance with ADA requirements or to advise a principal on the requirements of the ADA. Any principal who is a party to the above referenced agreement is advised to contact an attorney, contractor, architect, engineer or other qualified professional of his/her own choosing to determine to what degree, if at all, the ADA impacts upon that principal or this transaction.

The undersigned acknowledge that they have read and understand this agreement and have received a copy.

_____   _____
Buyer / Seller / Landlord / Tenant / Broker   Date

_____   _____
Buyer / Seller / Landlord / Tenant / Broker   Date

_____   _____
Buyer / Seller / Landlord / Tenant / Broker   Date

_____   _____
Buyer / Seller / Landlord / Tenant / Broker   Date

OFFICE USE ONLY
Reviewed by Broker or Designee _____
Date _____

FORM ADA-11

SPECIAL RULES FOR EXAMINERS AND COURSE PROVIDERS

Section 309 of Title III of the Americans with Disabilities Act applies to private entities that offer examinations or courses related to applications, licensing, certification or credentialling for secondary or postsecondary education, professional or trade purposes. Examinations or courses must be offered in a *place* and *manner* accessible to persons with disabilities, or alternative accessible arrangements must be offered to such persons.

The examiner must make sure that when an examination is administered to an individual with a disability that impairs sensory, manual or speaking skills, the examination results accurately reflect the individual's aptitude, achievement or other attribute the examination purports to measure, rather than the individual's impairment. ADA prohibits both public and private entities from basing decisions on test results that were obtained in a discriminatory fashion.

ADA places an affirmative obligation on an individual with a disability to make the need for an accommodation known; thus, it is critical that individuals with disabilities have the opportunity to do so. An examiner/course provider is permitted to request documentation of a claimed disability at the expense of the person making the request; however, the expense of making an accommodation must be borne by the examiner/course provider.

Architectural Accessibility

An individual with a mobility impairment may request that a course/examination site be architecturally accessible, with an unobstructed path of travel to the location and an accessible restroom and drinking fountain. If this is not possible, alternative arrangements may be made; for example, a proctor may give an examination at an individual's home.

Transferring Printed Materials to Alternate Media

Printed materials may need to be transferred to alternate media to accommodate individuals with sight, hearing, mobility or learning impairments. Alternate media include audiotape, computer disks, large-print and braille editions, among others.

Auxiliary Aids and Services

A *qualified reader* may be an option for an individual whose disability precludes independent reading, such as someone with a learning disability or visual impairment.

Use of a *sign language interpreter* during testing may be requested by a hearing-impaired individual; however, oral instructions can easily be given in writing instead.

The use of a *scribe* to record test answers might be an appropriate accommodation for an individual who has difficulty writing.

Adaptive equipment, such as computers and calculators with voice output, could be used to accommodate individuals with reading disabilities.

Common Testing Accommodations

Extended time is the most commonly requested testing accommodation. Whenever auxiliary aids or adaptive equipment are used, additional time should be allotted. Nevertheless, *unlimited* time is not a reasonable accommodation. *Test schedule variation* also may be necessary. The time of day could be critical to an individual with a particular disability, such as diabetes, or someone taking medication. An option in some situations could be to allow food to be taken into the testing site.

DEFENSES

Structural Modifications

A modification to an existing structure need not be made if it is not readily achievable. The change or improvement will be considered in light of its nature and cost as well as the entity's financial resources and overall operation. This is a lesser standard than the one imposed on employers by Title I, which requires all necessary reasonable accommodations be made to prevent discrimination unless to do so would impose an undue burden on the employer.

Nevertheless, just as with Title I, ADA Title III requires ongoing compliance. Circumstances affecting both the business climate and the state of technology are subject to change. Business operations may expand or contract in response to the economy and other factors, and new building products and techniques may be developed. In short, what was not readily achievable yesterday may be achievable tomorrow. Regular review of company policies, procedures and standards of practice, particularly in light of available technology, will help insure compliance with the law.

Auxiliary Aids or Services

If an auxiliary aid or service is required to prevent discrimination against an individual with a disability, it must be provided unless to do so would fundamentally alter the nature of a good, service or accommodation or would be an undue burden on the business or other entity. Here, the standard for compliance is similar to that of Title I.

Auxiliary aids or services do not include personal devices (such as a wheelchair), personally prescribed devices (such as a hearing aid) or personal services (such as assistance in eating, toileting or dressing). For example, a clothing store dressing room must be accessible to individuals with disabilities; however, the store is not required to provide an attendant to assist in trying on clothing.

New Construction and Alterations

New or remodeled public accommodations or commercial facilities must be made readily accessible to and usable by individuals with disabilities unless to do so would be structurally impractical.

This is an even higher level of compliance than the undue burden standard. The only exception to providing access by individuals with disabilities to new or remodeled facilities covered by Title III occurs when the nature or purpose of the structure prevents an accommodation from being made. An example of such a facility may be a sports or entertainment center, such as a water slide, that requires a certain level of physical ability for its use.

CERTIFICATION OF EQUIVALENCY

At the request of a state or local government, the U.S. Assistant Attorney General may certify that a state or local building code or similar ordinance meets or exceeds the minimum requirements of ADA by issuing a *certification of equivalency*.

In the event of litigation, certification of equivalency would be considered rebuttable evidence that the state law or local ordinance meets or exceeds the minimum requirements of ADA. In other words, the fact that a certification of equivalency has been issued and there has been compliance with the specified state or local law will *not* necessarily be adequate proof of compliance with ADA. An independent ADA compliance evaluation should always be made in addition to any steps taken to insure compliance with state and local requirements.

ENFORCEMENT

In general, a civil action for preventive relief, including application for a permanent or temporary injunction, may be brought by a person who is being subjected to discrimination on the basis of disability in violation of ADA or who has reasonable grounds for believing that he or she will be subjected to discrimination in violation of Section 303 of the Act, which regulates new construction and alterations in public accommodations and commercial facilities.

In a case brought under ADA, the court may grant any equitable relief that the court considers appropriate, which could include the providing of auxiliary aids or services, modifications of policies, practices or procedures and making facilities readily accessible to and usable by individuals with disabilities.

The Attorney General of the United States may bring a civil action if a "pattern or practice" of discrimination is believed to exist or if the alleged discrimination involves a matter of general public importance.

Compensatory damages may be awarded, as well as a reasonable attorney's fee, litigation expenses and costs.

CAUTION: A civil penalty of up to $50,000 may be assessed for a first violation of the law, and a penalty of up to $100,000 may be assessed for any subsequent violation. In deciding the appropriate amount of civil penalty, if any, the court is to give consideration to any good faith effort or attempt to comply with the law.

PUTTING IT ALL TOGETHER

Title III of the Americans with Disabilities Act applies to all places of public accommodation that affect commerce and all new commercial facilities, including those that are not open to the public.

Facilities must be accessible to and usable by individuals with disabilities whenever a necessary structural modification is readily achievable. Auxiliary aids and services must be provided whenever necessary to make the benefits of goods, services or accommodations available to individuals with disabilities unless doing so would impose an undue burden or would fundamentally alter the nature of the good, service or accommodation. All new or remodeled public accommodations or commercial facilities must comply with the law unless doing so would be structurally impractical.

Tax assistance is available for businesses that must comply with the Act. As discussed in Part I of this book, a tax *deduction* of up to $15,000 per year may be taken for expenses associated with the removal of qualified architectural and transportation barriers. A tax *credit* equal to 50% of allowable expenditures exceeding $250 but no more than $10,250, is available to eligible small businesses (defined on page 8). Allowable expenditures include necessary and reasonable costs incurred to remove barriers, provide auxiliary aids and acquire or modify equipment or devices.

The ongoing nature of ADA compliance is highlighted by the civil penalties that may be imposed for failure to comply. The amount of penalty, if any, will be determined by the evidence of a *good faith* effort to comply with the law. An initial consultation with an attorney, architect or other individual qualified to discuss the law must be followed not only by necessary compliance measures but also by regular review of policies, procedures and practices. Careful documentation of all consultations, information received and attempts at compliance will help insure that both the letter and the spirit of the law are followed.

UNDER ADA TITLE III, IT IS UNLAWFUL TO . . .

. . . utilize *standards* or *criteria* or *methods of administration* that have the effect of discriminating on the basis of disability or that perpetuate the discrimination of others who are subject to common administrative control.

. . . *deny the opportunity* to participate in or benefit from goods, services, facilities, privileges, advantages or accommodations to an individual or class of individuals on the basis of a disability or disabilities.

. . . provide an individual or class of individuals, on the basis of a disability or disabilities, with a good, service, facility, privilege, advantage or accommodation that is *not equal* to that provided to other individuals.

. . . provide an individual or class of individuals, on the basis of a disability or disabilities, with a good, service, facility, privilege, advantage or accommodation that is *different* or *separate from* that provided to other individuals, unless it is necessary to be as effective as that provided to others.

. . . deny an individual with a disability the opportunity to participate in a program or activity that is *not* separate or different, even if a separate or different program or activity is provided in accordance with the Act.

. . . deny equal goods, services, facilities, privileges, advantages, accommodations or other opportunities to an individual or entity because of the known disability of an individual with whom the individual or entity is known to have a relationship or association.

NOTE: The above activities are unlawful, whether carried out directly or through contractual, licensing or other arrangements.

EXAMPLES OF MODIFICATIONS MADE TO PUBLIC FACILITIES AND SERVICES:

• Rearranging clothing racks to provide enough aisle space for customers in wheelchairs

• Installing a buzzer at street level so that customers of a second-floor dry cleaner in a building with no elevator can signal for a clerk's assistance

• Altering the height of a pay telephone to make it accessible to a person in a wheelchair

• Providing a braille menu or having a server read food choices to a blind customer

• Installing automatic entry doors

• Adding grab bars to a restroom stall

• Providing information on real estate listings in large print or audio format

• Placing a ramp at the entrance to a residence used as a home office

• Allowing a companion to assist a person with a disability in a dressing room

COMPLIANCE CHECKLIST—BUILDING ACCESSIBILITY

EXISTING PLACES OF PUBLIC ACCOMMODATION

__ 1. Determine any architectural or structural communication barriers to full access to the facility by individuals with disabilities.

__ 2. Can barrier removal be readily achieved?

__ 3. If yes, remove the barrier.

   or

   If no, are there any planned alterations of the affected area?

__ 4. If no, no further action is required at this time.

   or

   If yes, would removal of the barrier be structurally impractical or change the fundamental nature of the operation?

__ 5. If yes, no further action is required at this time.

   or

   If no, add removal of the barrier to the anticipated alterations.

NEW PLACES OF PUBLIC ACCOMMODATION OR OTHER COMMERCIAL FACILITIES

__ 1. Determine structural modifications necessary to provide accessibility to the facility by individuals with disabilities.

__ 2. Is any required construction modification structurally impractical?

__ 3. If yes, the construction modification need not be made.

   or

   If no, the construction modification must be made.

CASE SITUATIONS

As with employment requirements, many questions regarding the building accessibility provisions of the Americans with Disabilities Act will be answered by the courts. The following hypothetical fact situations are based on issues that may be the subject of future cases. Use what you have learned in reading the law and the discussion in this book to help determine what you would do if you were the judge deciding these cases. In each situation you will be required to consider one or more of the following questions:

- Is the person bringing the complaint an individual protected by ADA?

- Is the person or company against whom the complaint is made a covered entity (someone who is required to comply with Title III of ADA)?

- Is an accommodation necessary?

- Is any necessary structural alteration also readily achievable?

- Would any necessary auxiliary aids or services create an undue burden or fundamentally alter the nature of the good, service or other benefit provided?

- If the complaint involves new construction, does the structure come under the rules of ADA?

- Would a modification of new construction be structurally impractical?

The Case of Harry's Haberdashery

Harry's Haberdashery, a retail outlet for men's shirts, ties and other apparel items, is located on Main Street in Pleasant Town, Anystate. Harry, the proprietor, has taken great pains to make his establishment accessible to disabled individuals. He has placed a small ramp at the one-step entryway and has installed an automatic sliding door. All aisles are spacious, and counters have been lowered to make their contents visible even to someone in a wheelchair. In addition, Harry carries all size ranges and can special order any item he does not currently have in stock.

One of Harry's customers is Marjorie, whose husband, Jeff, is known in the community to be suffering from auto-immune deficiency syndrome (AIDS). One day, Marjorie attempts to return a shirt she purchased for her husband, explaining to Harry that the sleeves are not long enough. Several other customers are present and can overhear Marjorie's conversation with Harry, which Harry realizes. Harry refuses to allow Marjorie to return the shirt because her husband has tried it on. He is very apologetic but explains that once a purchase has been made, the item cannot be returned if it has been worn. Marjorie points out that her husband is unable to come to the store to try on merchandise there, but Harry refuses to change his position.

Marjorie brings suit alleging that she has been discriminated against under Title III of the Americans with Disabilities Act. If you were the judge, what would be your decision?

The Case of XYZ Realty

XYZ Realty is a small office employing a receptionist and no more than ten sales agents at any one time. Paula, the broker and owner of XYZ, has attended a seminar at which several speakers discussed the requirements of the Americans with Disabilities Act. Paula, whose brother has suffered from a speech impediment for many years, is glad to hear that places of public accommodation must provide for the needs of the disabled. On her return from the conference, Paula suggests that all her sales agents attend a similar presentation.

The next afternoon, XYZ Realty receives a telephone call from someone interested in finding out more about a house that XYZ has advertised for sale. John, the agent on duty, discusses the house's size, location and price with the prospect and offers to meet him at the property for a showing. Mr. Klein, the prospect, declines the offer since the house has two stories. "I'm really looking for a one-story house," Mr. Klein explains. John then invites Mr. Klein to the office to discuss other listings the company has, but Mr. Klein says he is unable to do so because he is disabled and doesn't have anyone to assist him in getting to the office. John then offers to bring a computer printout of available one-story houses to Mr. Klein's home. Mr. Klein agrees to the idea but points out that because he has a "vision problem," he has difficulty reading anything other than large print. John, realizing that his computer printouts are in small type, apologizes to Mr. Klein for being unable to help him and suggests that Mr. Klein have someone else contact the XYZ office to set up an appointment.

Mr. Klein brings suit against John, Paula and XYZ Realty, alleging discrimination under the Americans with Disabilities Act.

The Case of Motorama Speedway

Motorama Speedway is a facility with a quarter-mile oval track that offers rides in customized miniature racing cars. Carol, who is a paraplegic and must use a wheelchair, would like to drive one of the cars. She visits Motorama Speedway and talks to Scott, the manager. Carol indicates that she can drive one of the cars if a hand-operated accelerator and brake (similar to devices in her car) are attached. Scott, who has promised the owner of Motorama Speedway that he will help control expenses, tells Carol that Motorama cannot afford to adapt any of its cars in the manner she has suggested.

Carol brings suit against Motorama Speedway, alleging discrimination.

The Case of Hot Dog Heaven

Hot Dog Heaven is a fast-food restaurant. Most orders are taken at the drive-up window. There is no table service and only one walk-up service window. Jim, who lives a few blocks from Hot Dog Heaven, is deaf and also has a speech impediment that makes it difficult for most people to understand him. He usually gets along very well in restaurants and stores by writing his requests on slips of paper.

One day when he has a taste for a hot dog "with everything," Jim writes his order on a notepad and takes it to the walk-up window at Hot Dog Heaven. The person taking orders at Hot Dog Heaven can speak English but cannot read English. Jim, who can only write in English, is unable to communicate his order. He gestures for the clerk to get someone else to help him, but the only other person on the premises is the cook, who also is unable to read English. The next day Jim writes to the owner of Hot Dog Heaven and relates his difficulty and requests that the restaurant find some way of making it possible for him to order food. The owner, who has difficulty finding good help, replies that he won't be able to comply with Jim's request because he can't afford to pay any additional workers.

Jim files a complaint with the Department of Justice charging Hot Dog Heaven with failure to comply with Title III of the Americans with Disabilities Act.

The Case of Music Mania

Louise is the executive director of Music Mania, a 3,000-seat outdoor amphitheater that showcases rock music groups. Bruce would like to attend a Music Mania concert, but he has a hearing disability that makes him extremely sensitive to loud sounds. Bruce contacts Louise and asks her to provide a special listening device that will allow him to hear a muted version of the concert. Louise refuses on the grounds that she can't accommodate such a personal request. Bruce responds by bringing suit against Music Mania, claiming violation of ADA.

RESOURCES

The following are just a few of the many resources available to help in complying with the Americans with Disabilities Act of 1990. Useful information may also be obtained from one of the sources listed on page 22, particularly the specialized agencies.

General information and enforcement:
Office on Americans with Disabilities Act
Civil Rights Division
U.S. Department of Justice
P.O. Box 66118
Washington, DC 20035-6118
202-514-0301, voice; 202-514-0381, TDD; 202-514-6193, modem

Copies of the Department of Justice's *Final Rule on Nondiscrimination on the Basis of Disability by Public Accommodations and in Commercial Facilities* (28 CFR 36) are available in regular print, large print, braille, electronic file on computer disk and audiotape formats. For a copy, call the Office on Americans with Disabilities Act at one of the numbers listed above; the Final Rule also appears on an electronic bulletin board that can be reached by calling the modem number.

Foundation on Employment & Disability, Inc., Torrance, California. See the listing on page 22 of the useful publications offered free of charge by this organization, which can take calls in many foreign languages in addition to English. Phone numbers for voice and TDD are given on page 22.

Examinations and courses:
Two publications of the Association on Handicapped Student Service Programs in Postsecondary Education (AHSSPPE) are available to assist agencies, institutions and organizations in complying with the specific provisions of ADA. They are *Testing Accommodations for Persons with Disabilities: A Guide for Licensure, Certification, and Credentialling*, by Warren L. King and Jane E. Jarrow, and *Making Your Association Accessible: A "How to" Guide*, by Jane E. Jarrow and Critta B. Park. In addition, AHSSPPE publishes *Accessible Meetings and Conventions*, also by Jarrow and Park, which explains how meeting planners can prepare for maximum accessibility of meeting places. All three manuals are available at a nominal charge from AHSSPPE, P.O. Box 21992, Columbus, OH 43221-0192.

Construction modifications:
Americans with Disabilities Act Compliance Evaluation Survey with Special California Title 24 Supplement: A Do-It-Yourself Assessment, put together by Production Consulting & Construction, Westlake Village, California, is available for $80 from CEEM Information Services, Fairfax, VA: 800-745-5565; 703-250-5900; 703-250-5313, fax. The ADAAG and California requirements are redrafted in a checklist format. A national edition and versions prepared for other states are also available from CEEM.

Betterway Publications, Inc., publishes *The Complete Guide to Barrier-Free Housing: Convenient Living for the Elderly and the Physically Handicapped*, by Gary D. Branson. Although written for residences rather than public accommodations, this book has many useful photos and illustrations showing how entries, stairs, halls, bathrooms and other areas can be modified to provide access to disabled individuals. There are also detailed listings of Independent Living Centers throughout the United States as well as organizations that can provide information on specific disabilities; companies that provide specialized products and services; and books, magazines and other published materials that deal with the issue of accessibility. The paperback book, priced at $14.95, is available from the publisher: P.O. Box 219, Crozet, VA 22032; 804-823-5661.

BUILDING ACCESSIBILITY REVIEW QUIZ

1. Title III of the Americans with Disabilities Act applies to all of the following *except*

    a. public accommodations.
    b. commercial facilities.
    c. private entities providing public transportation services.
    d. religious organizations.

2. Except for new construction designed for occupancy after January 1993, the effective date for implementation of Title III of ADA is

    a. July 26, 1990.   c. July 26, 1992.
    b. January 26, 1992.   d. January 26, 1993.

3. A business may deduct from taxable income its annual costs incurred in removing certain architectural or transportation barriers in an amount up to

    a. $5,000.   b. $10,000.   c. $15,000.   d. $20,000.

4. Title III of ADA prohibits all of the following *except*

    a. failure to undertake reasonable modifications of policies, practices and procedures.
    b. failure to provide auxiliary aids and services.
    c. failure to remove architectural and communication barriers if removal is readily achievable.
    d. failure to provide separate and different programs for individuals with disabilities.

5. In determining whether an accommodation would impose an undue burden, a court would consider all of the following *except*

    a. the nature and cost of the accommodation.
    b. the type of operation of the business.
    c. company policy.
    d. the overall size of the program or business.

6. The ADA Accessibility Guidelines cover all of the following *except*

    a. transient lodgings.   c. libraries.
    b. testing procedures.   d. alarms and detectable warnings.

7. Which of the following facilities would be exempt from the public accommodations requirements of Title III of ADA?

    a. A homeless shelter
    b. A senior citizens center
    c. An apartment building
    d. A health spa

8. Eligible small businesses may receive a tax credit for certain expenditures incurred in complying with ADA, in an amount up to

    a. $2,500.   b. $5,000.   c. $10,250.   d. $15,000.

9.   Which of the following statements is *false*?

     a.   The obligation to remove barriers is a continuing responsibility of public accommodations.
     b.   Failure to learn about ADA could be used as a defense for noncompliance.
     c.   In a civil action brought under ADA, courts will give consideration to good faith efforts to comply with the law.
     d.   A person with a disability cannot be charged the costs incurred in complying with the Act.

10. Which of the following actions is permissible under ADA?

     a.   Imposing administrative criteria that screen out individuals with disabilities
     b.   Denying individuals with disabilities the right to participate in or benefit from goods or services
     c.   Offering separate and unequal benefits to persons with disabilities
     d.   Providing goods, services and facilities in the most integrated setting appropriate to the needs of the individual

11. Elevators must be installed in facilities designed and constructed for first occupancy after January 26, 1993, unless the structure

     a.   is a shopping center or mall.
     b.   has fewer than three stories or less than 3,000 square feet per story.
     c.   houses a professional office of a health care provider.
     d.   is a public transportation facility.

12. If an entity undertakes an alteration to a primary function area, the path of travel to that area must be modified as well, unless the cost of modifying the path of travel would exceed what percentage of the cost of modifying the primary function area?

     a. 10 percent   b. 15 percent   c. 20 percent   d. 25 percent

13. Which of the following could *not* be a defense to enforcement of ADA's provisions regarding public accommodations?

     a.   An individual with a disability, if accommodated, would pose a direct threat to the health or safety of others.
     b.   Barrier removal in an existing facility is not readily achievable.
     c.   Provision of auxiliary aids and services constitutes an undue burden.
     d.   Modifying policies, practices and procedures would increase insurance costs.

14. In a civil action brought by the Attorney General, the court may assess a civil penalty for a first violation of ADA in an amount up to

     a. $25,000.   b. $50,000.   c. $75,000.   d. $100,000.

15. Which of the following statements regarding ADA's guidelines for new construction is *false*?

     a.   Facilities designed and constructed for occupancy after January 26, 1993, must be readily accessible to and usable by individuals with disabilities.
     b.   Elevators must be installed in all facilities.
     c.   The U.S. Architectural and Transportation Barriers Compliance Board has issued guidelines detailing building accessibility requirements.
     d.   A narrow exemption to the accessibility requirements exists if an entity can demonstrate structural impracticality.

Appendix A

Americans with Disabilities Act of 1990

AMERICANS WITH DISABILITIES ACT OF 1990
Public Law 101-336 [S. 933]; 42 U.S.C. 12101; July 26, 1990

An Act to establish a clear and comprehensive prohibition of discrimination on the basis of disability.

Be it enacted by the Senate and House of Representatives of the United States of America in Congress assembled,

SECTION 1. SHORT TITLE; TABLE OF CONTENTS.

(a) SHORT TITLE. This Act may be cited as the "Americans with Disabilities Act of 1990".

(b) TABLE OF CONTENTS. The table of contents is as follows:

SECTION 2. FINDINGS AND PURPOSES.

(a) FINDINGS. The Congress finds that:

(1)   some 43,000,000 Americans have one or more physical or mental disabilities, and this number is increasing as the population as a whole is growing older;

(2)   historically, society has tended to isolate and segregate individuals with disabilities, and, despite some improvements, such forms of discrimination against individuals with disabilities continue to be a serious and pervasive social problem;

(3)   discrimination against individuals with disabilities persists in such critical areas as employment, housing, public accommodations, education, transportation, communication, recreation, institutionalization, health services, voting, and access to public services;

(4)   unlike individuals who have experienced discrimination on the basis of race, color, sex, national origin, religion, or age, individuals who have experienced discrimination on the basis of disability have often had no legal recourse to redress such discrimination;

(5)   individuals with disabilities continually encounter various forms of discrimination, including outright intentional exclusion, the discriminatory effects of architectural, transportation, and communication barriers, overprotective rules and policies, failure to make modifications to existing facilities and practices, exclusionary qualification standards and criteria, segregation, and relegation to lesser services, programs, activities, benefits, jobs, or other opportunities;

(6)   census data, national polls, and other studies have documented that people with disabilities, as a group, occupy an inferior status in our society, and are severely disadvantaged socially, vocationally, economically, and educationally;

(7)   individuals with disabilities are a discrete and insular minority who have been faced with restrictions and limitations, subjected to a history of purposeful unequal treatment, and relegated to a position of political powerlessness in our society, based on characteristics that are beyond the control of such individuals and resulting from stereotypic assumptions not truly indicative of the individual ability of such individuals to participate in, and contribute to, society;

(8)   the Nation's proper goals regarding individuals with disabilities are to assure equality of opportunity, full participation, independent living, and economic self-sufficiency for such individuals; and

(9)   the continuing existence of unfair and unnecessary discrimination and prejudice denies people with disabilities the opportunity to compete on an equal basis and to pursue those opportunities for which our free society is justifiably famous, and costs the United States billions of dollars in unnecessary expenses resulting from dependency and nonproductivity.

(b) PURPOSE. It is the purpose of this Act:

(1)   to provide a clear and comprehensive national mandate for the elimination of discrimination against individuals with disabilities;

(2)   to provide clear, strong, consistent, enforceable standards addressing discrimination against individuals with disabilities;

(3)   to ensure that the Federal Government plays a central role in enforcing the standards established in this Act on behalf of individuals with disabilities; and

(4)   to invoke the sweep of congressional authority, including the power to enforce the fourteenth amendment and to regulate commerce, in order to address the major areas of discrimination faced day-to-day by people with disabilities.

SECTION 3. DEFINITIONS

As used in this Act:

(1)   AUXILIARY AIDS AND SERVICES. The term "auxiliary aids and services" includes

    (A)   qualified interpreters or other effective methods of making aurally delivered materials available to individuals with hearing impairments;

    (B)   qualified readers, taped texts, or other effective methods of making visually delivered materials available to individuals with visual impairments;

    (C)   acquisition or modification of equipment or devices; and

    (D)   other similar services and actions.

(2)   DISABILITY. The term "disability" means, with respect to an individual

    (A)   a physical or mental impairment that substantially limits one or more of the major life activities of such individual;

    (B)   a record of such an impairment; or

    (C)   being regarded as having such an impairment.

(3)   STATE. The term "State" means each of the several States, the District of Columbia, the Commonwealth of Puerto Rico, Guam, American Samoa, the Virgin Islands, the Trust Territory of the Pacific Islands, and the Commonwealth of the Northern Mariana Islands.

TITLE I. EMPLOYMENT

Section 101. DEFINITIONS.

As used in this title:

(1)   COMMISSION. The term "Commission" means the Equal Employment Opportunity Commission established by section 705 of the Civil Rights Act of 1964 (42 U.S.C. 2000e-4).

(2)   COVERED ENTITY. The term "covered entity" means an employer, employment agency, labor organization, or joint labor-management committee.

(3)   DIRECT THREAT. The term "direct threat" means a significant risk to the health or safety of others that cannot be eliminated by reasonable accommodation.

(4)   EMPLOYEE. The term "employee" means an individual employed by an employer.

(5)   EMPLOYER.

    (A)   IN GENERAL. The term "employer" means a person engaged in an industry affecting commerce who has 15 or more employees for each working day in each of 20 or more calendar weeks in the current or preceding calendar year, and any agent of such person, except that, for two years following the effective date of this title, an employer means a person engaged in an industry affecting commerce who has 25 or more employees for each working day in each of 20 or more calendar weeks in the current or preceding year, and any agent of such person.

    (B)   EXCEPTIONS. The term "employer" does not include

        (i)   the United States, a corporation wholly owned by the government of the United States, or an Indian tribe; or

        (ii)   a bona fide private membership club (other than a labor organization) that is exempt from taxation under section 501(c) of the Internal Revenue Code of 1986.

(6)   ILLEGAL USE OF DRUGS.

    (A)   IN GENERAL. The term "illegal use of drugs" means the use of drugs, the possession or distribution of which is unlawful under the Controlled Substances Act (21 U.S.C. 812). Such term does not include the use of a drug taken under supervision by a licensed health care professional, or other uses authorized by the Controlled Substances Act or other provisions of Federal law.

    (B)   DRUGS. The term "drug" means a controlled substance, as defined in schedules I through V of section 202 of the Controlled Substances Act.

(7)   PERSON, ETC. The terms "person", "labor organization", "employment agency", "commerce", and "industry affecting commerce", shall have the same meaning given such terms in section 701 of the Civil Rights Act of 1964 (42 U.S.C. 2000e).

(8)   QUALIFIED INDIVIDUAL WITH A DISABILITY. The term "qualified individual with a disability" means an individual with a disability who, with or without reasonable accommodation, can perform the essential functions of the employment position that such individual holds or desires. For the purposes of this title, consideration shall be given to the employer's judgment as to what functions of a job are essential, and if an employer has prepared a written description before advertising or interviewing applicants for the job, this description shall be considered evidence of the essential functions of the job.

(9)   REASONABLE ACCOMMODATION. The term "reasonable accommodation" may include:

    (A)   making existing facilities used by employees readily accessible to and usable by individuals with disabilities; and

    (B)   job restructuring, part-time or modified work schedules, reassignment to a vacant position, acquisition or modification of equipment or devices, appropriate adjustment or modifications of examinations, training materials or policies, the provision of qualified readers or interpreters, and other similar accommodations for individuals with disabilities.

(10) UNDUE HARDSHIP.

    (A) IN GENERAL. The term "undue hardship" means an action requiring significant difficulty or expense, when considered in light of the factors set forth in subparagraph (B).

    (B) FACTORS TO BE CONSIDERED. In determining whether an accommodation would impose an undue hardship on a covered entity, factors to be considered include:

        (i) the nature and cost of the accommodation needed under this Act;

        (ii) the overall financial resources of the facility or facilities involved in the provision of the reasonable accommodation; the number of persons employed at such facility; the effect on expenses and resources, or the impact otherwise of such accommodation upon the operation of the facility;

        (iii) the overall financial resources of the covered entity; the overall size of the business of a covered entity with respect to the number of its employees; the number, type, and location of its facilities; and

        (iv) the type of operation or operations of the covered entity, including the composition, structure, and functions of the workforce of such entity; the geographic separateness, administrative, or fiscal relationship of the facility or facilities in question to the covered entity.

Section 102. DISCRIMINATION.

(a) GENERAL RULE. No covered entity shall discriminate against a qualified individual with a disability because of the disability of such individual in regard to job application procedures, the hiring, advancement, or discharge of employees, employee compensation, job training, and other terms, conditions, and privileges of employment.

(b) CONSTRUCTION. As used in subsection (a), the term "discriminate" includes:

    (1) limiting, segregating, or classifying a job applicant or employee in a way that adversely affects the opportunities or status of such applicant or employee because of the disability of such applicant or employee;

    (2) participating in a contractual or other arrangement or relationship that has the effect of subjecting a covered entity's qualified applicant or employee with a disability to the discrimination prohibited by this title (such relationship includes a relationship with an employment or referral agency, labor union, an organization providing fringe benefits to an employee of the covered entity, or an organization providing training and apprenticeship programs);

    (3) utilizing standards, criteria, or methods of administration:

        (A) that have the effect of discrimination on the basis of disability; or

        (B) that perpetuate the discrimination of others who are subject to common administrative control;

(4)   excluding or otherwise denying equal jobs or benefits to a qualified individual because of the known disability of an individual with whom the qualified individual is known to have a relationship or association;

(5)   (A)   not making reasonable accommodations to the known physical or mental limitations of an otherwise qualified individual with a disability who is an applicant or employee, unless such covered entity can demonstrate that the accommodation would impose an undue hardship on the operation of the business of such covered entity; or

       (B)   denying employment opportunities to a job applicant or employee who is an otherwise qualified individual with a disability, if such denial is based on the need of such covered entity to make reasonable accommodation to the physical or mental impairments of the employee or applicant;

(6)   using qualification standards, employment tests or other selection criteria that screen out or tend to screen out an individual with a disability or a class of individuals with disabilities unless the standard, test or other selection criteria, as used by the covered entity, is shown to be job-related for the position in question and is consistent with business necessity; and

(7)   failing to select and administer tests concerning employment in the most effective manner to ensure that, when such test is administered to a job applicant or employee who has a disability that impairs sensory, manual, or speaking skills, such test results accurately reflect the skills, aptitude, or whatever other factor of such applicant or employee that such test purports to measure, rather than reflecting the impaired sensory, manual, or speaking skills of such employee or applicant (except where such skills are the factors that the test purports to measure).

(c)   MEDICAL EXAMINATIONS AND INQUIRIES.

       (1)   IN GENERAL. The prohibition against discrimination as referred to in subsection (a) shall include medical examinations and inquiries.

       (2)   PREEMPLOYMENT.

              (A)   PROHIBITED EXAMINATION OR INQUIRY. Except as provided in paragraph (3), a covered entity shall not conduct a medical examination or make inquiries of a job applicant as to whether such applicant is an individual with a disability or as to the nature or severity of such disability.

              (B)   ACCEPTABLE INQUIRY. A covered entity may make preemployment inquiries into the ability of an applicant to perform job-related functions.

       (3)   EMPLOYMENT ENTRANCE EXAMINATION. A covered entity may require a medical examination after an offer of employment has been made to a job applicant and prior to the commencement of the employment duties of such applicant, and may condition an offer of employment on the results of such examination, if:

              (A)   all entering employees are subjected to such an examination regardless of disability;

(B)   information obtained regarding the medical condition or history of the applicant is collected and maintained on separate forms and in separate medical files and is treated as a confidential medical record, except that

    (i)   supervisors and managers may be informed regarding necessary restrictions on the work or duties of the employee and necessary accommodations;

    (ii)   first aid and safety personnel may be informed, when appropriate, if the disability might require emergency treatment; and

    (iii) government officials investigating compliance with this Act shall be provided relevant information on request; and

(C)   the results of such examination are used only in accordance with this title.

(4)   EXAMINATION AND INQUIRY.

(A)   PROHIBITED EXAMINATIONS AND INQUIRIES. A covered entity shall not require a medical examination and shall not make inquiries of an employee as to whether such employee is an individual with a disability or as to the nature or severity of the disability, unless such examination or inquiry is shown to be job-related and consistent with business necessity.

(B)   ACCEPTABLE EXAMINATIONS AND INQUIRIES. A covered entity may conduct voluntary medical examinations, including voluntary medical histories, which are part of an employee health program available to employees at that work site. A covered entity may make inquiries into the ability of an employee to perform job-related functions.

(C)   REQUIREMENT. Information obtained under subparagraph (B) regarding the medical condition or history of any employee are subject to the requirements of subparagraphs (B) and (C) of paragraph (3).

SECTION 103. DEFENSES.

(a)   IN GENERAL. It may be a defense to a charge of discrimination under this Act that an alleged application of qualification standards, tests, or selection criteria that screen out or tend to screen out or otherwise deny a job or benefit to an individual with a disability has been shown to be job-related and consistent with business necessity, and such performance cannot be accomplished by reasonable accommodation, as required under this title.

(b)   QUALIFICATION STANDARDS. The term "qualification standards" may include a requirement that an individual shall not pose a direct threat to the health or safety of other individuals in the workplace.

(c)   RELIGIOUS ENTITIES.

(1)   IN GENERAL. This title shall not prohibit a religious corporation, association, educational institution, or society from giving preference in employment to individuals of a particular religion to perform work connected with the carrying on by such corporation, association, educational institution, or society of its activities.

(2) RELIGIOUS TENETS REQUIREMENT. Under this title, a religious organization may require that all applicants and employees conform to the religious tenets of such organization.

(d) LIST OF INFECTIOUS AND COMMUNICABLE DISEASES.

    (1) IN GENERAL. The Secretary of Health and Human Services, not later than 6 months after the date of enactment of this Act, shall:

        (A) review all infectious and communicable diseases which may be transmitted through handling the food supply;

        (B) publish a list of infectious and communicable diseases which are transmitted through handling the food supply;

        (C) publish the methods by which such diseases are transmitted; and

        (D) widely disseminate such information regarding the list of diseases and their modes of transmissibility to the general public.

    Such list shall be updated annually.

    (2) APPLICATIONS. In any case in which an individual has an infectious or communicable disease that is transmitted to others through the handling of food, that is included on the list developed by the Secretary of Health and Human Services under paragraph (1), and which cannot be eliminated by reasonable accommodation, a covered entity may refuse to assign or continue to assign such individual to a job involving food handling.

    (3) CONSTRUCTION. Nothing in this Act shall be construed to preempt, modify, or amend any State, county, or local law, ordinance, or regulation applicable to food handling which is designed to protect the public health from individuals who pose a significant risk to the health or safety of others, which cannot be eliminated by reasonable accommodation, pursuant to the list of infectious or communicable diseases and the modes of transmissability [sic] published by the Secretary of Health and Human Services.

SECTION 104. ILLEGAL USE OF DRUGS AND ALCOHOL.

(a) QUALIFIED INDIVIDUAL WITH A DISABILITY. For purposes of this title, the term "qualified individual with a disability" shall not include any employee or applicant who is currently engaging in the illegal use of drugs, when the covered entity acts on the basis of such use.

(b) RULES OF CONSTRUCTION. Nothing in subsection (a) shall be construed to exclude as a qualified individual with a disability an individual who:

    (1) has successfully completed a supervised drug rehabilitation program and is no longer engaging in the illegal use of drugs, or has otherwise been rehabilitated successfully and is no longer engaging in such use;

    (2) is participating in a supervised rehabilitation program and is no longer engaging in such use; or

    (3) is erroneously regarded as engaging in such use, but is not engaging in such use;

except that it shall not be a violation of this Act for a covered entity to adopt or administer reasonable policies or procedures, including but not limited to drug testing, designed to ensure that an individual described in paragraph (1) or (2) is no longer engaging in the illegal use of drugs.

(c)   AUTHORITY OF COVERED ENTITY. A covered entity:

(1)   may prohibit the illegal use of drugs and the use of alcohol at the workplace by all employees;

(2)   may require that employees shall not be under the influence of alcohol or be engaging in the illegal use of drugs at the workplace;

(3)   may require that employees behave in conformance with the requirements established under the Drug-Free Workplace Act of 1988 (41 U.S.C. 701 et seq.);

(4)   may hold an employee who engages in the illegal use of drugs or who is an alcoholic to the same qualification standards for employment or job performance and behavior that such entity holds other employees, even if any unsatisfactory performance or behavior is related to the drug use or alcoholism of such employee; and

(5)   may, with respect to Federal regulations regarding alcohol and the illegal use of drugs, require that:

(A)   employees comply with the standards established in such regulations of the Department of Defense, if the employees of the covered entity are employed in an industry subject to such regulations, including complying with regulations (if any) that apply to employment in sensitive positions in such an industry, in the case of employees of the covered entity who are employed in such positions (as defined in the regulations of the Department of Defense);

(B)   employees comply with the standards established in such regulations of the Nuclear Regulatory Commission, if the employees of the covered entity are employed in an industry subject to such regulations, including complying with regulations (if any) that apply to employment in sensitive positions in such an industry, in the case of employees of the covered entity who are employed in such positions (as defined in the regulations of the Nuclear Regulatory Commission); and

(C)   employees comply with the standards established in such regulations of the Department of Transportation, if the employees of the covered entity are employed in a transportation industry subject to such regulations, including complying with such regulations (if any) that apply to employment in sensitive positions in such an industry, in the case of employees of the covered entity who are employed in such positions (as defined in the regulations of the Department of Transportation).

(d)   DRUG TESTING.

(1)   IN GENERAL. For purposes of this title, a test to determine the illegal use of drugs shall not be considered a medical examination.

(2)   CONSTRUCTION. Nothing in this title shall be construed to encourage, prohibit, or authorize the conducting of drug testing for the illegal use of drugs by job applicants or employees or making employment decisions based on such test results.

(e) TRANSPORTATION EMPLOYEES. Nothing in this title shall be construed to encourage, prohibit, restrict, or authorize the otherwise lawful exercise by entities subject to the jurisdiction of the Department of Transportation of authority to:

   (1) test employees of such entities in, and applicants for, positions involving safety-sensitive duties for the illegal use of drugs and for on-duty impairment by alcohol; and

   (2) remove such persons who test positive for illegal use of drugs and on-duty impairment by alcohol pursuant to paragraph (1) from safety-sensitive duties in implementing subsection (c).

SECTION 105. POSTING NOTICES.

Every employer, employment agency, labor organization, or joint labor-management committee covered under this title shall post notices in an accessible format to applicants, employees, and members describing the applicable provisions of this Act, in the manner prescribed by section 711 of the Civil Rights Act of 1964 (42 U.S.C. 2000e-10).

SECTION 106. REGULATIONS.

Not later than 1 year after the date of enactment of this Act, the Commission shall issue regulations in an accessible format to carry out this title in accordance with subchapter II of chapter 5 of title 5, United States Code.

SECTION 107. ENFORCEMENT.

(a) POWERS, REMEDIES, AND PROCEDURES. The powers, remedies, and procedures set forth in sections 705, 706, 707, 709, and 710 of the Civil Rights Act of 1964 (42 U.S.C. 2000e-4, 2000e-5, 2000e-6, 2000e-8, and 2000e-9) shall be the powers, remedies, and procedures this title provides to the Commission, to the Attorney General, or to any person alleging discrimination on the basis of disability in violation of any provision of this Act, or regulations promulgated under section 106, concerning employment.

(b) COORDINATION. The agencies with enforcement authority for actions which allege employment discrimination under this title and under the Rehabilitation Act of 1973 shall develop procedures to ensure that administrative complaints filed under this title and under the Rehabilitation Act of 1973 are dealt with in a manner that avoids duplication of effort and prevents imposition of inconsistent or conflicting standards for the same requirements under this title and the Rehabilitation Act of 1973. The Commission, the Attorney General, and the Office of Federal Contract Compliance Programs shall establish such coordinating mechanisms (similar to provisions contained in the joint regulations promulgated by the Commission and the Attorney General at part 42 of title 28 and part 1691 of title 29, Code of Federal Regulations, and the Memorandum of Understanding between the Commission and the Office of Federal Contract Compliance Programs dated January 16, 1981 (46 Fed. Reg. 7435, January 23, 1981)) in regulations implementing this title and Rehabilitation Act of 1973 not later than 18 months after the date of enactment of this Act.

SECTION 108. EFFECTIVE DATE.

This title shall become effective 24 months after the date of enactment. [July 26, 1992, for employers with 25 or more employees; July 26, 1994, for employers with 15 to 24 employees.]

TITLE II. PUBLIC SERVICES

SUBTITLE A. PROHIBITION AGAINST DISCRIMINATION AND OTHER GENERALLY APPLICABLE PROVISIONS.

SECTION 201. DEFINITIONS.

As used in this title:

    (1)   PUBLIC ENTITY. The term "public entity" means:

        (A)   any State or local government;

        (B)   any department, agency, special purpose district, or other instrumentality of a State or States or local government; and

        (C)   the National Railroad Passenger Corporation, and any commuter authority (as defined in section 103(8) of the Rail Passenger Service Act).

    (2)   QUALIFIED INDIVIDUAL WITH A DISABILITY. The term "qualified individual with a disability" means an individual with a disability who, with or without reasonable modifications to rules, policies, or practices, the removal of architectural, communication, or transportation barriers, or the provision of auxiliary aids and services, meets the essential eligibility requirements for the receipt of services or the participation in programs or activities provided by a public entity.

SECTION 202. DISCRIMINATION.

Subject to the provisions of this title, no qualified individual with a disability shall, by reason of such disability, be excluded from participation in or be denied the benefits of the services, programs, or activities of a public entity, or be subjected to discrimination by any such entity.

SECTION 203. ENFORCEMENT.

The remedies, procedures, and rights set forth in section 505 of the Rehabilitation Act of 1973 (29 U.S.C. 794a) shall be the remedies, procedures, and rights this title provides to any person alleging discrimination on the basis of disability in violation of section 202.

SECTION 204. REGULATIONS.

    (a)   IN GENERAL. Not later than 1 year after the date of enactment of this Act, the Attorney General shall promulgate regulations in an accessible format that implement this subtitle. Such regulations shall not include any matter within the scope of the authority of the Secretary of Transportation under section 223, 229, or 244.

    (b)   RELATIONSHIP TO OTHER REGULATIONS. Except for "program accessibility, existing facilities", and "communications", regulations under subsection (a) shall be consistent with this Act and with the coordination regulations under part 41 of title 28, Code of Federal Regulations (as promulgated by the Department of Health, Education, and Welfare on January 13, 1978), applicable to recipients of Federal financial assistance under section 504 of the Rehabilitation Act of 1973 (29 U.S.C. 794). With respect to "program accessibility, existing facilities", and "communications", such regulations shall be consistent with regulations and analysis as in part 39 of title 28 of the Code of Federal Regulations, applicable to federally conducted activities under such section 504.

(c)   STANDARDS. Regulations under subsection (a) shall include standards applicable to facilities and vehicles covered by this subtitle, other than facilities, stations, rail passenger cars, and vehicles covered by subtitle B. Such standards shall be consistent with the minimum guidelines and requirements issued by the Architectural and Transportation Barriers Compliance Board in accordance with section 504(a) of this Act.

SECTION 205. EFFECTIVE DATE.

(a)   GENERAL RULE. Except as provided in subsection (b), this subtitle shall become effective 18 months after the date of enactment of this Act.

(b)   EXCEPTION. Section 204 shall become effective on the date of enactment of this Act.

SUBTITLE B. ACTIONS APPLICABLE TO PUBLIC TRANSPORTATION PROVIDED BY PUBLIC ENTITIES CONSIDERED DISCRIMINATORY.

PART 1. PUBLIC TRANSPORTATION OTHER THAN BY AIRCRAFT OR CERTAIN RAIL OPERATIONS.

SECTION 221. DEFINITIONS.

As used in this part:

(1)   DEMAND RESPONSIVE SYSTEM. The term "demand responsive system" means any system of providing designated public transportation which is not a fixed route system.

(2)   DESIGNATED PUBLIC TRANSPORTATION. The term "designated public transportation" means transportation (other than public school transportation) by bus, rail, or any other conveyance (other than transportation by aircraft or intercity or commuter rail transportation (as defined in section 241)) that provides the general public with general or special service (including charter service) on a regular and continuing basis.

(3)   FIXED ROUTE SYSTEM. The term "fixed route system" means a system of providing designated public transportation on which a vehicle is operated along a prescribed route according to a fixed schedule.

(4)   OPERATES. The term "operates", as used with respect to a fixed route system or demand responsive system, includes operation of such system by a person under a contractual or other arrangement or relationship with a public entity.

(5)   PUBLIC SCHOOL TRANSPORTATION. The term "public school transportation" means transportation by schoolbus vehicles of schoolchildren, personnel, and equipment to and from a public elementary or secondary school and school-related activities.

(6)   SECRETARY. The term "Secretary" means the Secretary of Transportation.

SECTION 222. PUBLIC ENTITIES OPERATING FIXED ROUTE SYSTEMS.

(a) PURCHASE AND LEASE OF NEW VEHICLES. It shall be considered discrimination for purposes of section 202 of this Act and section 504 of the Rehabilitation Act of 1973 (29 U.S.C. 794) for a public entity which operates a fixed route system to purchase or lease a new bus, a new rapid rail vehicle, a new light rail vehicle, or any other new vehicle to be used on such system, if the solicitation for such purchase or lease is made after the 30th day following the effective date of this subsection and if such bus, rail vehicle, or other vehicle is not readily accessible to and usable by individuals with disabilities, including individuals who use wheelchairs.

(b) PURCHASE AND LEASE OF USED VEHICLES. Subject to subsection (c)(1), it shall be considered discrimination for purposes of section 202 of this Act and section 504 of the Rehabilitation Act of 1973 (29 U.S.C. 794) for a public entity which operates a fixed route system to purchase or lease, after the 30th day following the effective date of this subsection, a used vehicle for use on such system unless such entity makes demonstrated good faith efforts to purchase or lease a used vehicle for use on such system that is readily accessible to and usable by individuals with disabilities, including individuals who use wheelchairs.

(c) REMANUFACTURED VEHICLES.

    (1) GENERAL RULE. Except as provided in paragraph (2), it shall be considered discrimination for purposes of section 202 of this Act and section 504 of the Rehabilitation Act of 1973 (29 U.S.C. 794) for a public entity which operates a fixed route system:

        (A) to remanufacture a vehicle for use on such system so as to extend its usable life for 5 years or more, which remanufacture begins (or for which the solicitation is made) after the 30th day following the effective date of this subsection; or

        (B) to purchase or lease for use on such system a remanufactured vehicle which has been remanufactured so as to extend its usable life for 5 years or more, which purchase or lease occurs after such 30th day and during the period in which the usable life is extended;

    unless, after remanufacture, the vehicle is, to the maximum extent feasible, readily accessible to and usable by individuals with disabilities, including individuals who use wheelchairs.

    (2) EXCEPTION FOR HISTORIC VEHICLES.

        (A) GENERAL RULE. If a public entity operates a fixed route system any segment of which is included on the National Register of Historic Places and if making a vehicle of historic character to be used solely on such segment readily accessible to and usable by individuals with disabilities would significantly alter the historic character of such vehicle, the public entity only has to make (or to purchase or lease a remanufactured vehicle with) those modifications which are necessary to meet the requirements of paragraph (1) and which do not significantly alter the historic character of such vehicle.

        (B) VEHICLES OF HISTORIC CHARACTER DEFINED BY REGULATIONS. For purposes of this paragraph and section 228(b), a vehicle of historic character shall be defined by the regulations issued by the Secretary to carry out this subsection.

SECTION 223. PARATRANSIT AS A COMPLEMENT TO FIXED ROUTE SERVICE.

(a)   GENERAL RULE. It shall be considered discrimination for purposes of section 202 of this Act and section 504 of the Rehabilitation Act of 1973 (29 U.S.C. 794) for a public entity which operates a fixed route system (other than a system which provides solely commuter bus service) to fail to provide with respect to the operations of its fixed route system, in accordance with this section, paratransit and other special transportation services to individuals with disabilities, including individuals who use wheelchairs, that are sufficient to provide to such individuals a level of service

      (1)   which is comparable to the level of designated public transportation services provided to individuals without disabilities using such system; or

      (2)   in the case of response time, which is comparable, to the extent practicable, to the level of designated public transportation services provided to individuals without disabilities using such system.

(b)   ISSUANCE OF REGULATIONS. Not later than 1 year after the effective date of this subsection, the Secretary shall issue final regulations to carry out this section.

(c)   REQUIRED CONTENTS OF REGULATIONS.

      (1)   ELIGIBLE RECIPIENTS OF SERVICE. The regulations issued under this section shall require each public entity which operates a fixed route system to provide the paratransit and other special transportation services required under this section:

            (A)   (i)   to any individual with a disability who is unable, as a result of a physical or mental impairment (including a vision impairment) and without the assistance of another individual (except an operator of a wheelchair lift or other boarding assistance device), to board, ride, or disembark from any vehicle on the system which is readily accessible to and usable by individuals with disabilities;

                  (ii)   to any individual with a disability who needs the assistance of a wheelchair lift or other boarding assistance device (and is able with such assistance) to board, ride, and disembark from any vehicle which is readily accessible to and usable by individuals with disabilities if the individual wants to travel on a route on the system during the hours of operation of the system at a time (or within a reasonable period of such time) when such a vehicle is not being used to provide designated public transportation on the route; and

                  (iii)   to any individual with a disability who has a specific impairment-related condition which prevents such individual from traveling to a boarding location or from a disembarking location on such system;

            (B)   to one other individual accompanying the individual with the disability; and

            (C)   to other individuals, in addition to the one individual described in subparagraph (B), accompanying the individual with a disability provided that space for these additional individuals is available on the paratransit vehicle carrying the individual with a disability and that the transportation of such additional individuals will not result in a denial of service to individuals with disabilities.

For purposes of clauses (i) and (ii) of subparagraph (A), boarding or disembarking from a vehicle does not include travel to the boarding location or from the disembarking location.

(2)   SERVICE AREA. The regulations issued under this section shall require the provision of paratransit and special transportation services required under this section in the service area of each public entity which operates a fixed route system, other than any portion of the service area in which the public entity solely provides commuter bus service.

(3)   SERVICE CRITERIA. Subject to paragraphs (1) and (2), the regulations issued under this section shall establish minimum service criteria for determining the level of services to be required under this section.

(4)   UNDUE FINANCIAL BURDEN LIMITATION. The regulations issued under this section shall provide that, if the public entity is able to demonstrate to the satisfaction of the Secretary that the provision of paratransit and other special transportation services otherwise required under this section would impose an undue financial burden on the public entity, the public entity, notwithstanding any other provision of this section (other than paragraph (5)), shall only be required to provide such services to the extent that providing such services would not impose such a burden.

(5)   ADDITIONAL SERVICES. The regulations issued under this section shall establish circumstances under which the Secretary may require a public entity to provide, notwithstanding paragraph (4), paratransit and other special transportation services under this section beyond the level of paratransit and other special transportation services which would otherwise be required under paragraph (4).

(6)   PUBLIC PARTICIPATION. The regulations issued under this section shall require that each public entity which operates a fixed route system hold a public hearing, provide an opportunity for public comment, and consult with individuals with disabilities in preparing its plan under paragraph (7).

(7)   PLANS. The regulations issued under this section shall require that each public entity which operates a fixed route system:

  (A)   within 18 months after the effective date of this subsection, submit to the Secretary, and commence implementation of, a plan for providing paratransit and other special transportation services which meets the requirements of this section; and

  (B)   on an annual basis thereafter, submit to the Secretary, and commence implementation of, a plan for providing such services.

(8)   PROVISION OF SERVICES BY OTHERS. The regulations issued under this section shall:

  (A)   require that a public entity submitting a plan to the Secretary under this section identify in the plan any person or other public entity which is providing a paratransit or other special transportation service for individuals with disabilities in the service area to which the plan applies; and

  (B)   provide that the public entity submitting the plan does not have to provide under the plan such service for individuals with disabilities.

(9)   OTHER PROVISIONS. The regulations issued under this section shall include such other provisions and requirements as the Secretary determines are necessary to carry out the objectives of this section.

(d)   REVIEW OF PLAN.

(1)   GENERAL RULE. The Secretary shall review a plan submitted under this section for the purpose of determining whether or not such plan meets the requirements of this section, including the regulations issued under this section.

(2)   DISAPPROVAL. If the Secretary determines that a plan reviewed under this subsection fails to meet the requirements of this section, the Secretary shall disapprove the plan and notify the public entity which submitted the plan of such disapproval and the reasons therefor.

(3)   MODIFICATION OF DISAPPROVED PLAN. Not later than 90 days after the date of disapproval of a plan under this subsection, the public entity which submitted the plan shall modify the plan to meet the requirements of this section and shall submit to the Secretary, and commence implementation of, such modified plan.

(e)   DISCRIMINATION DEFINED. As used in subsection (a), the term "discrimination" includes:

(1)   a failure of a public entity to which the regulations issued under this section apply to submit, or commence implementation of, a plan in accordance with subsections (c)(6) and (c)(7);

(2)   a failure of such entity to submit, or commence implementation of, a modified plan in accordance with subsection (d)(3);

(3)   submission to the Secretary of a modified plan under subsection (d)(3) which does not meet the requirements of this section; or

(4)   a failure of such entity to provide paratransit or other special transportation services in accordance with the plan or modified plan the public entity submitted to the Secretary under this section.

(f)   STATUTORY CONSTRUCTION.   Nothing in this section shall be construed as preventing a public entity:

(1)   from providing paratransit or other special transportation services at a level which is greater than the level of such services which are required by this section,

(2)   from providing paratransit or other special transportation services in addition to those paratransit and special transportation services required by this section, or

(3)   from providing such services to individuals in addition to those individuals to whom such services are required to be provided by this section.

SECTION 224. PUBLIC ENTITY OPERATING A DEMAND RESPONSIVE SYSTEM.

If a public entity operates a demand responsive system, it shall be considered discrimination, for purposes of section 202 of this Act and section 504 of the Rehabilitation Act of 1973 (29 U.S.C. 794), for such entity to purchase or lease a new vehicle for use on such system, for which a solicitation is made after the 30th day following the effective date of this section, that is not readily accessible to and usable by individuals with disabilities, including individuals who use wheelchairs, unless such system, when viewed in its entirety, provides a level of service to such individuals equivalent to the level of service such system provides to individuals without disabilities.

SECTION 225. TEMPORARY RELIEF WHERE LIFTS ARE UNAVAILABLE.

(a) GRANTING. With respect to the purchase of new buses, a public entity may apply for, and the Secretary may temporarily relieve such public entity from the obligation under section 222(a) or 224 to purchase new buses that are readily accessible to and usable by individuals with disabilities if such public entity demonstrates to the satisfaction of the Secretary:

    (1) that the initial solicitation for new buses made by the public entity specified that all new buses were to be lift-equipped and were to be otherwise accessible to and usable by individuals with disabilities;

    (2) the unavailability from any qualified manufacturer of hydraulic, electromechanical, or other lifts for such new buses;

    (3) that the public entity seeking temporary relief has made good faith efforts to locate a qualified manufacturer to supply the lifts to the manufacturer of such buses in sufficient time to comply with such solicitation; and

    (4) that any further delay in purchasing new buses necessary to obtain such lifts would significantly impair transportation services in the community served by the public entity.

(b) DURATION AND NOTICE TO CONGRESS. Any relief granted under subsection (a) shall be limited in duration by a specified date, and the appropriate committees of Congress shall be notified of any such relief granted.

(c) FRAUDULENT APPLICATION. If, at any time, the Secretary has reasonable cause to believe that any relief granted under subsection (a) was fraudulently applied for, the Secretary shall:

    (1) cancel such relief if such relief is still in effect; and

    (2) take such other action as the Secretary considers appropriate.

SECTION 226. NEW FACILITIES.

For purposes of section 202 of this Act and section 504 of the Rehabilitation Act of 1973 (29 U.S.C. 794), it shall be considered discrimination for a public entity to construct a new facility to be used in the provision of designated public transportation services unless such facility is readily accessible to and usable by individuals with disabilities, including individuals who use wheelchairs.

SECTION 227. ALTERATIONS OF EXISTING FACILITIES.

(a) GENERAL RULE. With respect to alterations of an existing facility or part thereof used in the provision of designated public transportation services that affect or could affect the usability of the facility or part thereof, it shall be considered discrimination, for purposes of section 202 of this Act and section 504 of the Rehabilitation Act of 1973 (29 U.S.C. 794), for a public entity to fail to make such alterations (or to ensure that the alterations are made) in such a manner that, to the maximum extent feasible, the altered portions of the facility are readily accessible to and usable by individuals with disabilities, including individuals who use wheelchairs, upon the completion of such alterations. Where the public entity is undertaking an alteration that affects or could affect usability of or access to an area of the facility containing a primary function, the entity shall also make the alterations in such a manner that, to the maximum extent feasible, the path of travel to the altered area and the bathrooms, telephones, and drinking fountains serving the altered area, are readily accessible to and usable by individuals with disabilities, including individuals who use wheelchairs, upon completion of such alterations, where such alterations to the path of travel or the bathrooms, telephones, and drinking fountains serving the altered area are not disproportionate to the overall alterations in terms of cost and scope (as determined under criteria established by the Attorney General).

(b)   SPECIAL RULE FOR STATIONS.

(1)   GENERAL RULE. For purposes of section 202 of this Act and section 504 of the Rehabilitation Act of 1973 (29 U.S.C. 794), it shall be considered discrimination for a public entity that provides designated public transportation to fail, in accordance with the provisions of this subsection, to make key stations (as determined under criteria established by the Secretary by regulation) in rapid rail and light rail systems readily accessible to and usable by individuals with disabilities, including individuals who use wheelchairs.

(2)   RAPID RAIL AND LIGHT RAIL KEY STATIONS.

(A)   ACCESSIBILITY. Except as otherwise provided in this paragraph, all key stations (as determined under criteria established by the Secretary by regulation) in rapid rail and light rail systems shall be made readily accessible to and usable by individuals with disabilities, including individuals who use wheelchairs, as soon as practicable but in no event later than the last day of the 3-year period beginning on the effective date of this paragraph.

(B)   EXTENSION FOR EXTRAORDINARILY EXPENSIVE STRUCTURAL CHANGES.   The Secretary may extend the 3-year period under subparagraph (A) up to a 30-year period for key stations in a rapid rail or light rail system which stations need extraordinarily expensive structural changes to, or replacement of, existing facilities; except that by the last day of the 20th year following the date of the enactment of this Act at least 2/3 of such key stations must be readily accessible to and usable by individuals with disabilities.

(3)   PLANS AND MILESTONES. The Secretary shall require the appropriate public entity to develop and submit to the Secretary a plan for compliance with this subsection:

(A)   that reflects consultation with individuals with disabilities affected by such plan and the results of a public hearing and public comments on such plan, and

(B)   that establishes milestones for achievement of the requirements of this subsection.

SECTION 228. PUBLIC TRANSPORTATION PROGRAMS AND ACTIVITIES IN EXISTING FACILITIES AND ONE CAR PER TRAIN RULE.

(a) PUBLIC TRANSPORTATION PROGRAMS AND ACTIVITIES IN EXISTING FACILITIES.

    (1) IN GENERAL. With respect to existing facilities used in the provision of designated public transportation services, it shall be considered discrimination, for purposes of section 202 of this Act and section 504 of the Rehabilitation Act of 1973 (29 U.S.C. 794), for a public entity to fail to operate a designated public transportation program or activity conducted in such facilities so that, when viewed in the entirety, the program or activity is readily accessible to and usable by individuals with disabilities.

    (2) EXCEPTION. Paragraph (1) shall not require a public entity to make structural changes to existing facilities in order to make such facilities accessible to individuals who use wheelchairs, unless and to the extent required by section 227(a) (relating to alterations) or section 227(b) (relating to key stations).

    (3) UTILIZATION. Paragraph (1) shall not require a public entity to which paragraph (2) applies, to provide to individuals who use wheelchairs services made available to the general public at such facilities when such individuals could not utilize or benefit from such services provided at such facilities.

(b) ONE CAR PER TRAIN RULE.

    (1) GENERAL RULE. Subject to paragraph (2), with respect to 2 or more vehicles operated as a train by a light or rapid rail system, for purposes of section 202 of this Act and section 504 of the Rehabilitation Act of 1973 (29 U.S.C. 794), it shall be considered discrimination for a public entity to fail to have at least 1 vehicle per train that is accessible to individuals with disabilities, including individuals who use wheelchairs, as soon as practicable but in no event later than the last day of the 5-year period beginning on the effective date of this section.

    (2) HISTORIC TRAINS. In order to comply with paragraph (1) with respect to the remanufacture of a vehicle of historic character which is to be used on a segment of a light or rapid rail system which is included on the National Register of Historic Places, if making such vehicle readily accessible to and usable by individuals with disabilities would significantly alter the historic character of such vehicle, the public entity which operates such system only has to make (or to purchase or lease a remanufactured vehicle with) those modifications which are necessary to meet the requirements of section 222(c)(1) and which do not significantly alter the historic character of such vehicle.

SECTION 229. REGULATIONS.

(a) IN GENERAL. Not later than 1 year after the date of enactment of this Act, the Secretary of Transportation shall issue regulations, in an accessible format, necessary for carrying out this part (other than section 223).

(b) STANDARDS. The regulations issued under this section and section 223 shall include standards applicable to facilities and vehicles covered by this subtitle. The standards shall be consistent with the minimum guidelines and requirements issued by the Architectural and Transportation Barriers Compliance Board in accordance with section 504 of this Act.

SECTION 230. INTERIM ACCESSIBILITY REQUIREMENTS.

If final regulations have not been issued pursuant to section 229, for new construction or alterations for which a valid and appropriate State or local building permit is obtained prior to the issuance of final regulations under such section, and for which the construction or alteration authorized by such permit begins within one year of the receipt of such permit and is completed under the terms of such permit, compliance with the Uniform Federal Accessibility Standards in effect at the time the building permit is issued shall suffice to satisfy the requirement that facilities be readily accessible to and usable by persons with disabilities as required under sections 226 and 227, except that, if such final regulations have not been issued one year after the Architectural and Transportation Barriers Compliance Board has issued the supplemental minimum guidelines required under section 504(a) of this Act, compliance with such supplemental minimum guidelines shall be necessary to satisfy the requirement that facilities be readily accessible to and usable by persons with disabilities prior to issuance of the final regulations.

SECTION 231. EFFECTIVE DATE.

(a)   GENERAL RULE. Except as provided in subsection (b), this part shall become effective 18 months after the date of enactment of this Act.

(b)   EXCEPTION. Sections 222, 223 (other than subsection (a)), 224, 225, 227(b), 228(b), and 229 shall become effective on the date of enactment of this Act.

PART II. PUBLIC TRANSPORTATION BY INTERCITY AND COMMUTER RAIL.

SECTION 241. DEFINITIONS.

As used in this part:

(1)   COMMUTER AUTHORITY. The term "commuter authority" has the meaning given such term in section 103(8) of the Rail Passenger Service Act (45 U.S.C. 502(8)).

(2)   COMMUTER RAIL TRANSPORTATION. The term "commuter rail transportation" has the meaning given the term "commuter service" in section 103(9) of the Rail Passenger Service Act (45 U.S.C. 502(9)).

(3)   INTERCITY RAIL TRANSPORTATION. The term "intercity rail transportation" means transportation provided by the National Railroad Passenger Corporation.

(4)   RAIL PASSENGER CAR. The term "rail passenger car" means, with respect to intercity rail transportation, single-level and bi-level coach cars, single-level and bi-level dining cars, single-level and bi-level sleeping cars, single-level and bi-level lounge cars, and food service cars.

(5)   RESPONSIBLE PERSON. The term "responsible person" means:

(A)   in the case of a station more than 50 percent of which is owned by a public entity, such public entity;

(B)   in the case of a station more than 50 percent of which is owned by a private party, the persons providing intercity or commuter rail transportation to such station, as allocated on an equitable basis by regulation by the Secretary of Transportation; and

(C)   in a case where no party owns more than 50 percent of a station, the persons providing intercity or commuter rail transportation to such station and the owners of the station, other than private party owners, as allocated on an equitable basis by regulation by the Secretary of Transportation.

(6)   STATION.   The term "station" means the portion of a property located appurtenant to a right-of-way on which intercity or commuter rail transportation is operated, where such portion is used by the general public and is related to the provision of such transportation, including passenger platforms, designated waiting areas, ticketing areas, restrooms, and, where a public entity providing rail transportation owns the property, concession areas, to the extent that such public entity exercises control over the selection, design, construction, or alteration of the property, but such term does not include flag stops.

SECTION 242. INTERCITY AND COMMUTER RAIL ACTIONS CONSIDERED DISCRIMINATORY.

(a)   INTERCITY RAIL TRANSPORTATION.

(1)   ONE CAR PER TRAIN RULE.   It shall be considered discrimination for purposes of section 202 of this Act and section 504 of the Rehabilitation Act of 1973 (29 U.S.C. 794) for a person who provides intercity rail transportation to fail to have at least one passenger car per train that is readily accessible to and usable by individuals with disabilities, including individuals who use wheelchairs, in accordance with regulations issued under section 244, as soon as practicable, but in no event later than 5 years after the date of enactment of this Act.

(2)   NEW INTERCITY CARS.

(A)   GENERAL RULE.   Except as otherwise provided in this subsection with respect to individuals who use wheelchairs, it shall be considered discrimination for purposes of section 202 of this Act and section 504 of the Rehabilitation Act of 1973 (29 U.S.C. 794) for a person to purchase or lease any new rail passenger cars for use in intercity rail transportation, and for which a solicitation is made later than 30 days after the effective date of this section, unless all such rail cars are readily accessible to and usable by individuals with disabilities, including individuals who use wheelchairs, as prescribed by the Secretary of Transportation in regulations issued under section 244.

(B)   SPECIAL RULE FOR SINGLE-LEVEL PASSENGER COACHES FOR INDIVIDUALS WHO USE WHEELCHAIRS.   Single-level passenger coaches shall be required to:

(i)   be able to be entered by an individual who uses a wheelchair;
(ii)   have space to park and secure a wheelchair;
(iii)   have a seat to which a passenger in a wheelchair can transfer, and a space to fold and store such passenger's wheelchair; and
(iv)   have a restroom usable by an individual who uses a wheelchair,

only to the extent provided in paragraph (3).

(C)   SPECIAL RULE FOR SINGLE-LEVEL DINING CARS FOR INDIVID-UALS WHO USE WHEELCHAIRS. Single-level dining cars shall not be required to:

   (i)   be able to be entered from the station platform by an individu-al who uses a wheelchair; or

   (ii) have a restroom usable by an individual who uses a wheelchair if no restroom is provided in such car for any passenger.

(D)   SPECIAL RULE FOR BI-LEVEL DINING CARS FOR INDIVIDUALS WHO USE WHEELCHAIRS. Bi-level dining cars shall not be required to:

   (i)   be able to be entered by an individual who uses a wheelchair;

   (ii) have space to park and secure a wheelchair;

   (iii) have a seat to which a passenger in a wheelchair can transfer, or a space to fold and store such passenger's wheelchair; or

   (iv) have a restroom usable by an individual who uses a wheel-chair.

(3)   ACCESSIBILITY OF SINGLE-LEVEL COACHES.

(A)   GENERAL RULE. It shall be considered discrimination for purposes of section 202 of this Act and section 504 of the Rehabilitation Act of 1973 (29 U.S.C. 794) for a person who provides intercity rail transporta-tion to fail to have on each train which includes one or more single-level rail passenger coaches:

   (i)   a number of spaces
      (I)   to park and secure wheelchairs (to accommodate individuals who wish to remain in their wheelchairs) equal to not less than one-half of the number of single-level rail passenger coaches in such train; and
      (II) to fold and store wheelchairs (to accommodate individu-als who wish to transfer to coach seats) equal to not less than one-half of the number of single-level rail passenger coaches in such train,
   as soon as practicable, but in no event later than 5 years after the date of enactment of this Act; and

   (ii) a number of spaces
      (I)   to park and secure wheelchairs (to accommodate individuals who wish to remain in their wheelchairs) equal to not less than the total number of single-level rail passenger coaches in such train; and
      (II) to fold and store wheelchairs (to accommodate individu-als who wish to transfer to coach seats) equal to not less than the total number of single-level rail passenger coaches in such train,
   as soon as practicable, but in no event later than 10 years after the date of enactment of this Act.

(B)   LOCATION. Spaces required by subparagraph (A) shall be located in single-level rail passenger coaches or food service cars.

(C)   LIMITATION.   Of the number of spaces required on a train by subparagraph (A), not more than two spaces to park and secure wheelchairs nor more than two spaces to fold and store wheelchairs shall be located in any one coach or food service car.

(D)   OTHER ACCESSIBILITY FEATURES. Single-level rail passenger coaches and food service cars on which the spaces required by subparagraph (A) are located shall have a restroom usable by an individual who uses a wheelchair and shall be able to be entered from the station platform by an individual who uses a wheelchair.

(4)   FOOD SERVICE.

(A)   SINGLE-LEVEL DINING CARS. On any train in which a single-level dining car is used to provide food service:

(i)   if such single-level dining car was purchased after the date of enactment of this Act, table service in such car shall be provided to a passenger who uses a wheelchair if
(I)   the car adjacent to the end of the dining car through which a wheelchair may enter is itself accessible to a wheelchair;
(II)   such passenger can exit to the platform from the car such passenger occupies, move down the platform, and enter the adjacent accessible car described in subclause (I) without the necessity of the train being moved within the station; and
(III)   space to park and secure a wheelchair is available in the dining car at the time such passenger wishes to eat (if such passenger wishes to remain in a wheelchair), or space to store and fold a wheelchair is available in the dining car at the time such passenger wishes to eat (if such passenger wishes to transfer to a dining car seat); and

(ii)   appropriate auxiliary aids and services, including a hard surface on which to eat, shall be provided to ensure that other equivalent food service is available to individuals with disabilities, including individuals who use wheelchairs, and to passengers traveling with such individuals.

Unless not practicable, a person providing intercity rail transportation shall place an accessible car adjacent to the end of a dining car described in clause (i) through which an individual who uses a wheelchair may enter.

(B)   BI-LEVEL DINING CARS. On any train in which a bi-level dining car is used to provide food service:

(i)   if such train includes a bi-level lounge car purchased after the date of enactment of this Act, table service in such lounge car shall be provided to individuals who use wheelchairs and to other passengers; and
(ii)   appropriate auxiliary aids and services, including a hard surface on which to eat, shall be provided to ensure that other equivalent food service is available to individuals with disabilities, including individuals who use wheelchairs, and to passengers traveling with such individuals.

(b)   COMMUTER RAIL TRANSPORTATION.

(1)   ONE CAR PER TRAIN RULE. It shall be considered discrimination for purposes of section 202 of this Act and section 504 of the Rehabilitation Act of 1973 (29 U.S.C. 794) for a person who provides commuter rail transportation

to fail to have at least one passenger car per train that is readily accessible to and usable by individuals with disabilities, including individuals who use wheelchairs, in accordance with regulations issued under section 244, as soon as practicable, but in no event later than 5 years after the date of enactment of this Act.

(2) NEW COMMUTER RAIL CARS.

(A) GENERAL RULE. It shall be considered discrimination for purposes of section 202 of this Act and section 504 of the Rehabilitation Act of 1973 (29 U.S.C. 794) for a person to purchase or lease any new rail passenger cars for use in commuter rail transportation, and for which a solicitation is made later than 30 days after the effective date of this section, unless all such rail cars are readily accessible to and usable by individuals with disabilities, including individuals who use wheelchairs, as prescribed by the Secretary of Transportation in regulations issued under section 244.

(B) ACCESSIBILITY. For purposes of section 202 of this Act and section 504 of the Rehabilitation Act of 1973 (29 U.S.C. 794), a requirement that a rail passenger car used in commuter rail transportation be accessible to or readily accessible to and usable by individuals with disabilities, including individuals who use wheelchairs, shall not be construed to require:

(i) a restroom usable by an individual who uses a wheelchair if no restroom is provided in such car for any passenger;

(ii) space to fold and store a wheelchair; or

(iii) a seat to which a passenger who uses a wheelchair can transfer.

(c) USED RAIL CARS. It shall be considered discrimination for purposes of section 202 of this Act and section 504 of the Rehabilitation Act of 1973 (29 U.S.C. 794) for a person to purchase or lease a used rail passenger car for use in intercity or commuter rail transportation, unless such person makes demonstrated good faith efforts to purchase or lease a used rail car that is readily accessible to and usable by individuals with disabilities, including individuals who use wheelchairs, as prescribed by the Secretary of Transportation in regulations issued under section 244.

(d) REMANUFACTURED RAIL CARS.

(1) REMANUFACTURING. It shall be considered discrimination for purposes of section 202 of this Act and section 504 of the Rehabilitation Act of 1973 (29 U.S.C. 794) for a person to remanufacture a rail passenger car for use in intercity or commuter rail transportation so as to extend its usable life for 10 years or more, unless the rail car, to the maximum extent feasible, is made readily accessible to and usable by individuals with disabilities, including individuals who use wheelchairs, as prescribed by the Secretary of Transportation in regulations issued under section 244.

(2) PURCHASE OR LEASE. It shall be considered discrimination for purposes of section 202 of this Act and section 504 of the Rehabilitation Act of 1973 (29 U.S.C. 794) for a person to purchase or lease a remanufactured rail passenger car for use in intercity or commuter rail transportation unless such car was remanufactured in accordance with paragraph (1).

(e)   STATIONS.

(1)   NEW STATIONS. It shall be considered discrimination for purposes of section 202 of this Act and section 504 of the Rehabilitation Act of 1973 (29 U.S.C. 794) for a person to build a new station for use in intercity or commuter rail transportation that is not readily accessible to and usable by individuals with disabilities, including individuals who use wheelchairs, as prescribed by the Secretary of Transportation in regulations issued under section 244.

(2)   EXISTING STATIONS.

(A)   FAILURE TO MAKE READILY ACCESSIBLE.

(i)   GENERAL RULE. It shall be considered discrimination for purposes of section 202 of this Act and section 504 of the Rehabilitation Act of 1973 (29 U.S.C. 794) for a responsible person to fail to make existing stations in the intercity rail transportation system, and existing key stations in commuter rail transportation systems, readily accessible to and usable by individuals with disabilities, including individuals who use wheelchairs, as prescribed by the Secretary of Transportation in regulations issued under section 244.

(ii)   PERIOD FOR COMPLIANCE.

(I)   INTERCITY RAIL. All stations in the intercity rail transportation system shall be made readily accessible to and usable by individuals with disabilities, including individuals who use wheelchairs, as soon as practicable, but in no event later than 20 years after the date of enactment of this Act.

(II)   COMMUTER RAIL. Key stations in commuter rail transportation systems shall be made readily accessible to and usable by individuals with disabilities, including individuals who use wheelchairs, as soon as practicable but in no event later than 3 years after the date of enactment of this Act, except that the time limit may be extended by the Secretary of Transportation up to 20 years after the date of enactment of this Act in a case where the raising of the entire passenger platform is the only means available of attaining accessibility or where other extraordinarily expensive structural changes are necessary to attain accessibility.

(iii)   DESIGNATION OF KEY STATIONS. Each commuter authority shall designate the key stations in its commuter rail transportation system, in consultation with individuals with disabilities and organizations representing such individuals, taking into consideration such factors as high ridership and whether such station serves as a transfer or feeder station. Before the final designation of key stations under this clause, a commuter authority shall hold a public hearing.

(iv)   PLANS AND MILESTONES. The Secretary of Transportation shall require the appropriate person to develop a plan for carrying out this subparagraph that reflects consultation with individuals with disabilities affected by such plan and that establishes milestones for achievement of the requirements of this subparagraph.

(B) REQUIREMENT WHEN MAKING ALTERATIONS.

(i) GENERAL RULE. It shall be considered discrimination, for purposes of section 202 of this Act and section 504 of the Rehabilitation Act of 1973 (29 U.S.C. 794), with respect to alterations of an existing station or part thereof in the intercity or commuter rail transportation systems that affect or could affect the usability of the station or part thereof, for the responsible person, owner, or person in control of the station to fail to make the alterations in such a manner that, to the maximum extent feasible, the altered portions of the station are readily accessible to and usable by individuals with disabilities, including individuals who use wheelchairs, upon completion of such alterations.

(ii) ALTERATIONS TO A PRIMARY FUNCTION AREA. It shall be considered discrimination, for purposes of section 202 of this Act and section 504 of the Rehabilitation Act of 1973 (29 U.S.C. 794), with respect to alterations that affect or could affect the usability of or access to an area of the station containing a primary function, for the responsible person, owner, or person in control of the station to fail to make the alterations in such a manner that, to the maximum extent feasible, the path of travel to the altered area, and the bathrooms, telephones, and drinking fountains serving the altered area, are readily accessible to and usable by individuals with disabilities, including individuals who use wheelchairs, upon completion of such alterations, where such alterations to the path of travel or the bathrooms, telephones, and drinking fountains serving the altered area are not disproportionate to the overall alterations in terms of cost and scope (as determined under criteria established by the Attorney General).

(C) REQUIRED COOPERATION. It shall be considered discrimination for purposes of section 202 of this Act and section 504 of the Rehabilitation Act of 1973 (29 U.S.C. 794) for an owner, or person in control, of a station governed by subparagraph (A) or (B) to fail to provide reasonable cooperation to a responsible person with respect to such station in that responsible person's efforts to comply with such subparagraph. An owner, or person in control, of a station shall be liable to a responsible person for any failure to provide reasonable cooperation as required by this subparagraph. Failure to receive reasonable cooperation required by this subparagraph shall not be a defense to a claim of discrimination under this Act.

SECTION 243. CONFORMANCE OF ACCESSIBILITY STANDARDS.

Accessibility standards included in regulations issued under this part shall be consistent with the minimum guidelines issued by the Architectural and Transportation Barriers Compliance Board under section 504(a) of this Act.

SECTION 244. REGULATIONS.

Not later than 1 year after the date of enactment of this Act, the Secretary of Transportation shall issue regulations, in an accessible format, necessary for carrying out this part.

SECTION 245. INTERIM ACCESSIBILITY REQUIREMENTS.

(a)   STATIONS. If final regulations have not been issued pursuant to section 244, for new construction or alterations for which a valid and appropriate State or local building permit is obtained prior to the issuance of final regulations under such section, and for which the construction or alteration authorized by such permit begins within one year of the receipt of such permit and is completed under the terms of such permit, compliance with the Uniform Federal Accessibility Standards in effect at the time the building permit is issued shall suffice to satisfy the requirement that stations be readily accessible to and usable by persons with disabilities as required under section 242(e), except that, if such final regulations have not been issued one year after the Architectural and Transportation Barriers Compliance Board has issued the supplemental minimum guidelines required under section 504(a) of this Act, compliance with such supplemental minimum guidelines shall be necessary to satisfy the requirement that stations be readily accessible to and usable by persons with disabilities prior to issuance of the final regulations.

(b)   RAIL PASSENGER CARS. If final regulations have not been issued pursuant to section 244, a person shall be considered to have complied with the requirements of section 242(a) through (d) that a rail passenger car be readily accessible to and usable by individuals with disabilities, if the design for such car complies with the laws and regulations (including the Minimum Guidelines and Requirements for Accessible Design and such supplemental minimum guidelines as are issued under section 504(a) of this Act) governing accessibility of such cars, to the extent that such laws and regulations are not inconsistent with this part and are in effect at the time such design is substantially completed.

SECTION 246. EFFECTIVE DATE.

(a)   GENERAL RULE. Except as provided in subsection (b), this part shall become effective 18 months after the date of enactment of this Act.

(b)   EXCEPTION. Sections 242 and 244 shall become effective on the date of enactment of this Act.

TITLE III. PUBLIC ACCOMMODATIONS AND SERVICES OPERATED BY PRIVATE ENTITIES

SECTION 301. DEFINITIONS.

As used in this title:

(1)   COMMERCE. The term "commerce" means travel, trade, commerce, transportation, or communication

(A)   among the several States;

(B)   between any foreign country or any territory or possession and any State; or

(C)   between points in the same State but through another State or foreign country.

(2) COMMERCIAL FACILITIES. The term "commercial facilities" means facilities

   (A) that are intended for nonresidential use; and

   (B) whose operations will affect commerce.

Such term shall not include railroad locomotives, railroad freight cars, railroad cabooses, railroad cars described in section 242 or covered under this title, railroad rights-of-way, or facilities that are covered or expressly exempted from coverage under the Fair Housing Act of 1968 (42 U.S.C. 3601 et seq.).

(3) DEMAND RESPONSIVE SYSTEM. The term "demand responsive system" means any system of providing transportation of individuals by a vehicle, other than a system which is a fixed route system.

(4) FIXED ROUTE SYSTEM. The term "fixed route system" means a system of providing transportation of individuals (other than by aircraft) on which a vehicle is operated along a prescribed route according to a fixed schedule.

(5) OVER-THE-ROAD BUS. The term "over-the-road bus" means a bus characterized by an elevated passenger deck located over a baggage compartment.

(6) PRIVATE ENTITY. The term "private entity" means any entity other than a public entity (as defined in section 201(1)).

(7) PUBLIC ACCOMMODATION. The following private entities are considered public accommodations for purposes of this title, if the operations of such entities affect commerce—

   (A) an inn, hotel, motel, or other place of lodging, except for an establishment located within a building that contains not more than five rooms for rent or hire and that is actually occupied by the proprietor of such establishment as the residence of such proprietor;

   (B) a restaurant, bar, or other establishment serving food or drink;

   (C) a motion picture house, theater, concert hall, stadium, or other place of exhibition or entertainment;

   (D) an auditorium, convention center, lecture hall, or other place of public gathering;

   (E) a bakery, grocery store, clothing store, hardware store, shopping center, or other sales or rental establishment;

   (F) a laundromat, dry-cleaner, bank, barber shop, beauty shop, travel service, shoe repair service, funeral parlor, gas station, office of an accountant or lawyer, pharmacy, insurance office, professional office of a health care provider, hospital, or other secure establishment;

   (G) a terminal, depot, or other station used for specified public transportation;

   (H) a museum, library, gallery, or other place of public display or collection;

   (I) a park, zoo, amusement park, or other place of recreation;

      (J)   a nursery, elementary, secondary, undergraduate, or postgraduate private school, or other place of education;

      (K)   a day care center, senior citizen center, homeless shelter, food bank, adoption agency, or other social service center establishment; and

      (L)   a gymnasium, health spa, bowling alley, golf course, or other place of exercise or recreation.

(8)   RAIL AND RAILROAD. The terms "rail" and "railroad" have the meaning given the term "railroad" in section 202(e) of the Federal Railroad Safety Act of 1970 (45 U.S.C. 431 (e)).

(9)   READILY ACHIEVABLE. The term "readily achievable" means easily accomplishable and able to be carried out without much difficulty or expense. In determining whether an action is readily achievable, factors to be considered include

      (A)   the nature and cost of the action needed under this Act:

      (B)   the overall financial resources of the facility or facilities involved in the action; the number of persons employed at such facility; the effect on expenses and resources, or the impact otherwise of such action upon the operation of the facility;

      (C)   the overall financial resources of the covered entity; the overall size of the business of a covered entity with respect to the number of its employees; the number, type and location of its facilities; and

      (D)   the type of operation or operations of the covered entity, including the composition, structure, and functions of the workforce of such entity; the geographic separateness, administrative or fiscal relationship of the facility or facilities in question to the covered entity.

(10)   SPECIFIED PUBLIC TRANSPORTATION. The term "specified public transportation" means transportation by bus, rail, or any other conveyance (other than by aircraft) that provides the general public with general or special service (including charter service) on a regular and continuing basis.

(11)   VEHICLE. The term "vehicle" does not include a rail passenger car, railroad locomotive, railroad freight car, railroad caboose, or a railroad car described in section 242 or covered under this title.

SECTION 302. PROHIBITION OF DISCRIMINATION BY PUBLIC ACCOMMODATIONS.

(a)   GENERAL RULE. No individual shall be discriminated against on the basis of disability in the full and equal enjoyment of the goods, services, facilities, privileges, advantages, or accommodations of any place of public accommodation by any person who owns, leases (or leases to), or operates a place of public accommodation.

(b)   CONSTRUCTION.

    (1)   GENERAL PROHIBITION.

      (A)   ACTIVITIES.

          (i)   DENIAL OF PARTICIPATION. It shall be discriminatory to subject an individual or class of individuals on the basis of a disability or disabilities of such individual or class, directly, or through contractual, licensing, or other arrangements, to a denial of the opportunity of the individual or class to participate in or benefit from the goods, services, facilities, privileges, advantages, or accommodations of an entity.

(ii) PARTICIPATION IN UNEQUAL BENEFIT. It shall be discriminatory to afford an individual or class of individuals, on the basis of a disability or disabilities of such individual or class, directly, or through contractual, licensing, or other arrangements with the opportunity to participate in or benefit from a good, service, facility, privilege, advantage, or accommodation that is not equal to that afforded to other individuals.

(iii) SEPARATE BENEFIT. It shall be discriminatory to provide an individual or class of individuals, on the basis of a disability or disabilities of such individual or class, directly, or through contractual, licensing, or other arrangements with a good, service, facility, privilege, advantage, or accommodation that is different or separate from that provided to other individuals, unless such action is necessary to provide the individual or class of individuals with a good, service, facility, privilege, advantage, or accommodation, or other opportunity that is as effective as that provided to others.

(iv) INDIVIDUAL OR CLASS OF INDIVIDUALS. For purposes of clauses (i) through (iii) of this subparagraph, the term "individual or class of individuals" refers to the clients or customers of the covered public accommodation that enters into the contractual, licensing or other arrangement.

(B) INTEGRATED SETTINGS. Goods, services, facilities, privileges, advantages, and accommodations shall be afforded to an individual with a disability in the most integrated setting appropriate to the needs of the individual.

(C) OPPORTUNITY TO PARTICIPATE. Notwithstanding the existence of separate or different programs or activities provided in accordance with this section, an individual with a disability shall not be denied the opportunity to participate in such programs or activities that are not separate or different.

(D) ADMINISTRATIVE METHODS. An individual or entity shall not, directly or through contractual or other arrangement, utilize standards or criteria or methods of administration

(i) that have the effect of discriminating on the basis of disability; or

(ii) that perpetuate the discrimination of others who are subject to common administrative control.

(E) ASSOCIATION. It shall be discriminatory to exclude or otherwise deny equal goods, services, facilities, privileges, advantages, accommodations, or other opportunities to an individual or entity because of the known disability of an individual with whom the individual or entity is known to have a relationship or association.

(2)   SPECIFIC PROHIBITIONS.

    (A)   DISCRIMINATION. For purposes of subsection (a), discrimination includes:

        (i)   the imposition or application of eligibility criteria that screen out or tend to screen out an individual with a disability or any class of individuals with disabilities from fully and equally enjoying any goods, services, facilities, privileges, advantages, or accommodations, unless such criteria can be shown to be necessary for the provision of the goods, services, facilities, privileges, advantages, or accommodations being offered;

        (ii)   a failure to make reasonable modifications in policies, practices, or procedures, when such modifications are necessary to afford such goods, services, facilities, privileges, advantages, or accommodations to individuals with disabilities, unless the entity can demonstrate that making such modifications would fundamentally alter the nature of such goods, services, facilities, privileges, advantages, or accommodations;

        (iii)   a failure to take such steps as may be necessary to ensure that no individual with a disability is excluded, denied services, segregated or otherwise treated differently than other individuals because of the absence of auxiliary aids and services, unless the entity can demonstrate that taking such steps would fundamentally alter the nature of the good, service, facility, privilege, advantage, or accommodation being offered or would result in an undue burden;

        (iv)   a failure to remove architectural barriers, and communication barriers that are structural in nature, in existing facilities, and transportation barriers in existing vehicles and rail passenger cars used by an establishment for transporting individuals (not including barriers that can only be removed through the retrofitting of vehicles or rail passenger cars by the installation of a hydraulic or other lift), where such removal is readily achievable; and

        (v)   where an entity can demonstrate that the removal of a barrier under clause (iv) is not readily achievable, a failure to make such goods, services, facilities, privileges, advantages, or accommodations available through alternative methods if such methods are readily achievable.

    (B)   FIXED ROUTE SYSTEM.

        (i)   ACCESSIBILITY. It shall be considered discrimination for a private entity which operates a fixed route system and which is not subject to section 304 to purchase or lease a vehicle with a seating capacity in excess of 16 passengers (including the driver) for use on such system, for which a solicitation is made after the 30th day following the effective date of this subparagraph, that is not readily accessible to and usable by individuals with disabilities, including individuals who use wheelchairs.

        (ii)   EQUIVALENT SERVICE. If a private entity which operates a fixed route system and which is not subject to section 304 purchases or leases a vehicle with a seating capacity of 16 passengers or less (including the driver) for use on such system after the effective date of this subparagraph that is not readily accessible to or usable by individuals with disabilities, it shall be considered discrimination for such entity to fail to operate such system so that, when viewed in its entirety, such system ensures a level of service to individuals with disabilities, including individuals who use wheelchairs, equivalent to the level of service provided to individuals without disabilities.

    (C)   DEMAND RESPONSIVE SYSTEM. For purposes of subsection (a), discrimination includes:

        (i)   a failure of a private entity which operates a demand responsive system and which is not subject to section 304 to operate such system so that, when viewed in its entirety, such system ensures a level of service to individuals with disabilities, including individuals who use wheelchairs, equivalent to the level of service provided to individuals without disabilities; and

        (ii)   the purchase or lease by such entity for use on such system of a vehicle with a seating capacity in excess of 16 passengers (including the driver), for which solicitations are made after the 30th day following the effective date of this subparagraph, that is not readily accessible to and usable by individuals with disabilities (including individuals who use wheelchairs) unless such entity can demonstrate that such system, when viewed in its entirety, provides a level of service to individuals with disabilities equivalent to that provided to individuals without disabilities.

    (D)   OVER-THE-ROAD BUSES.

        (i)   LIMITATION ON APPLICABILITY. Subparagraphs (B) and (C) do not apply to over-the-road buses.

        (ii)   ACCESSIBILITY REQUIREMENTS. For purposes of subsection (a), discrimination includes

            (I)   the purchase or lease of an over-the-road bus which does not comply with the regulations issued under section 306(a)(2) by a private entity which provides transportation of individuals and which is not primarily engaged in the business of transporting people, and

            (II)   any other failure of such entity to comply with such regulations.

  (3)   SPECIFIC CONSTRUCTION. Nothing in this title shall require an entity to permit an individual to participate in or benefit from the goods, services, facilities, privileges, advantages and accommodations of such entity where such individual poses a direct threat to the health or safety of others. The term "direct threat" means a significant risk to the health or safety of others that cannot be eliminated by a modification of policies, practices, or procedures or by the provision of auxiliary aids or services.

SECTION 303. NEW CONSTRUCTION AND ALTERATIONS IN PUBLIC ACCOMMODATIONS AND COMMERCIAL FACILITIES.

(a)   APPLICATION OF TERM. Except as provided in subsection (b), as applied to public accommodations and commercial facilities, discrimination for purposes of section 302(a) includes:

  (1)   a failure to design and construct facilities for first occupancy later than 30 months after the date of enactment of this Act that are readily accessible to and usable by individuals with disabilities, except where an entity can demonstrate that it is structurally impracticable to meet the requirements of

such subsection in accordance with standards set forth or incorporated by reference in regulations issued under this title; and

(2)   with respect to a facility or part thereof that is altered by, on behalf of, or for the use of an establishment in a manner that affects or could affect the usability of the facility or part thereof, a failure to make alterations in such a manner that, to the maximum extent feasible, the altered portions of the facility are readily accessible to and usable by individuals with disabilities, including individuals who use wheelchairs. Where the entity is undertaking an alteration that affects or could affect usability of or access to an area of the facility containing a primary function, the entity shall also make the alterations in such a manner that, to the maximum extent feasible, the path of travel to the altered area and the bathrooms, telephones, and drinking fountains serving the altered area, are readily accessible to and usable by individuals with disabilities where such alterations to the path of travel or the bathrooms, telephones, and drinking fountains serving the altered area are not disproportionate to the overall alterations in terms of cost and scope (as determined under criteria established by the Attorney General).

(b)   ELEVATOR. Subsection (a) shall not be construed to require the installation of an elevator for facilities that are less than three stories or have less than 3,000 square feet per story unless the building is a shopping center, a shopping mall, or the professional office of a health care provider or unless the Attorney General determines that a particular category of such facilities requires the installation of elevators based on the usage of such facilities.

SECTION 304. PROHIBITION OF DISCRIMINATION IN SPECIFIED PUBLIC TRANSPORTATION SERVICES PROVIDED BY PRIVATE ENTITIES.

(a)   GENERAL RULE. No individual shall be discriminated against on the basis of disability in the full and equal enjoyment of specified public transportation services provided by a private entity that is primarily engaged in the business of transporting people and whose operations affect commerce.

(b)   CONSTRUCTION. For purposes of subsection (a), discrimination includes:

(1)   the imposition or application by an entity described in subsection (a) of eligibility criteria that screen out or tend to screen out an individual with a disability or any class of individuals with disabilities from fully enjoying the specified public transportation services provided by the entity, unless such criteria can be shown to be necessary for the provision of the services being offered;

(2)   the failure of such entity to

(A)   make reasonable modifications consistent with those required under section 302(b)(2)(A)(ii);

(B)   provide auxiliary aids and services consistent with the requirements of section 302(b)(2)(A)(iii); and

(C)   remove barriers consistent with the requirements of section 302(b)(2)(A) and with the requirements of section 303(a)(2);

(3)   the purchase or lease by such entity of a new vehicle (other than an automobile, a van with a seating capacity of less than 8 passengers, including the driver, or an over-the-road bus) which is to be used to provide specified public transportation and for which a solicitation is made after the 30th day following

the effective date of this section, that is not readily accessible to and usable by individuals with disabilities, including individuals who use wheelchairs; except that the new vehicle need not be readily accessible to and usable by such individuals if the new vehicle is to be used solely in a demand responsive system and if the entity can demonstrate that such system, when viewed in its entirety, provides a level of service to such individuals equivalent to the level of service provided to the general public;

(4)   (A)   the purchase or lease by such entity of an over-the-road bus which does not comply with the regulations issued under section 306(a)(2); and

        (B)   any other failure of such entity to comply with such regulations; and

(5)   the purchase or lease by such entity of a new van with a seating capacity of less than 8 passengers, including the driver, which is to be used to provide specified public transportation and for which a solicitation is made after the 30th day following the effective date of this section that is not readily accessible to or usable by individuals with disabilities, including individuals who use wheelchairs; except that the new van need not be readily accessible to and usable by such individuals if the entity can demonstrate that the system for which the van is being purchased or leased, when viewed in its entirety, provides a level of service to such individuals equivalent to the level of service provided to the general public;

(6)   the purchase or lease by such entity of a new rail passenger car that is to be used to provide specified public transportation, and for which a solicitation is made later than 30 days after the effective date of this paragraph, that is not readily accessible to and usable by individuals with disabilities, including individuals who use wheelchairs; and

(7)   the remanufacture by such entity of a rail passenger car that is to be used to provide specified public transportation so as to extend its usable life for 10 years or more, or the purchase or lease by such entity of such a rail car, unless the rail car, to the maximum extent feasible, is made readily accessible to and usable by individuals with disabilities, including individuals who use wheelchairs.

(c)   HISTORICAL OR ANTIQUATED CARS.

    (1)   EXCEPTION. To the extent that compliance with subsection (b)(2)(C) or (b)(7) would significantly alter the historic or antiquated character of a historical or antiquated rail passenger car, or a rail station served exclusively by such cars, or would result in violation of any rule, regulation, standard, or order issued by the Secretary of Transportation under the Federal Railroad Safety Act of 1970, such compliance shall not be required.

    (2)   DEFINITION. As used in this subsection, the term "historical or antiquated rail passenger car" means a rail passenger car:

        (A)   which is not less than 30 years old at the time of its use for transporting individuals;

        (B)   the manufacturer of which is no longer in the business of manufacturing rail passenger cars; and

        (C)   which

            (i)   has a consequential association with events or persons significant to the past; or

            (ii)   embodies, or is being restored to embody, the distinctive characteristics of a type of rail passenger car used in the past, or to represent a time period which has passed.

SECTION 305. STUDY.

(a)   PURPOSES.   The Office of Technology Assessment shall undertake a study to determine:

    (1)   the access needs of individuals with disabilities to over-the-road buses and over-the-road bus service; and

    (2)   the most cost-effective methods for providing access to over-the-road buses and over-the-road bus service to individuals with disabilities, particularly individuals who use wheelchairs, through all forms of boarding options.

(b)   CONTENTS. The study shall include, at a minimum, an analysis of the following:

    (1)   The anticipated demand by individuals with disabilities for accessible over-the-road buses and over-the-road bus service.

    (2)   The degree to which such buses and service, including any service required under sections 304(b)(4) and 306(a)(2), are readily accessible to and usable by individuals with disabilities.

    (3)   The effectiveness of various methods of providing accessibility to such buses and service to individuals with disabilities.

    (4)   The cost of providing accessible over-the-road buses and bus service to individuals with disabilities, including consideration of recent technological and cost saving developments in equipment and devices.

    (5)   Possible design changes in over-the-road buses that could enhance accessibility, including the installation of accessible restrooms which do not result in a loss of seating capacity.

    (6)   The impact of accessibility requirements on the continuation of over-the-road bus service, with particular consideration of the impact of such requirements on such service to rural communities.

(c)   ADVISORY COMMITTEE. In conducting the study required by subsection (a), the Office of Technology Assessment shall establish an advisory committee, which shall consist of:

    (1)   members selected from among private operators and manufacturers of over-the-road buses;

    (2)   members selected from among individuals with disabilities, particularly individuals who use wheelchairs, who are potential riders of such buses; and

    (3)   members selected for their technical expertise on issues included in the study, including manufacturers of boarding assistance equipment and devices.

The members selected under each of paragraphs (1) and (2) shall be equal, and the total number of members selected under paragraphs (1) and (2) shall exceed the number of members selected under paragraph (3).

(d)   DEADLINE. The study required by subsection (a), along with recommendations by the Office of Technology Assessment, including any policy options for legislative action, shall be submitted to the President and Congress within 36 months after the date of the enactment of this Act. If the President determines that compliance with the regulations issued pursuant to section 306(a)(2)(B) on or before the applicable deadlines specified in section 306(a)(2)(B) will result in a significant reduction in intercity over-the-road bus service, the President shall extend each such deadline by 1 year.

(e)   REVIEW. In developing the study required by subsection (a), the Office of Technology Assessment shall provide a preliminary draft of such study to the Architectural and Transportation Barriers Compliance Board established under section 502 of the Rehabilitation Act of 1973 (29 U.S.C. 792). The Board shall have an opportunity to comment on such draft study, and any such comments by the Board made in writing within 120 days after the Board's receipt of the draft study shall be incorporated as part of the final study required to be submitted under subsection (d).

SECTION 306. REGULATIONS.

(a)   TRANSPORTATION PROVISIONS.

       (1)   GENERAL RULE. Not later than 1 year after the date of the enactment of this Act, the Secretary of Transportation shall issue regulations in an accessible format to carry out sections 302(b)(2)(B) and (C) and to carry out section 304 (other than subsection (b)(4)).

       (2)   SPECIAL RULES FOR PROVIDING ACCESS TO OVER-THE-ROAD BUSES.

             (A)   INTERIM REQUIREMENTS.

                   (i)   ISSUANCE. Not later than 1 year after the date of the enactment of this Act, the Secretary of Transportation shall issue regulations in an accessible format to carry out sections 304(b)(4) and 302(b)(2)(D)(ii) that require each private entity which uses an over-the-road bus to provide transportation of individuals to provide accessibility to such bus; except that such regulations shall not require any structural changes in over-the-road buses in order to provide access to individuals who use wheelchairs during the effective period of such regulations and shall not require the purchase of boarding assistance devices to provide access to such individuals.

                   (ii)   EFFECTIVE PERIOD. The regulations issued pursuant to this subparagraph shall be effective until the effective date of the regulations issued under subparagraph (B).

             (B)   FINAL REQUIREMENT.

                   (i)   REVIEW OF STUDY AND INTERIM REQUIREMENTS. The Secretary shall review the study submitted under section 305 and the regulations issued pursuant to subparagraph (A).

                   (ii)   ISSUANCE. Not later than 1 year after the date of the submission of the study under section 305, the Secretary shall issue in an accessible format new regulations to carry out sections 304(b)(4) and 302(b)(2)(D)(ii) that require, taking into account the purposes of the study under section 305 and any recommendations resulting from such study, each private entity which uses an over-the-road bus to provide transportation to individuals to provide accessibility to such bus to individuals with disabilities, including individuals who use wheelchairs.

                  (iii)   EFFECTIVE PERIOD. Subject to section 305(d), the regulations issued pursuant to this subparagraph shall take effect:

                       (I)   with respect to small providers of transportation (as defined by the Secretary), 7 years after the date of the enactment of this Act; and

           (II)   with respect to other providers of transportation, 6 years after such date of enactment.

    (C)   LIMITATION ON REQUIRING INSTALLATION OF ACCESSIBLE RESTROOMS. The regulations issued pursuant to this paragraph shall not require the installation of accessible restrooms in over-the-road buses if such installation would result in a loss of seating capacity.

  (3)   STANDARDS. The regulations issued pursuant to this subsection shall include standards applicable to facilities and vehicles covered by sections 302(b)(2) and 304.

(b)   OTHER PROVISIONS. Not later than 1 year after the date of the enactment of this Act, the Attorney General shall issue regulations in an accessible format to carry out the provisions of this title not referred to in subsection (a) that include standards applicable to facilities and vehicles covered under section 302.

(c)   CONSISTENCY WITH ATBCB GUIDELINES. Standards included in regulations issued under subsections (a) and (b) shall be consistent with the minimum guidelines and requirements issued by the Architectural and Transportation Barriers Compliance Board in accordance with section 504 of this Act.

(d)   INTERIM ACCESSIBILITY STANDARDS.

  (1)   FACILITIES. If final regulations have not been issued pursuant to this section, for new construction or alterations for which a valid and appropriate State or local building permit is obtained prior to the issuance of final regulations under this section, and for which the construction or alteration authorized by such permit begins within one year of the receipt of such permit and is completed under the terms of such permit, compliance with the Uniform Federal Accessibility Standards in effect at the time the building permit is issued shall suffice to satisfy the requirement that facilities be readily accessible to and usable by persons with disabilities as required under section 303, except that, if such final regulations have not been issued one year after the Architectural and Transportation Barriers Compliance Board has issued the supplemental minimum guidelines required under section 504(a) of this Act, compliance with such supplemental minimum guidelines shall be necessary to satisfy the requirement that facilities be readily accessible to and usable by persons with disabilities prior to issuance of the final regulations.

  (2)   VEHICLES AND RAIL PASSENGER CARS. If final regulations have not been issued pursuant to this section, a private entity shall be considered to have complied with the requirements of this title, if any, that a vehicle or rail passenger car be readily accessible to and usable by individuals with disabilities, if the design for such vehicle or car complies with the laws and regulations (including the Minimum Guidelines and Requirements for Accessible Design and such supplemental minimum guidelines as are issued under section 504(a) of this Act) governing accessibility of such vehicles or cars, to the extent that such laws and regulations are not inconsistent with this title and are in effect at the time such design is substantially completed.

SECTION 307. EXEMPTIONS FOR PRIVATE CLUBS AND RELIGIOUS ORGANIZATIONS.

The provisions of this title shall not apply to private clubs or establishments exempted from coverage under title II of the Civil Rights Act of 1964 (42 U.S.C. 2000-a(e)) or to religious organizations or entities controlled by religious organizations, including places of worship.

SECTION 308. ENFORCEMENT.

(a) IN GENERAL.

  (1) AVAILABILITY OF REMEDIES AND PROCEDURES. The remedies and procedures set forth in section 204(a) of the Civil Rights Act of 1964 (42 U.S.C. 2000a-3(a)) are the remedies and procedures this title provides to any person who is being subjected to discrimination on the basis of disability in violation of this title or who has reasonable grounds for believing that such person is about to be subjected to discrimination in violation of section 303. Nothing in this section shall require a person with a disability to engage in a futile gesture if such person has actual notice that a person or organization covered by this title does not intend to comply with its provisions.

  (2) INJUNCTIVE RELIEF. In the case of violations of sections 302(b)(2)(A)(iv) and section 303(a), injunctive relief shall include an order to alter facilities to make such facilities readily accessible to and usable by individuals with disabilities to the extent required by this title. Where appropriate, injunctive relief shall also include requiring the provision of an auxiliary aid or service, modification of a policy, or provision of alternative methods, to the extent required by this title.

(b) ENFORCEMENT BY THE ATTORNEY GENERAL

  (1) DENIAL OF RIGHTS.

    (A) DUTY TO INVESTIGATE.

      (i) IN GENERAL. The Attorney General shall investigate alleged violations of this title, and shall undertake periodic reviews of compliance of covered entities under this title.

      (ii) ATTORNEY GENERAL CERTIFICATION. On the application of a State or local government, the Attorney General may, in consultation with the Architectural and Transportation Barriers Compliance Board, and after prior notice and a public hearing at which persons, including individuals with disabilities, are provided an opportunity to testify against such certification, certify that a State law or local building code or similar ordinance that establishes accessibility requirements meets or exceeds the minimum requirements of this Act for the accessibility and usability of covered facilities under this title. At any enforcement proceeding under this section, such certification by the Attorney General shall be rebuttable evidence that such State law or local ordinance does meet or exceed the minimum requirements of this Act.

    (B) POTENTIAL VIOLATION. If the Attorney General has reasonable cause to believe that:

      (i) any person or group of persons is engaged in a pattern or practice of discrimination under this title; or

      (ii) any person or group of persons has been discriminated against under this title and such discrimination raises an issue of general public importance,

the Attorney General may commence a civil action in any appropriate United States district court.

(2)   AUTHORITY OF COURT. In a civil action under paragraph (1)(B), the court:

    (A)   may grant any equitable relief that such court considers to be appropriate, including, to the extent required by this title

        (i)   granting temporary, preliminary, or permanent relief;

        (ii)   providing an auxiliary aid or service, modification of policy, practice, or procedure, or alternative method; and

        (iii)   making facilities readily accessible to and usable by individuals with disabilities;

    (B)   may award such other relief as the court considers to be appropriate, including monetary damages to persons aggrieved when requested by the Attorney General; and

    (C)   may, to vindicate the public interest, assess a civil penalty against the entity in an amount

        (i)   not exceeding $50,000 for a first violation; and

        (ii)   not exceeding $100,000 for any subsequent violation.

(3)   SINGLE VIOLATION. For purposes of paragraph (2)(C), in determining whether a first or subsequent violation has occurred, a determination in a single action, by judgment or settlement, that the covered entity has engaged in more than one discriminatory act shall be counted as a single violation.

(4)   PUNITIVE DAMAGES. For purposes of subsection (b)(2)(B), the term "monetary damages" and "such other relief" does not include punitive damages. [NOTE: The Civil Rights Act of 1991 amends ADA to allow punitive damages within certain limits in Title I actions.]

(5)   JUDICIAL CONSIDERATION. In a civil action under paragraph (1)(B), the court, when considering what amount of civil penalty, if any, is appropriate, shall give consideration to any good faith effort or attempt to comply with this Act by the entity. In evaluating good faith, the court shall consider, among other factors it deems relevant, whether the entity could have reasonably anticipated the need for an appropriate type of auxiliary aid needed to accommodate the unique needs of a particular individual with a disability.

SECTION 309. EXAMINATIONS AND COURSES.

Any person that offers examinations or courses related to applications, licensing, certification, or credentialing for secondary or post-secondary education, professional, or trade purposes shall offer such examinations or courses in a place and manner accessible to persons with disabilities or offer alternative accessible arrangements for such individuals.

SECTION 310. EFFECTIVE DATE.

(a)   Except as provided in subsections (b) and (c), this title shall become effective 18 months after the date of the enactment of this Act. [Effective January 26, 1992, for the most part. January 26, 1993, is the deadline for new construction designed for occupancy after January, 1993.]

(b)   CIVIL ACTIONS. Except for any civil action brought for a violation of section 303, no civil action shall be brought for any act or omission described in section 302 which occurs:

    (1)   during the first 6 months after the effective date, against businesses that employ 25 or fewer employees and have gross receipts of $1,000,000 or less; and

(2)   during the first year after the effective date, against businesses that employ 10 or fewer employees and have gross receipts of $500,000 or less.

(c)   EXCEPTION. Sections 302(a) for purposes of section 302(b)(2)(B) and (C) only, 304(a) for purposes of section 304(b)(3) only, 304(b)(3), 305, and 306 shall take effect on the date of the enactment of this Act.

TITLE IV. TELECOMMUNICATIONS

SECTION 401. TELECOMMUNICATIONS RELAY SERVICES FOR HEARING-IMPAIRED AND SPEECH-IMPAIRED INDIVIDUALS.

(A)   TELECOMMUNICATIONS. Title II of the Communications Act of 1934 (47 U.S.C. 201 et seq.) is amended by adding at the end thereof the following new section [shown below in italic type]:

SECTION 225. TELECOMMUNICATIONS SERVICES FOR HEARING-IMPAIRED AND SPEECH-IMPAIRED INDIVIDUALS.

(a)   DEFINITIONS. As used in this section:

   (1)   COMMON CARRIER OR CARRIER. The term "common carrier" or "carrier" includes any common carrier engaged in interstate communication by wire or radio as defined in section 3(h) and any common carrier engaged in intrastate communication by wire or radio, notwithstanding sections 2(b) and 221(b).

   (2)   TDD. The term "TDD" means a Telecommunications Device for the Deaf, which is a machine that employs graphic communication in the transmission of coded signals through a wire or radio communication system.

   (3)   TELECOMMUNICATIONS RELAY SERVICES. The term "telecommunications relay services" means telephone transmission services that provide the ability for an individual who has a hearing impairment or speech impairment to engage in communication by wire or radio with a hearing individual in a manner that is functionally equivalent to the ability of an individual who does not have a hearing impairment or speech impairment to communicate using voice communication services by wire or radio. Such term includes services that enable two-way communication between an individual who uses a TDD or other nonvoice terminal device and an individual who does not use such a device.

(b)   AVAILABILITY OF TELECOMMUNICATIONS RELAY SERVICES.

   (1)   IN GENERAL. In order to carry out the purposes established under section 1, to make available to all individuals in the United States a rapid, efficient nationwide communication service, and to increase the utility of the telephone system of the Nation, the Commission shall ensure that interstate and intrastate telecommunications relay services are available, to the extent possible and in the most efficient manner, to hearing-impaired and speech-impaired individuals in the United States.

   (2)   USE OF GENERAL AUTHORITY AND REMEDIES. For the purposes of administering and enforcing the provisions of this section and the regulations prescribed thereunder, the Commission shall have the same authority, power, and functions with respect to common carriers engaged in intrastate communication as the Commission has in administering and enforcing the provisions of this title with respect to any common carrier engaged in interstate communication. Any violation of this section by an common carrier engaged in intrastate

communication shall be subject to the same remedies, penalties, and procedures as are applicable to a violation of this Act by a common carrier engaged in interstate communication.

(c)   *PROVISION OF SERVICES.   Each common carrier providing telephone voice transmission services shall, not later than 3 years after the date of enactment of this section, provide in compliance with the regulations prescribed under this section, throughout the area in which it offers service, telecommunications relay services, individually, through designees, through a competitively selected vendor, or in concert with other carriers.   A common carrier shall be considered to be in compliance with such regulations:*

    (1)   *with respect to intrastate telecommunications relay services in any State that does not have a certified program under subsection (f) and with respect to interstate telecommunications relay services, if such common carrier (or other entity through which the carrier is providing such relay services) is in compliance with the Commission's regulations under subsection (d); or*

    (2)   *with respect to intrastate telecommunications relay services in any State that has a certified program under subsection (f) for such State, if such common carrier (or other entity through which the carrier is providing such relay services) is in compliance with the program certified under subsection (f) for such State.*

(d)   *REGULATIONS.*

    (1)   *IN GENERAL.   The commission shall, not later than 1 year after the date of enactment of this section, prescribe regulations to implement this section, including regulations that:*

        (A)   *establish functional requirements, guidelines, and operations procedures for telecommunications relay services;*

        (B)   *establish minimum standards that shall be met in carrying out subsection (c);*

        (C)   *require that telecommunications relay services operate every day for 24 hours per day;*

        (D)   *require that users of telecommunications relay services pay rates no greater than the rates paid for functionally equivalent voice communication services with respect to such factors as the duration of the call, the time of day, and the distance from point of origination to point of termination.*

        (E)   *prohibit relay operators from failing to fulfill the obligations of common carriers by refusing calls or limiting the length of calls that use telecommunications relay services;*

        (F)   *prohibit relay operators from disclosing the content of any relayed conversation and from keeping records of the content of any such conversation beyond the duration of the call; and*

        (G)   *prohibit relay operators from intentionally altering a relayed conversation.*

    (2)   *TECHNOLOGY.   The Commission shall ensure that regulations prescribed to implement this section encourage, consistent with section 7(a) of this Act, the use of existing technology and do not discourage or impair the development of improved technology.*

(3) *JURISDICTIONAL SEPARATION OF COSTS.*

(A) *IN GENERAL. Consistent with the provisions of section 410 of this Act, the Commission shall prescribe regulations governing the jurisdictional separation of costs for the services provided pursuant to this section.*

(B) *RECOVERING COSTS. Such regulations shall generally provide that costs caused by interstate telecommunications relay services shall be recovered from all subscribers for every interstate service and costs caused by intrastate telecommunications relay services shall be recovered from the intrastate jurisdiction. In a State that has a certified program under subsection (f), a State commission shall permit a common carrier to recover the costs incurred in providing intrastate telecommunications relay services by a method consistent with the requirements of this section.*

(e) *ENFORCEMENT.*

(1) *IN GENERAL. Subject to subsections (f) and (g), the Commission shall enforce this section.*

(2) *COMPLAINT. The Commission shall resolve, by final order, a complaint alleging a violation of this section within 180 days after the date such complaint is filed.*

(f) *CERTIFICATION.*

(1) *STATE DOCUMENTATION. Any State desiring to establish a State program under this section shall submit documentation to the Commission that describes the program of such State for implementing intrastate telecommunications relay services and the procedures and remedies available for enforcing any requirements imposed by the State program.*

(2) *REQUIREMENTS FOR CERTIFICATION. After review of such documentation, the Commission shall certify the State program if the Commission determines that:*

(A) *the program makes available to hearing-impaired and speech-impaired individuals, either directly, through designees, through a competitively selected vendor, or through regulation of intrastate common carriers, intrastate telecommunications relay services in such State in a manner that meets or exceeds the requirements of regulations prescribed by the Commission under subsection (d); and*

(B) *the program makes available adequate procedures and remedies for enforcing the requirements of the State program.*

(3) *METHOD OF FUNDING. Except as provided in subsection (d), the Commission shall not refuse to certify a State program based solely on the method such State will implement for funding intrastate telecommunication relay services.*

(4) *SUSPENSION OR REVOCATION OF CERTIFICATION. The Commission may suspend or revoke such certification if, after notice and opportunity for hearing, the Commission determines that such certification is no longer warranted. In a State whose program has been suspended or revoked, the Commission shall take such steps as may be necessary, consistent with this section, to ensure continuity of telecommunications relay services.*

(g)   *COMPLAINT.*

    (1)   *REFERRAL OF COMPLAINT. If a complaint to the Commission alleges a violation of this section with respect to intrastate telecommunications relay services within a State and certification of the program of such State under subsection (f) is in effect, the Commission shall refer such complaint to such State.*

    (2)   *JURISDICTION OF COMMISSION. After referring a complaint to a State under paragraph (1), the Commission shall exercise jurisdiction over such complaint only if:*

        (A)   *final action under such State program has not been taken on such complaint by such State*

            (i)   *within 180 days after the complaint is filed with such State; or*
            (ii)   *within a shorter period as prescribed by the regulations of such State; or*

        (B)   *the Commission determines that such State program is no longer qualified for certification under subsection (f).*

(b)   CONFORMING AMENDMENTS. The Communications Act of 1934 (47 U.S.C. 151 et seq.) is amended:

    (1)   in section 2(b) (47 U.S.C. 152(b)), by striking "section 224" and inserting "sections 224 and 225"; and

    (2)   in section 221(b) (47 U.S.C. 221(b)), by striking "section 301" and inserting "sections 225 and 301".

SECTION 402. CLOSED-CAPTIONING OF PUBLIC SERVICE ANNOUNCEMENTS.

Section 711 of the Communications Act of 1934 is amended to read as follows [shown below in italic type]:

SECTION 711. CLOSED-CAPTIONING OF PUBLIC SERVICE ANNOUNCEMENTS.

Any television public service announcement that is produced or funded in whole or in part by any agency or instrumentality of Federal Government shall include closed captioning of the verbal content of such announcement. A television broadcast station licensee

    (1)   *shall not be required to supply closed captioning for any such announcement that fails to include it; and*

    (2)   *shall not be liable for broadcasting any such announcement without transmitting a closed caption unless the licensee intentionally fails to transmit the closed caption that was included with the announcement.*

TITLE V. MISCELLANEOUS PROVISIONS.

SECTION 501. CONSTRUCTION.

(a)   IN GENERAL. Except as otherwise provided in this Act, nothing in this Act shall be construed to apply a lesser standard than the standards applied under title V of the Rehabilitation Act of 1973 (29 U.S.C. 790 et seq.) or the regulations issued by Federal agencies pursuant to such title.

(b) RELATIONSHIP TO OTHER LAWS. Nothing in this Act shall be construed to invalidate or limit the remedies, rights, and procedures of any Federal law or law of any State or political subdivision of any State or jurisdiction that provides greater or equal protection for the rights of individuals with disabilities than are afforded by this Act. Nothing in this Act shall be construed to preclude the prohibition of, or the imposition of restrictions on, smoking in places of employment covered by title I, in transportation covered by title II or III, or in places of public accommodation covered by title III.

(c) INSURANCE. Titles I through IV of this Act shall not be construed to prohibit or restrict:

(1) an insurer, hospital or medical service company, health maintenance organization, or any agent, or entity that administers benefit plans, or similar organizations from underwriting risks, classifying risks, or administering such risks that are based on or not inconsistent with State law; or

(2) a person or organization covered by this Act from establishing, sponsoring, observing or administering the terms of a bona fide benefit plan that are based on underwriting risks, classifying risks, or administering such risks that are based on or not inconsistent with State law; or

(3) a person or organization covered by this Act from establishing, sponsoring, observing or administering the terms of a bona fide benefit plan that is not subject to State laws that regulate insurance.

Paragraphs (1), (2), and (3) shall not be used as a subterfuge to evade the purposes of title I and III.

(d) ACCOMMODATIONS AND SERVICES. Nothing in this Act shall be construed to require an individual with a disability to accept an accommodation, aid, service, opportunity, or benefit which such individual chooses not to accept.

SECTION 502. STATE IMMUNITY.

A state shall not be immune under the eleventh amendment to the Constitution of the United States from an action in Federal or State court of competent jurisdiction for a violation of this Act. In any action against a State for a violation of the requirements of this Act, remedies (including remedies both at law and in equity) are available for such a violation to the same extent as such remedies are available for such a violation in an action against any public or private entity other than a State.

SECTION 503. PROHIBITION AGAINST RETALIATION AND COERCION.

(a) RETALIATION. No person shall discriminate against any individual because such individual has opposed any act or practice made unlawful by this Act or because such individual made a charge, testified, assisted, or participated in any manner in an investigation, proceeding, or hearing under this Act.

(b) INTERFERENCE, COERCION, OR INTIMIDATION. It shall be unlawful to coerce, intimidate, threaten, or interfere with any individual in the exercise or enjoyment of, or on account of his or her having exercised or enjoyed, or on account of his or her having aided or encouraged any other individual in the exercise or enjoyment of, any right granted or protected by this Act.

(c) REMEDIES AND PROCEDURES. The remedies and procedures available under sections 107, 203, and 308 of this Act shall be available to aggrieved persons for violations of subsections (a) and (b), with respect to title I, title II and title III, respectively.

SECTION 504. REGULATIONS BY THE ARCHITECTURAL AND TRANSPORTATION BARRIERS COMPLIANCE BOARD.

(a)   ISSUANCE OF GUIDELINES. Not later than 9 months after the date of enactment of this Act, the Architectural and Transportation Barriers Compliance Board shall issue minimum guidelines that shall supplement the existing Minimum Guidelines and Requirements for Accessible Design for purposes of titles II and III of this Act.

(b)   CONTENTS OF GUIDELINES. The supplemental guidelines issued under subsection (a) shall establish additional requirements, consistent with this Act, to ensure that buildings, facilities, rail passenger cars, and vehicles are accessible, in terms of architecture and design, transportation, and communication, to individuals with disabilities.

(c)   QUALIFIED HISTORIC PROPERTIES.

   (1)   IN GENERAL. The supplemental guidelines issued under subsection (a) shall include procedures and requirements for alterations that will threaten or destroy the historic significance of qualified historic buildings and facilities as defined in 4.1.7(1)(a) of the Uniform Federal Accessibility Standards.

   (2)   SITES ELIGIBLE FOR LISTING IN NATIONAL REGISTER. With respect to alterations of buildings or facilities that are eligible for listing in the National Register of Historic Places under the National Historic Preservation Act (16 U.S.C. 470 et seq.), the guidelines described in paragraph (1) shall, at a minimum, maintain the procedures and requirements established in 4.1.7(1) and (2) of the Uniform Federal Accessibility Standards.

   (3)   OTHER SITES. With respect to alterations of buildings or facilities designated as historic under State or local law, the guidelines described in paragraph (1) shall establish procedures equivalent to those established by 4.1.7(1)(b) and (c) of the Uniform Federal Accessibility Standards, and shall require, at a minimum, compliance with the requirements established in 4.1.7(2) of such standards.

SECTION 505. ATTORNEY'S FEES.

In any action or administrative proceeding commenced pursuant to this Act, the court or agency, in its discretion, may allow the prevailing party, other than the United States, a reasonable attorney's fee, including litigation expenses, and costs, and the United States shall be liable for the foregoing the same as a private individual.

SECTION 506. TECHNICAL ASSISTANCE.

(a)   PLAN FOR ASSISTANCE.

   (1)   IN GENERAL. Not later than 180 days after the date of enactment of this Act, the Attorney General, in consultation with the Chair of the Equal Employment Opportunity Commission, the Secretary of Transportation, the Chair of the Architectural and Transportation Barriers Compliance Board, and the Chairman of the Federal Communications Commission, shall develop a plan to assist entities covered under this Act, and other Federal agencies, in understanding the responsibility of such entities and agencies under this Act.

   (2)   PUBLICATION OF PLAN. The Attorney General shall publish the plan referred to in paragraph (1) for public comment in accordance with subchapter II of chapter 5 of title 5, United States Code (commonly known as the Administrative Procedure Act).

(b) AGENCY AND PUBLIC ASSISTANCE. The Attorney General may obtain the assistance of other Federal agencies in carrying out subsection (a), including the National Council on Disability, the President's Committee on Employment of People with Disabilities, the Small Business Administration, and the Department of Commerce.

(c) IMPLEMENTATION.

   (1) RENDERING ASSISTANCE. Each Federal agency that has responsibility under paragraph (2) for implementing this Act may render technical assistance to individuals and institutions that have rights or duties under the respective title or titles for which such agency has responsibility.

   (2) IMPLEMENTATION OF TITLES.

      (A) TITLE I. The Equal Employment Opportunity Commission and the Attorney General shall implement the plan for assistance developed under subsection (a), for title I.

      (B) TITLE II.

         (i)   SUBTITLE A. The Attorney General shall implement such plan for assistance for subtitle A of title II.
         (ii) SUBTITLE B. The Secretary of Transportation shall implement such plan for assistance for subtitle B of title II.

      (C) TITLE III. The Attorney General, in coordination with the Secretary of Transportation and the Chair of the Architectural Transportation Barriers Compliance Board, shall implement such plan for assistance for title III, except for section 304, the plan for assistance for which shall be implemented by the Secretary of Transportation.

      (D) TITLE IV. The Chairman of the Federal Communications Commission, in coordination with the Attorney General, shall implement such plan for assistance for title IV.

   (3) TECHNICAL ASSISTANCE MANUALS. Each Federal agency that has responsibility under paragraph (2) for implementing this Act shall, as part of its implementation responsibilities, ensure the availability and provision of appropriate technical assistance manuals to individuals or entities with rights or duties under this Act no later than six months after applicable final regulations are published under titles I, II, III, and IV.

(d) GRANTS AND CONTRACTS.

   (1) IN GENERAL. Each Federal agency that has responsibility under subsection (c)(2) for implementing this Act may make grants or award contracts to effectuate the purposes of this section, subject to the availability of appropriations. Such grants and contracts may be awarded to individuals, institutions not organized for profit and no part of the net earnings of which inures to the benefit of any private shareholder or individual (including educational institutions), and associations representing individuals who have rights or duties under this Act. Contracts may be awarded to entities organized for profit, but such entities may not be the recipients of grants described in this paragraph.

   (2) DISSEMINATION OF INFORMATION. Such grants and contracts, among other uses, may be designed to ensure wide dissemination of information about

the rights and duties established by this Act and to provide information and technical assistance about techniques for effective compliance with this Act.

(e)   FAILURE TO RECEIVE ASSISTANCE. An employer, public accommodation, or other entity covered under this Act shall not be excused from compliance with the requirements of this Act because of any failure to receive technical assistance under this section, including any failure in the development or dissemination of any technical assistance manual authorized by this section.

SECTION 507. FEDERAL WILDERNESS AREAS.

(a)   STUDY. The National Council on Disability shall conduct a study and report on the effect that wilderness designations and wilderness land management practices have on the ability of individuals with disabilities to use and enjoy the National Wilderness Preservation System as established under the Wilderness Act (16 U.S.C. 1131 et seq.).

(b)   SUBMISSION OF REPORT. Not later than 1 year after the enactment of this Act, the National Council on Disability shall submit the report required under subsection (a) to Congress.

(c)   SPECIFIC WILDERNESS ACCESS.

    (1)   IN GENERAL. Congress reaffirms that nothing in the Wilderness Act is to be construed as prohibiting the use of a wheelchair in a wilderness area by an individual whose disability requires use of a wheelchair, and consistent with the Wilderness Act no agency is required to provide any form of special treatment or accommodation, or to construct any facilities or modify any conditions of lands within a wilderness area in order to facilitate such use.

    (2)   DEFINITION. For purposes of paragraph (1), the term "wheelchair' means a device designed solely for use by a mobility-impaired person for locomotion, that is suitable for use in an indoor pedestrian area.

SECTION 508. TRANSVESTITES.

For the purposes of this Act, the term "disabled" or "disability" shall not apply to an individual solely because that individual is a transvestite.

SECTION 509. COVERAGE OF CONGRESS AND THE AGENCIES OF THE LEGISLATIVE BRANCH.

(a)   COVERAGE OF THE SENATE.

    (1)   COMMITMENT TO RULE XLII. The Senate reaffirms its commitment to Rule XLII of the Standing Rules of the Senate which provides as follows [in italic]:

    No member, officer, or employee of the Senate shall, with respect to employment by the Senate or any office thereof:

        (a)   fail or refuse to hire an individual;
        (b)   discharge an individual; or
        (c)   otherwise discriminate against an individual with respect to promotion, compensation, or terms, conditions, or privileges of employment
    on the basis of such individual's race, color, religion, sex, national origin, age, or state of physical handicap.

    (2)   APPLICATION TO SENATE EMPLOYMENT. The rights and protections provided pursuant to this Act, the Civil Rights Act of 1990 (S. 2104, 101st

Congress), the Civil Rights Act of 1964, the Age Discrimination in Employment Act of 1967, and the Rehabilitation Act of 1973 shall apply with respect to employment by the United States Senate.

(3)   INVESTIGATION AND ADJUDICATION OF CLAIMS. All claims raised by any individual with respect to Senate employment, pursuant to the Acts referred to in paragraph (2), shall be investigated and adjudicated by the Select Committee on Ethics, pursuant to S. Res. 338, 88th Congress, as amended, or such other entity as the Senate may designate.

(4)   RIGHTS OF EMPLOYEES. The Committee on Rules and Administration shall ensure that Senate employees are informed of their rights under the Acts referred to in paragraph (2).

(5)   APPLICABLE REMEDIES. When assigning remedies to individuals found to have a valid claim under the Acts referred to in paragraph (2), the Select Committee on Ethics, or such other entity as the Senate may designate, should to the extent practicable apply the same remedies applicable to all other employees covered by the Acts referred to in paragraph (2). Such remedies shall apply exclusively.

(6)   MATTERS OTHER THAN EMPLOYMENT.

    (A)   IN GENERAL. The rights and protections under this Act shall, subject to subparagraph (B), apply with respect to the conduct of the Senate regarding matters other than employment.

    (B)   REMEDIES. The Architect of the Capitol shall establish remedies and procedures to be utilized with respect to the rights and protections provided pursuant to subparagraph (A). Such remedies and procedures shall apply exclusively, after approval in accordance with subparagraph (C).

    (C)   PROPOSED REMEDIES AND PROCEDURES. For purposes of subparagraph (B), the Architect of the Capitol shall submit proposed remedies and procedures to the Senate Committee on Rules and Administration. The remedies and procedures shall be effective upon the approval of the Committee on Rules and Administration.

(7)   EXERCISE OF RULEMAKING POWER. Notwithstanding any other provision of law, enforcement and adjudication of the rights and protections referred to in paragraph (2) and (6)(A) shall be within the exclusive jurisdiction of the United States Senate. The provisions of paragraph (1), (3), (4), (5), (6)(B), and (6)(C) are enacted by the Senate as an exercise of the rulemaking power of the Senate, with full recognition of the right of the Senate to change its rules, in the same manner, and to the same extent, as in the case of any other rule of the Senate.

(b)   COVERAGE OF THE HOUSE OF REPRESENTATIVES.

(1)   IN GENERAL. Notwithstanding any other provision of this Act or of law, the purposes of this Act shall, subject to paragraphs (2) and (3), apply in their entirety to the House of Representatives.

(2)   EMPLOYMENT IN THE HOUSE.

    (A)   APPLICATION. The rights and protections under this Act shall, subject to subparagraph (B), apply with respect to any employee in an employment position in the House of Representatives and any employing authority of the House of Representatives.

(B)   ADMINISTRATION.

(i)   IN GENERAL. In the administration of this paragraph, the remedies and procedures made applicable pursuant to the resolution described in clause (ii) shall apply exclusively.

(ii)   RESOLUTION. The resolution referred to in clause (i) is House Resolution 15 of the One Hundredth First Congress, as agreed to January 3, 1989, or any other provision that continues in effect the provisions of, or is a successor to, the Fair Employment Practices Resolution (House Resolution 558 of the One Hundredth Congress, as agreed to October 4, 1988).

(C)   EXERCISE OF RULEMAKING POWER. The provisions of subparagraph (B) are enacted by the House of Representatives as an exercise of the rulemaking power of the House of Representatives, with full recognition of the right of the House to change its rules, in the same manner, and to the same extent as in the case of any other rule of the House.

(3)   MATTERS OTHER THAN EMPLOYMENT.

(A)   IN GENERAL. The rights and protections under this Act shall, subject to subparagraph (B), apply with respect to the conduct of the House of Representatives regarding matters other than employment.

(B)   REMEDIES. The Architect of the Capitol shall establish remedies and procedures to be utilized with respect to the rights and protections provided pursuant to subparagraph (A). Such remedies and procedures shall apply exclusively, after approval in accordance with subparagraph (C).

(C)   APPROVAL. For purposes of subparagraph (B), the Architect of the Capitol shall submit proposed remedies and procedures to the Speaker of the House of Representatives. The remedies and procedures shall be effective upon the approval of the Speaker, after consultation with the House Office Building Commission.

(c)   INSTRUMENTALITIES OF CONGRESS.

(1)   IN GENERAL. The rights and protections under this Act shall, subject to paragraph (2), apply with respect to the conduct of each instrumentality of the Congress.

(2)   ESTABLISHMENT OF REMEDIES AND PROCEDURES BY INSTRUMEN-TALITIES. The chief official of each instrumentality of the Congress shall establish remedies and procedures to be utilized with respect to the rights and protections provided pursuant to paragraph (1). Such remedies and procedures shall apply exclusively.

(3)   REPORT TO CONGRESS. The chief official of each instrumentality of the Congress shall, after establishing remedies and procedures for purposes of paragraph (2), submit to the Congress a report describing the remedies and procedures.

(4) DEFINITION OF INSTRUMENTALITIES. For purposes of this section, instrumentalities of the Congress include the following: the Architect of the Capitol, the Congressional Budget Office, the General Accounting Office, the Government Printing Office, the Library of Congress, the Office of Technology Assessment, and the United States Botanic Garden.

(5) CONSTRUCTION. Nothing in this section shall alter the enforcement procedures for individuals with disabilities provided in the General Accounting Office Personnel Act of 1980 and regulations promulgated pursuant to that Act.

SECTION 510. ILLEGAL USE OF DRUGS.

(a) IN GENERAL. For purposes of this Act, the term "individual with a disability" does not include an individual who is currently engaging in the illegal use of drugs, when the covered entity acts on the basis of such use.

(b) RULES OF CONSTRUCTION. Nothing in subsection (a) shall be construed to exclude as an individual with a disability an individual who:

(1) has successfully completed a supervised drug rehabilitation program and is no longer engaging in the illegal use of drugs, or has otherwise been rehabilitated successfully and is no longer engaging in such use;

(2) is participating in a supervised rehabilitation program and is no longer engaging in such use; or

(3) is erroneously regarded as engaging in such use, but is not engaging in such use;

except that it shall not be a violation of this Act for a covered entity to adopt or administer reasonable policies or procedures, including but not limited to drug testing, designed to ensure that an individual described in paragraph (1) or (2) is no longer engaging in the illegal use of drugs; however, nothing in this section shall be construed to encourage, prohibit, restrict, or authorize the conducting of testing for the illegal use of drugs.

(c) HEALTH AND OTHER SERVICES. Notwithstanding subsection (a) and section 511(b)(3), an individual shall not be denied health services, or services provided in connection with drug rehabilitation, on the basis of the current illegal use of drugs if the individual is otherwise entitled to such services.

(d) DEFINITION OF ILLEGAL USE OF DRUGS.

(1) IN GENERAL. The term "illegal use of drugs" means the use of drugs, the possession or distribution of which is unlawful under the Controlled Substances Act (21 U.S.C. 812). Such term does not include the use of a drug taken under supervision by a licensed health care professional, or other uses authorized by the Controlled Substances Act or other provisions of Federal law.

(2) DRUGS. The term "drug" means a controlled substance, as defined in schedules I through V of section 202 of the Controlled Substances Act.

SECTION 511. DEFINITIONS.

(a) HOMOSEXUALITY AND BISEXUALITY. For purposes of the definition of "disability" in section 3(2), homosexuality and bisexuality are not impairments and as such are not disabilities under this Act.

(b)   CERTAIN CONDITIONS. Under this Act, the term "disability" shall not include:

(1)   transvestism, transsexualism, pedophilia, exhibitionism, voyeurism, gender identity disorders not resulting from physical impairments, or other sexual behavior disorders;

(2)   compulsive gambling, kleptomania, or pyromania; or

(3)   psychoactive substance use disorders resulting from current illegal use of drugs.

SECTION 512. AMENDMENTS TO THE REHABILITATION ACT.

(a)   DEFINITION OF HANDICAPPED INDIVIDUAL. Section 7(8) of the Rehabilitation Act of 1973 (29 U.S.C. 706(8)) is amended by redesignating subparagraph (C) as subparagraph (D) and by inserting after subparagraph (B) the following subparagraph [shown below in italic type]:

(C)   (i)   *For purposes of title V, the term "individual with handicaps" does not include an individual who is currently engaging in the illegal use of drugs, when a covered entity acts on the basis of such use.*

(ii)   *Nothing in clause (i) shall be construed to exclude as an individual with handicaps an individual who*

(I)   *has successfully completed a supervised drug rehabilitation program and is no longer engaging in the illegal use of drugs, or has otherwise been rehabilitated successfully and is no longer engaging in such use;*

(II)   *is participating in a supervised rehabilitation program and is no longer engaging in such use; or*

(III)   *is erroneously regarded as engaging in such use, but is not engaging in such use; except that it shall not be a violation of this Act for a covered entity to adopt or administer reasonable policies or procedures, including but not limited to drug testing, designed to ensure that an individual described in subclause (I) or (II) is no longer engaging in the illegal use of drugs.*

(iii)   *Notwithstanding clause (i), for purposes of programs and activities providing health services and services provided under titles I, II, and III, an individual shall not be excluded from the benefits of such programs or activities on the basis of his or her current illegal use of drugs if he or she is otherwise entitled to such services.*

(iv)   *For purposes of programs and activities providing educational services, local educational agencies may take disciplinary action pertaining to the use or possession of illegal drugs or alcohol against any handicapped student who currently is engaging in the illegal use of drugs or in the use of alcohol to the same extent that such disciplinary action is taken against nonhandicapped students. Furthermore, the due process procedures at 34 CFR 104.36 shall not apply to such disciplinary actions.*

(v)   *For purposes of sections 503 and 504 as such sections relate to employment, the term "individual with handicaps" does not include any individual who is an alcoholic whose current use of alcohol prevents such individual from performing the duties of the job in question or whose employment, by reason of such current alcohol abuse, would constitute a direct threat to property or the safety of others.*

(b)   DEFINITION OF ILLEGAL DRUGS. Section 7 of the Rehabilitation Act of 1973 (29 U.S.C. 706) is amended by adding at the end the following new paragraph [shown below in italic type]:

    (22)   *(A)*   *The term "drug" means a controlled substance, as defined in schedules I through V of section 202 of the Controlled Substances Act (21 U.S.C. 812).*

            (B)   *The term "illegal use of drugs" means the use of drugs, the possession or distribution of which is unlawful under the Controlled Substances Act. Such term does not include the use of a drug taken under supervision by a licensed health care professional, or other uses authorized by the Controlled Substances Act or other provisions of Federal law.*

(c)   CONFORMING AMENDMENTS. Section 7(8)(B) of the Rehabilitation Act of 1973 (29 U.S.C. 706(8)(B)) is amended:

    (1)   in the first sentence, by striking "Subject to the second sentence of this subparagraph," and inserting "Subject to subparagraphs (C) and (D),"; and

    (2)   by striking the second sentence.

SECTION 513. ALTERNATIVE MEANS OF DISPUTE RESOLUTION.

Where appropriate and to the extent authorized by law, the use of alternative means of dispute resolution, including settlement negotiations, conciliation, facilitation, mediation, factfinding, minitrials, and arbitration, is encouraged to resolve disputes arising under this Act.

SECTION 514. SEVERABILITY.

Should any provision in this Act be found to be unconstitutional by a court of law, such provision shall be severed from the remainder of the Act, and such action shall not affect the enforceability of the remaining provisions of the Act.

Appendix B
ADA Accessibility Guidelines

Federal Register / Vol. 56, No. 144 / Friday, July 26, 1991 / Rules and Regulations   **35605**

Appendix A to Part 36—Standards for Accessible Design

ADA ACCESSIBILITY GUIDELINES
FOR BUILDINGS AND FACILITIES
TABLE OF CONTENTS

Federal Register / Vol. 56, No. 144 / Friday, July 26, 1991 / Rules and Regulations **35607**

1. PURPOSE.

This document sets guidelines for accessibility to places of public accommodation and commercial facilities by individuals with disabilities. These guidelines are to be applied during the design, construction, and alteration of such buildings and facilities to the extent required by regulations issued by Federal agencies, including the Department of Justice, under the Americans with Disabilities Act of 1990.

The technical specifications 4.2 through 4.35, of these guidelines are the same as those of the American National Standard Institute's document A117.1-1980, except as noted in this text by italics. However, sections 4.1.1 through 4.1.7 and sections 5 through 10 are different from ANSI A117.1 in their entirety and are printed in standard type.

The illustrations and text of ANSI A117.1 are reproduced with permission from the American National Standards Institute. Copies of the standard may be purchased from the American National Standards Institute at 1430 Broadway, New York, New York 10018.

2. GENERAL.

2.1 Provisions for Adults. *The specifications in these guidelines are based upon adult dimensions and anthropometrics.*

2.2* Equivalent Facilitation. *Departures from particular technical and scoping requirements of this guideline by the use of other designs and technologies are permitted where the alternative designs and technologies used will provide substantially equivalent or greater access to and usability of the facility.*

3. MISCELLANEOUS INSTRUCTIONS AND DEFINITIONS.

3.1 Graphic Conventions. Graphic conventions are shown in Table 1. Dimensions that are not marked minimum or maximum are absolute, unless otherwise indicated in the text or captions.

Table 1
Graphic Conventions

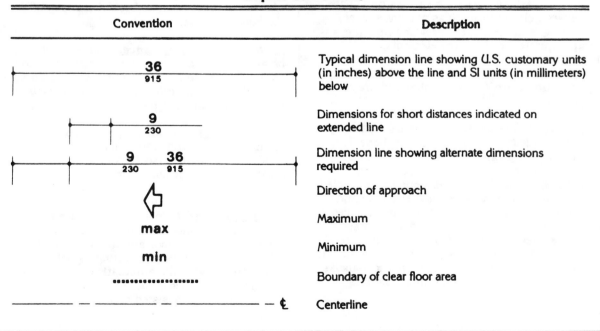

Convention	Description
36 / 915	Typical dimension line showing U.S. customary units (in inches) above the line and SI units (in millimeters) below
9 / 230	Dimensions for short distances indicated on extended line
9 36 / 230 915	Dimension line showing alternate dimensions required
	Direction of approach
max	Maximum
min	Minimum
	Boundary of clear floor area
₵	Centerline

35608   Federal Register / Vol. 56, No. 144 / Friday, July 26, 1991 / Rules and Regulations

3.4 General Terminology

3.2 Dimensional Tolerances. All dimensions are subject to conventional building industry tolerances for field conditions.

3.3 Notes. The text of *these guidelines* does not contain notes or footnotes. Additional information, explanations, and advisory materials are located in the Appendix. Paragraphs marked with an asterisk have related, non-mandatory material in the Appendix. In the Appendix, the corresponding paragraph numbers are preceded by an A.

3.4 General Terminology.

comply with. Meet one or more specifications of *these guidelines*.

if, if ... then. Denotes a specification that applies only when the conditions described are present.

may. Denotes an option or alternative.

shall. Denotes a mandatory specification or requirement.

should. Denotes an advisory specification or recommendation.

3.5 Definitions.

Access Aisle. An accessible pedestrian space between elements, such as parking spaces, seating, and desks, that provides clearances appropriate for use of the elements.

Accessible. Describes a site, building, facility, or portion thereof that complies with *these guidelines*.

Accessible Element. An *element* specified by *these guidelines* (for example, telephone, controls, and the like).

Accessible Route. A continuous unobstructed path connecting all accessible elements and spaces of a building or facility. Interior accessible routes may include corridors, floors, ramps, elevators, lifts, and clear floor space at fixtures. Exterior accessible routes may include parking access aisles, curb ramps, *crosswalks at vehicular ways*, walks, ramps, and lifts.

Accessible Space. *Space that complies with these guidelines.*

Adaptability. The ability of certain building spaces and elements, such as kitchen counters, sinks, and grab bars, to be added or altered so as to accommodate the needs of *individuals with or without disabilities* or to accommodate the needs of persons with different types or degrees of disability.

Addition. *An expansion, extension, or increase in the gross floor area of a building or facility.*

Administrative Authority. A governmental agency that adopts or enforces regulations and *guidelines* for the design, construction, or *alteration* of buildings and facilities.

Alteration. *An alteration is a change to a building or facility made by, on behalf of, or for the use of a public accommodation or commercial facility, that affects or could affect the usability of the building or facility or part thereof. Alterations include, but are not limited to, remodeling, renovation, rehabilitation, reconstruction, historic restoration, changes or rearrangement of the structural parts or elements, and changes or rearrangement in the plan configuration of walls and full-height partitions. Normal maintenance, reroofing, painting or wallpapering, or changes to mechanical and electrical systems are not alterations unless they affect the usability of the building or facility.*

Area of Rescue Assistance. *An area, which has direct access to an exit, where people who are unable to use stairs may remain temporarily in safety to await further instructions or assistance during emergency evacuation.*

Assembly Area. A room or space accommodating a *group of* individuals for recreational, educational, political, social, or amusement purposes, or for the consumption of food and drink.

Automatic Door. A door equipped with a power-operated mechanism and controls that open and close the door automatically upon receipt of a momentary actuating signal. The switch that begins the automatic cycle may be a photoelectric device, floor mat, or manual switch (see power-assisted door).

Federal Register / Vol. 56, No. 144 / Friday, July 26, 1991 / Rules and Regulations   **35609**

3.5 Definitions

Building. Any structure used and intended for supporting or sheltering any use or occupancy.

Circulation Path. An exterior or interior way of passage from one place to another for pedestrians, including, but not limited to, walks, hallways, courtyards, stairways, and stair landings.

Clear. Unobstructed.

Clear Floor Space. *The minimum unobstructed floor or ground space required to accommodate a single, stationary wheelchair and occupant.*

Closed Circuit Telephone. *A telephone with dedicated line(s) such as a house phone, courtesy phone or phone that must be used to gain entrance to a facility.*

Common Use. Refers to those interior and exterior rooms, spaces, or elements that are made available for the use of a restricted group of people (for example, *occupants of a homeless shelter*, the occupants of an office building, or the guests of such occupants).

Cross Slope. The slope that is perpendicular to the direction of travel (see running slope).

Curb Ramp. A short ramp cutting through a curb or built up to it.

Detectable Warning. *A standardized surface feature built in or applied to walking surfaces or other elements to warn visually impaired people of hazards on a circulation path.*

Dwelling Unit. A single unit which provides a kitchen or food preparation area, in addition to rooms and spaces for living, bathing, sleeping, and the like. *Dwelling units include a single family home or a townhouse used as a transient group home; an apartment building used as a shelter; guestrooms in a hotel that provide sleeping accommodations and food preparation areas; and other similar facilities used on a transient basis. For purposes of these guidelines, use of the term "Dwelling Unit" does not imply the unit is used as a residence.*

Egress, Means of. *A continuous and unobstructed way of exit travel from any point in a building or facility to a public way. A means of egress comprises vertical and horizontal travel and may include intervening room spaces, doorways, hallways, corridors, passageways, balconies, ramps, stairs, enclosures, lobbies, horizontal exits, courts and yards. An accessible means of egress is one that complies with these guidelines and does not include stairs, steps, or escalators. Areas of rescue assistance or evacuation elevators may be included as part of accessible means of egress.*

Element. *An architectural or mechanical component of a building, facility, space, or site, e.g., telephone, curb ramp, door, drinking fountain, seating, or water closet.*

Entrance. *Any access point to a building or portion of a building or facility used for the purpose of entering. An entrance includes the approach walk, the vertical access leading to the entrance platform, the entrance platform itself, vestibules if provided, the entry door(s) or gate(s), and the hardware of the entry door(s) or gate(s).*

Facility. *All or any portion of buildings, structures, site improvements, complexes, equipment, roads, walks, passageways, parking lots, or other real or personal property located on a site.*

Ground Floor. *Any occupiable floor less than one story above or below grade with direct access to grade. A building or facility always has at least one ground floor and may have more than one ground floor as where a split level entrance has been provided or where a building is built into a hillside.*

Mezzanine or Mezzanine Floor. *That portion of a story which is an intermediate floor level placed within the story and having occupiable space above and below its floor.*

Marked Crossing. A crosswalk or other identified path intended for pedestrian use in crossing a vehicular way.

Multifamily Dwelling. Any building containing more than two dwelling units.

Occupiable. *A room or enclosed space designed for human occupancy in which individuals congregate for amusement, educational or similar purposes, or in which occupants are engaged at labor, and which is equipped with means of egress, light, and ventilation.*

35610   Federal Register / Vol. 56, No. 144 / Friday, July 26, 1991 / Rules and Regulations

3.5 Definitions

Operable Part. A part of a piece of equipment or appliance used to insert or withdraw objects, or to activate, deactivate, or adjust the equipment or appliance (for example, coin slot, pushbutton, handle).

Path of Travel. (Reserved).

Power-assisted Door. A door used *for human passage* with a mechanism that helps to open the door, or relieves the opening resistance of a door, upon the activation of a switch or a continued force applied to the door itself.

Public Use. Describes interior or exterior rooms or spaces that are made available to the general public. Public use may be provided at a building or facility that is privately or publicly owned.

Ramp. A walking surface which has a running slope greater than 1:20.

Running Slope. The slope that is parallel to the direction of travel (see cross slope).

Service Entrance. An entrance intended primarily for delivery of goods or services.

Signage. *Displayed* verbal, symbolic, *tactile*, and pictorial information.

Site. A parcel of land bounded by a property line or a designated portion of a public right-of-way.

Site Improvement. Landscaping, paving for pedestrian and vehicular ways, outdoor lighting, recreational facilities, and the like, added to a site.

Sleeping Accommodations. Rooms in which people sleep; for example, dormitory and hotel or motel guest rooms or suites.

Space. A definable area, e.g., room, toilet room, hall, assembly area, entrance, storage room, alcove, courtyard, or lobby.

Story. That portion of a building included between the upper surface of a floor and upper surface of the floor or roof next above. If such

portion of a building does not include occupiable space, it is not considered a story for purposes of these guidelines. There may be more than one floor level within a story as in the case of a mezzanine or mezzanines.

Structural Frame. The structural frame shall be considered to be the columns and the girders, beams, trusses and spandrels having direct connections to the columns and all other members which are essential to the stability of the building as a whole.

Tactile. Describes an object that can be perceived using the sense of touch.

Text Telephone. Machinery or equipment that employs interactive graphic (i.e., typed) communications through the transmission of coded signals across the standard telephone network. Text telephones can include, for example, devices known as TDD's (telecommunication display devices or telecommunication devices for deaf persons) or computers.

Transient Lodging. A building, facility, or portion thereof, excluding inpatient medical care facilities, that contains one or more dwelling units or sleeping accommodations. Transient lodging may include, but is not limited to, resorts, group homes, hotels, motels, and dormitories.

Vehicular Way. A route intended for vehicular traffic, such as a street, driveway, or parking lot.

Walk. An exterior pathway with a prepared surface intended for pedestrian use, including general pedestrian areas such as plazas and courts.

NOTE: Sections 4.1.1 through 4.1.7 are different from ANSI A117.1 in their entirety and are printed in standard type (ANSI A117.1 does not include scoping provisions).

4.0 Accessible Elements and Spaces: Scope and Technical Requirements

4. ACCESSIBLE ELEMENTS AND SPACES: SCOPE AND TECHNICAL REQUIREMENTS.

4.1 Minimum Requirements

4.1.1* Application.

(1) General. All areas of newly designed or newly constructed buildings and facilities required to be accessible by 4.1.2 and 4.1.3 and altered portions of existing buildings and facilities required to be accessible by 4.1.6 shall comply with these guidelines, 4.1 through 4.35, unless otherwise provided in this section or as modified in a special application section.

(2) Application Based on Building Use. Special application sections 5 through 10 provide additional requirements for restaurants and cafeterias, medical care facilities, business and mercantile, libraries, accessible transient lodging, and transportation facilities. When a building or facility contains more than one use covered by a special application section, each portion shall comply with the requirements for that use.

(3)* Areas Used Only by Employees as Work Areas. Areas that are used only as work areas shall be designed and constructed so that individuals with disabilities can approach, enter, and exit the areas. These guidelines do not require that any areas used only as work areas be constructed to permit maneuvering within the work area or be constructed or equipped (i.e., with racks or shelves) to be accessible.

(4) Temporary Structures. These guidelines cover temporary buildings or facilities as well as permanent facilities. Temporary buildings and facilities are not of permanent construction but are extensively used or are essential for public use for a period of time. Examples of temporary buildings or facilities covered by these guidelines include, but are not limited to: reviewing stands, temporary classrooms, bleacher areas, exhibit areas, temporary banking facilities, temporary health screening services, or temporary safe pedestrian passageways around a construction site. Structures,

sites and equipment directly associated with the actual processes of construction, such as scaffolding, bridging, materials hoists, or construction trailers are not included.

(5) General Exceptions.

(a) In new construction, a person or entity is not required to meet fully the requirements of these guidelines where that person or entity can demonstrate that it is structurally impracticable to do so. Full compliance will be considered structurally impracticable only in those rare circumstances when the unique characteristics of terrain prevent the incorporation of accessibility features. If full compliance with the requirements of these guidelines is structurally impracticable, a person or entity shall comply with the requirements to the extent it is not structurally impracticable. Any portion of the building or facility which can be made accessible shall comply to the extent that it is not structurally impracticable.

(b) Accessibility is not required to (i) observation galleries used primarily for security purposes; or (ii) in non-occupiable spaces accessed only by ladders, catwalks, crawl spaces, very narrow passageways, or freight (non-passenger) elevators, and frequented only by service personnel for repair purposes; such spaces include, but are not limited to, elevator pits, elevator penthouses, piping or equipment catwalks.

4.1.2 Accessible Sites and Exterior Facilities: New Construction. An accessible site shall meet the following minimum requirements:

(1) At least one accessible route complying with 4.3 shall be provided within the boundary of the site from public transportation stops, accessible parking spaces, passenger loading zones if provided, and public streets or sidewalks, to an accessible building entrance.

(2) At least one accessible route complying with 4.3 shall connect accessible buildings, accessible facilities, accessible elements, and accessible spaces that are on the same site.

(3) All objects that protrude from surfaces or posts into circulation paths shall comply with 4.4.

35612   Federal Register / Vol. 56, No. 144 / Friday, July 26, 1991 / Rules and Regulations

4.1.2 Accessible Sites and Exterior Facilities: New Construction

(4) Ground surfaces along accessible routes and in accessible spaces shall comply with 4.5.

(5) (a) If parking spaces are provided for self-parking by employees or visitors, or both, then accessible spaces complying with 4.6 shall be provided in each such parking area in conformance with the table below. Spaces required by the table need not be provided in the particular lot. They may be provided in a different location if equivalent or greater accessibility, in terms of distance from an accessible entrance, cost and convenience is ensured.

Total Parking in Lot	Required Minimum Number of Accessible Spaces
1 to 25	1
26 to 50	2
51 to 75	3
76 to 100	4
101 to 150	5
151 to 200	6
201 to 300	7
301 to 400	8
401 to 500	9
501 to 1000	2 percent of total
1001 and over	20 plus 1 for each 100 over 1000

Except as provided in (b), access aisles adjacent to accessible spaces shall be 60 in (1525 mm) wide minimum.

(b) One in every eight accessible spaces, but not less than one, shall be served by an access aisle 96 in (2440 mm) wide minimum and shall be designated "van accessible" as required by 4.6.4. The vertical clearance at such spaces shall comply with 4.6.5. All such spaces may be grouped on one level of a parking structure.

EXCEPTION: Provision of all required parking spaces in conformance with "Universal Parking Design" (see appendix A4.6.3) is permitted.

(c) If passenger loading zones are provided, then at least one passenger loading zone shall comply with 4.6.6.

(d) At facilities providing medical care and other services for persons with mobility impairments, parking spaces complying with 4.6 shall

be provided in accordance with 4.1.2(5)(a) except as follows:

(i) Outpatient units and facilities: 10 percent of the total number of parking spaces provided serving each such outpatient unit or facility;

(ii) Units and facilities that specialize in treatment or services for persons with mobility impairments: 20 percent of the total number of parking spaces provided serving each such unit or facility.

(e)*Valet parking: Valet parking facilities shall provide a passenger loading zone complying with 4.6.6 located on an accessible route to the entrance of the facility. Paragraphs 5(a), 5(b), and 5(d) of this section do not apply to valet parking facilities.

(6) If toilet facilities are provided on a site, then each such public or common use toilet facility shall comply with 4.22. If bathing facilities are provided on a site, then each such public or common use bathing facility shall comply with 4.23.

For single user portable toilet or bathing units clustered at a single location, at least 5% but no less than one toilet unit or bathing unit complying with 4.22 or 4.23 shall be installed at each cluster whenever typical inaccessible units are provided. Accessible units shall be identified by the International Symbol of Accessibility.

EXCEPTION: Portable toilet units at construction sites used exclusively by construction personnel are not required to comply with 4.1.2(6).

(7) Building Signage. Signs which designate permanent rooms and spaces shall comply with 4.30.1, 4.30.4, 4.30.5 and 4.30.6. Other signs which provide direction to, or information about, functional spaces of the building shall comply with 4.30.1, 4.30.2, 4.30.3, and 4.30.5. Elements and spaces of accessible facilities which shall be identified by the International Symbol of Accessibility and which shall comply with 4.30.7 are:

(a) Parking spaces designated as reserved for individuals with disabilities;

Federal Register / Vol. 56, No. 144 / Friday, July 26, 1991 / Rules and Regulations   35613

4.1.3 Accessible Buildings: New Construction

(b) Accessible passenger loading zones;

(c) Accessible entrances when not all are accessible (inaccessible entrances shall have directional signage to indicate the route to the nearest accessible entrance);

(d) Accessible toilet and bathing facilities when not all are accessible.

4.1.3 Accessible Buildings: New Construction. Accessible buildings and facilities shall meet the following minimum requirements:

(1) At least one accessible route complying with 4.3 shall connect accessible building or facility entrances with all accessible spaces and elements within the building or facility.

(2) All objects that overhang or protrude into circulation paths shall comply with 4.4.

(3) Ground and floor surfaces along accessible routes and in accessible rooms and spaces shall comply with 4.5.

(4) Interior and exterior stairs connecting levels that are not connected by an elevator, ramp, or other accessible means of vertical access shall comply with 4.9.

(5)* One passenger elevator complying with 4.10 shall serve each level, including mezzanines, in all multi-story buildings and facilities unless exempted below. If more than one elevator is provided, each full passenger elevator shall comply with 4.10.

EXCEPTION 1: Elevators are not required in facilities that are less than three stories or that have less than 3000 square feet per story unless the building is a shopping center, a shopping mall, or the professional office of a health care provider, or another type of facility as determined by the Attorney General. The elevator exemption set forth in this paragraph does not obviate or limit in any way the obligation to comply with the other accessibility requirements established in section 4.1.3. For example, floors above or below the accessible ground floor must meet the requirements of this section except for elevator service. If toilet or bathing facilities are provided on a level not served by an elevator, then toilet or bathing facilities must be provided on the accessible

ground floor. In new construction if a building or facility is eligible for this exemption but a full passenger elevator is nonetheless planned, that elevator shall meet the requirements of 4.10 and shall serve each level in the building. A full passenger elevator that provides service from a garage to only one level of a building or facility is not required to serve other levels.

EXCEPTION 2: Elevator pits, elevator penthouses, mechanical rooms, piping or equipment catwalks are exempted from this requirement.

EXCEPTION 3: Accessible ramps complying with 4.8 may be used in lieu of an elevator.

EXCEPTION 4: Platform lifts (wheelchair lifts) complying with 4.11 of this guideline and applicable state or local codes may be used in lieu of an elevator only under the following conditions:

(a) To provide an accessible route to a performing area in an assembly occupancy.

(b) To comply with the wheelchair viewing position line-of-sight and dispersion requirements of 4.33.3.

(c) To provide access to incidental occupiable spaces and rooms which are not open to the general public and which house no more than five persons, including but not limited to equipment control rooms and projection booths.

(d) To provide access where existing site constraints or other constraints make use of a ramp or an elevator infeasible.

(6) Windows: (Reserved).

(7) Doors:

(a) At each accessible entrance to a building or facility, at least one door shall comply with 4.13.

(b) Within a building or facility, at least one door at each accessible space shall comply with 4.13.

(c) Each door that is an element of an accessible route shall comply with 4.13.

35614   Federal Register / Vol. 56, No. 144 / Friday, July 26, 1991 / Rules and Regulations

4.1.3 Accessible Buildings: New Construction

(d) Each door required by 4.3.10, Egress, shall comply with 4.13.

(8) In new construction, at a minimum, the requirements in (a) and (b) below shall be satisfied independently:

(a)(i) At least 50% of all public entrances (excluding those in (b) below) must be accessible. At least one must be a ground floor entrance. Public entrances are any entrances that are not loading or service entrances.

(ii) Accessible entrances must be provided in a number at least equivalent to the number of exits required by the applicable building/fire codes. (This paragraph does not require an increase in the total number of entrances planned for a facility.)

(iii) An accessible entrance must be provided to each tenancy in a facility (for example, individual stores in a strip shopping center).

One entrance may be considered as meeting more than one of the requirements in (a). Where feasible, accessible entrances shall be the entrances used by the majority of people visiting or working in the building.

(b)(i) In addition, if direct access is provided for pedestrians from an enclosed parking garage to the building, at least one direct entrance from the garage to the building must be accessible.

(ii) If access is provided for pedestrians from a pedestrian tunnel or elevated walkway, one entrance to the building from each tunnel or walkway must be accessible.

One entrance may be considered as meeting more than one of the requirements in (b).

Because entrances also serve as emergency exits whose proximity to all parts of buildings and facilities is essential, it is preferable that all entrances be accessible.

(c) If the only entrance to a building, or tenancy in a facility, is a service entrance, that entrance shall be accessible.

(d) Entrances which are not accessible shall have directional signage complying with 4.30.1,

4.30.2, 4.30.3, and 4.30.5, which indicates the location of the nearest accessible entrance.

(9)* In buildings or facilities, or portions of buildings or facilities, required to be accessible, accessible means of egress shall be provided in the same number as required for exits by local building/life safety regulations. Where a required exit from an occupiable level above or below a level of accessible exit discharge is not accessible, an area of rescue assistance shall be provided on each such level (in a number equal to that of inaccessible required exits). Areas of rescue assistance shall comply with 4.3.11. A horizontal exit, meeting the requirements of local building/life safety regulations, shall satisfy the requirement for an area of rescue assistance.

EXCEPTION: Areas of rescue assistance are not required in buildings or facilities having a supervised automatic sprinkler system.

(10)* Drinking Fountains:

(a) Where only one drinking fountain is provided on a floor there shall be a drinking fountain which is accessible to individuals who use wheelchairs in accordance with 4.15 and one accessible to those who have difficulty bending or stooping. (This can be accommodated by the use of a "hi-lo" fountain; by providing one fountain accessible to those who use wheelchairs and one fountain at a standard height convenient for those who have difficulty bending; by providing a fountain accessible under 4.15 and a water cooler; or by such other means as would achieve the required accessibility for each group on each floor.)

(b) Where more than one drinking fountain or water cooler is provided on a floor, 50% of those provided shall comply with 4.15 and shall be on an accessible route.

(11) Toilet Facilities: If toilet rooms are provided, then each public and common use toilet room shall comply with 4.22. Other toilet rooms provided for the use of occupants of specific spaces (i.e., a private toilet room for the occupant of a private office) shall be adaptable. If bathing rooms are provided, then each public and common use bathroom shall comply with 4.23. Accessible toilet rooms and bathing facilities shall be on an accessible route.

Federal Register / Vol. 56, No. 144 / Friday, July 26, 1991 / Rules and Regulations   **35615**

4.1.3 Accessible Buildings: New Construction

(12) Storage, Shelving and Display Units:

(a) If fixed or built-in storage facilities such as cabinets, shelves, closets, and drawers are provided in accessible spaces, at least one of each type provided shall contain storage space complying with 4.25. Additional storage may be provided outside of the dimensions required by 4.25.

(b) Shelves or display units allowing self-service by customers in mercantile occupancies shall be located on an accessible route complying with 4.3. Requirements for accessible reach range do not apply.

(13) Controls and operating mechanisms in accessible spaces, along accessible routes, or as parts of accessible elements (for example, light switches and dispenser controls) shall comply with 4.27.

(14) If emergency warning systems are provided, then they shall include both audible alarms and visual alarms complying with 4.28. Sleeping accommodations required to comply with 9.3 shall have an alarm system complying with 4.28. Emergency warning systems in medical care facilities may be modified to suit standard health care alarm design practice.

(15) Detectable warnings shall be provided at locations as specified in 4.29.

(16) Building Signage:

(a) Signs which designate permanent rooms and spaces shall comply with 4.30.1, 4.30.4, 4.30.5 and 4.30.6.

(b) Other signs which provide direction to or information about functional spaces of the building shall comply with 4.30.1, 4.30.2, 4.30.3, and 4.30.5.

EXCEPTION: Building directories, menus, and all other signs which are temporary are not required to comply.

(17) Public Telephones:

(a) If public pay telephones, public closed circuit telephones, or other public telephones are provided, then they shall comply with 4.31.2 through 4.31.8 to the extent required by the following table:

Number of each type of telephone provided on each floor	Number of telephones required to comply with 4.31.2 through 4.31.8[1]
1 or more single unit	1 per floor
1 bank[2]	1 per floor
2 or more banks[2]	1 per bank. Accessible unit may be installed as a single unit in proximity (either visible or with signage) to the bank. At least one public telephone per floor shall meet the requirements for a forward reach telephone[3].

[1] Additional public telephones may be installed at any height. Unless otherwise specified, accessible telephones may be either forward or side reach telephones.

[2] A bank consists of two or more adjacent public telephones, often installed as a unit.

[3] EXCEPTION: For exterior installations only, if dial tone first service is available, then a side reach telephone may be installed instead of the required forward reach telephone (i.e., one telephone in proximity to each bank shall comply with 4.31).

(b)* All telephones required to be accessible and complying with 4.31.2 through 4.31.8 shall be equipped with a volume control. In addition, 25 percent, but never less than one, of all other public telephones provided shall be equipped with a volume control and shall be dispersed among all types of public telephones, including closed circuit telephones, throughout the building or facility. Signage complying with applicable provisions of 4.30.7 shall be provided.

(c) The following shall be provided in accordance with 4.31.9:

(i) if a total number of four or more public pay telephones (including both interior and exterior phones) is provided at a site, and at least one is in an interior location, then at least one interior public text telephone shall be provided.

(ii) if an interior public pay telephone is provided in a stadium or arena, in a convention center, in a hotel with a convention center, or

35616   Federal Register / Vol. 56, No. 144 / Friday, July 26, 1991 / Rules and Regulations

4.1.3 Accessible Buildings: New Construction

in a covered mall, at least one interior public text telephone shall be provided in the facility.

(iii) if a public pay telephone is located in or adjacent to a hospital emergency room, hospital recovery room, or hospital waiting room, one public text telephone shall be provided at each such location.

(d) Where a bank of telephones in the interior of a building consists of three or more public pay telephones, at least one public pay telephone in each such bank shall be equipped with a shelf and outlet in compliance with 4.31.9(2).

(18) If fixed or built-in seating or tables (including, but not limited to, study carrels and student laboratory stations), are provided in accessible public or common use areas, at least five percent (5%), but not less than one, of the fixed or built-in seating areas or tables shall comply with 4.32. An accessible route shall lead to and through such fixed or built-in seating areas, or tables.

(19)* Assembly areas:

(a) In places of assembly with fixed seating accessible wheelchair locations shall comply with 4.33.2, 4.33.3, and 4.33.4 and shall be provided consistent with the following table:

Capacity of Seating in Assembly Areas	Number of Required Wheelchair Locations
4 to 25	1
26 to 50	2
51 to 300	4
301 to 500	6
over 500	6, plus 1 additional space for each total seating capacity increase of 100

In addition, one percent, but not less than one, of all fixed seats shall be aisle seats with no armrests on the aisle side, or removable or folding armrests on the aisle side. Each such seat shall be identified by a sign or marker. Signage notifying patrons of the availability of such seats shall be posted at the ticket office. Aisle seats are not required to comply with 4.33.4.

(b) This paragraph applies to assembly areas where audible communications are integral to the use of the space (e.g., concert and lecture halls, playhouses and movie theaters, meeting rooms, etc.). Such assembly areas, if (1) they accommodate at least 50 persons, or if they have audio-amplification systems, and (2) they have fixed seating, shall have a permanently installed assistive listening system complying with 4.33. For other assembly areas, a permanently installed assistive listening system, or an adequate number of electrical outlets or other supplementary wiring necessary to support a portable assistive listening system shall be provided. The minimum number of receivers to be provided shall be equal to 4 percent of the total number of seats, but in no case less than two. Signage complying with applicable provisions of 4.30 shall be installed to notify patrons of the availability of a listening system.

(20) Where automated teller machines (ATMs) are provided, each ATM shall comply with the requirements of 4.34 except where two or more are provided at a location. then only one must comply.

EXCEPTION: Drive-up-only automated teller machines are not required to comply with 4.27.2, 4.27.3 and 4.34.3.

(21) Where dressing and fitting rooms are provided for use by the general public, patients, customers or employees, 5 percent, but never less than one, of dressing rooms for each type of use in each cluster of dressing rooms shall be accessible and shall comply with 4.35.

Examples of types of dressing rooms are those serving different genders or distinct and different functions as in different treatment or examination facilities.

4.1.4 (Reserved).

4.1.5 Accessible Buildings: Additions.
Each addition to an existing building or facility shall be regarded as an alteration. Each space or element added to the existing building or facility shall comply with the applicable provisions of 4.1.1 to 4.1.3, Minimum Requirements (for New Construction) and the applicable technical specifications of 4.2 through 4.35 and sections 5 through 10. Each addition that

Federal Register / Vol. 56, No. 144 / Friday, July 26, 1991 / Rules and Regulations
35617

affects or could affect the usability of an area containing a primary function shall comply with 4.1.6(2).

4.1.6 Accessible Buildings: Alterations.

(1) General. Alterations to existing buildings and facilities shall comply with the following:

(a) No alteration shall be undertaken which decreases or has the effect of decreasing accessibility or usability of a building or facility below the requirements for new construction at the time of alteration.

(b) If existing elements, spaces, or common areas are altered, then each such altered element, space, feature, or area shall comply with the applicable provisions of 4.1.1 to 4.1.3 Minimum Requirements (for New Construction). If the applicable provision for new construction requires that an element, space, or common area be on an accessible route, the altered element, space, or common area is not required to be on an accessible route except as provided in 4.1.6(2) (Alterations to an Area Containing a Primary Function.)

(c) If alterations of single elements, when considered together, amount to an alteration of a room or space in a building or facility, the entire space shall be made accessible.

(d) No alteration of an existing element, space, or area of a building or facility shall impose a requirement for greater accessibility than that which would be required for new construction. For example, if the elevators and stairs in a building are being altered and the elevators are, in turn, being made accessible, then no accessibility modifications are required to the stairs connecting levels connected by the elevator. If stair modifications to correct unsafe conditions are required by other codes, the modifications shall be done in compliance with these guidelines unless technically infeasible.

(e) At least one interior public text telephone complying with 4.31.9 shall be provided if:

(i) alterations to existing buildings or facilities with less than four exterior or interior public pay telephones would increase the total number to four or more telephones with at least one in an interior location; or

(ii) alterations to one or more exterior or interior public pay telephones occur in an existing building or facility with four or more public telephones with at least one in an interior location.

(f) If an escalator or stair is planned or installed where none existed previously and major structural modifications are necessary for such installation, then a means of accessible vertical access shall be provided that complies with the applicable provisions of 4.7, 4.8, 4.10, or 4.11.

(g) In alterations, the requirements of 4.1.3(9), 4.3.10 and 4.3.11 do not apply.

(h)*Entrances: If a planned alteration entails alterations to an entrance, and the building has an accessible entrance, the entrance being altered is not required to comply with 4.1.3(8), except to the extent required by 4.1.6(2). If a particular entrance is not made accessible, appropriate accessible signage indicating the location of the nearest accessible entrance(s) shall be installed at or near the inaccessible entrance, such that a person with disabilities will not be required to retrace the approach route from the inaccessible entrance.

(i) If the alteration work is limited solely to the electrical, mechanical, or plumbing system, or to hazardous material abatement, or automatic sprinkler retrofitting, and does not involve the alteration of any elements or spaces required to be accessible under these guidelines, then 4.1.6(2) does not apply.

(j) EXCEPTION: In alteration work, if compliance with 4.1.6 is technically infeasible, the alteration shall provide accessibility to the maximum extent feasible. Any elements or features of the building or facility that are being altered and can be made accessible shall be made accessible within the scope of the alteration.

Technically Infeasible. Means, with respect to an alteration of a building or a facility, that it has little likelihood of being accomplished because existing structural conditions would require removing or altering a load-bearing member which is an essential part of the structural frame; or because other existing physical or site constraints prohibit modification or

35618   Federal Register / Vol. 56, No. 144 / Friday, July 26, 1991 / Rules and Regulations

4.1.6 Accessible Buildings: Alterations

addition of elements, spaces, or features which are in full and strict compliance with the minimum requirements for new construction and which are necessary to provide accessibility.

(k) EXCEPTION:

(i) These guidelines do not require the installation of an elevator in an altered facility that is less than three stories or has less than 3,000 square feet per story unless the building is a shopping center, a shopping mall, the professional office of a health care provider, or another type of facility as determined by the Attorney General.

(ii) The exemption provided in paragraph (i) does not obviate or limit in any way the obligation to comply with the other accessibility requirements established in these guidelines. For example, alterations to floors above or below the ground floor must be accessible regardless of whether the altered facility has an elevator. If a facility subject to the elevator exemption set forth in paragraph (i) nonetheless has a full passenger elevator, that elevator shall meet, to the maximum extent feasible, the accessibility requirements of these guidelines.

(2) Alterations to an Area Containing a Primary Function: In addition to the requirements of 4.1.6(1), an alteration that affects or could affect the usability of or access to an area containing a primary function shall be made so as to ensure that, to the maximum extent feasible, the path of travel to the altered area and the restrooms, telephones, and drinking fountains serving the altered area, are readily accessible to and usable by individuals with disabilities, unless such alterations are disproportionate to the overall alterations in terms of cost and scope (as determined under criteria established by the Attorney General).

(3) Special Technical Provisions for Alterations to Existing Buildings and Facilities:

(a) Ramps: Curb ramps and interior or exterior ramps to be constructed on sites or in existing buildings or facilities where space limitations prohibit the use of a 1:12 slope or less may have slopes and rises as follows:

(i) A slope between 1:10 and 1:12 is allowed for a maximum rise of 6 inches.

(ii) A slope between 1:8 and 1:10 is allowed for a maximum rise of 3 inches. A slope steeper than 1:8 is not allowed.

(b) Stairs: Full extension of handrails at stairs shall not be required in alterations where such extensions would be hazardous or impossible due to plan configuration.

(c) Elevators:

(i) If safety door edges are provided in existing automatic elevators, automatic door reopening devices may be omitted (see 4.10.6).

(ii) Where existing shaft configuration or technical infeasibility prohibits strict compliance with 4.10.9, the minimum car plan dimensions may be reduced by the minimum amount necessary, but in no case shall the inside car area be smaller than 48 in by 48 in.

(iii) Equivalent facilitation may be provided with an elevator car of different dimensions when usability can be demonstrated and when all other elements required to be accessible comply with the applicable provisions of 4.10. For example, an elevator of 47 in by 69 in (1195 mm by 1755 mm) with a door opening on the narrow dimension, could accommodate the standard wheelchair clearances shown in Figure 4.

(d) Doors:

(i) Where it is technically infeasible to comply with clear opening width requirements of 4.13.5, a projection of 5/8 in maximum will be permitted for the latch side stop.

(ii) If existing thresholds are 3/4 in high or less, and have (or are modified to have) a beveled edge on each side, they may remain.

(e) Toilet Rooms:

(i) Where it is technically infeasible to comply with 4.22 or 4.23, the installation of at least one unisex toilet/bathroom per floor, located in the same area as existing toilet facilities, will be permitted in lieu of modifying existing toilet facilities to be accessible. Each unisex toilet room shall contain one water closet complying with 4.16 and one lavatory complying with 4.19, and the door shall have a privacy latch.

Federal Register / Vol. 56, No. 144 / Friday, July 26, 1991 / Rules and Regulations   35619

4.1.7 Accessible Buildings: Historic Preservation

(ii) Where it is technically infeasible to install a required standard stall (Fig. 30(a)), or where other codes prohibit reduction of the fixture count (i.e., removal of a water closet in order to create a double-wide stall), either alternate stall (Fig.30(b)) may be provided in lieu of the standard stall.

(iii) When existing toilet or bathing facilities are being altered and are not made accessible, signage complying with 4.30.1, 4.30.2, 4.30.3, 4.30.5, and 4.30.7 shall be provided indicating the location of the nearest accessible toilet or bathing facility within the facility.

(f) Assembly Areas:

(i) Where it is technically infeasible to disperse accessible seating throughout an altered assembly area, accessible seating areas may be clustered. Each accessible seating area shall have provisions for companion seating and shall be located on an accessible route that also serves as a means of emergency egress.

(ii) Where it is technically infeasible to alter all performing areas to be on an accessible route, at least one of each type of performing area shall be made accessible.

(g) Platform Lifts (Wheelchair Lifts): In alterations, platform lifts (wheelchair lifts) complying with 4.11 and applicable state or local codes may be used as part of an accessible route. The use of lifts is not limited to the four conditions in exception 4 of 4.1.3(5).

(h) Dressing Rooms: In alterations where technical infeasibility can be demonstrated, one dressing room for each sex on each level shall be made accessible. Where only unisex dressing rooms are provided, accessible unisex dressing rooms may be used to fulfill this requirement.

4.1.7 Accessible Buildings: Historic Preservation.

(1) Applicability:

(a) General Rule. Alterations to a qualified historic building or facility shall comply with 4.1.6 Accessible Buildings: Alterations, the applicable technical specifications of 4.2 through 4.35 and the applicable special application sections 5 through 10 unless it is determined in accordance with the procedures in 4.1.7(2) that compliance with the requirements for accessible routes (exterior and interior), ramps, entrances, or toilets would threaten or destroy the historic significance of the building or facility in which case the alternative requirements in 4.1.7(3) may be used for the feature.

EXCEPTION: (Reserved).

(b) Definition. A qualified historic building or facility is a building or facility that is:

(i) Listed in or eligible for listing in the National Register of Historic Places; or

(ii) Designated as historic under an appropriate State or local law.

(2) Procedures:

(a) Alterations to Qualified Historic Buildings and Facilities Subject to Section 106 of the National Historic Preservation Act:

(i) Section 106 Process. Section 106 of the National Historic Preservation Act (16 U.S.C. 470 f) requires that a Federal agency with jurisdiction over a Federal, federally assisted, or federally licensed undertaking consider the effects of the agency's undertaking on buildings and facilities listed in or eligible for listing in the National Register of Historic Places and give the Advisory Council on Historic Preservation a reasonable opportunity to comment on the undertaking prior to approval of the undertaking.

(ii) ADA Application. Where alterations are undertaken to a qualified historic building or facility that is subject to section 106 of the National Historic Preservation Act, the Federal agency with jurisdiction over the undertaking shall follow the section 106 process. If the State Historic Preservation Officer or Advisory Council on Historic Preservation agrees that compliance with the requirements for accessible routes (exterior and interior), ramps, entrances, or toilets would threaten or destroy the historic significance of the building or facility, the alternative requirements in 4.1.7(3) may be used for the feature.

35620   Federal Register / Vol. 56, No. 144 / Friday, July 26, 1991 / Rules and Regulations

4.2 Space Allowance and Reach Ranges

(b) Alterations to Qualified Historic Buildings and Facilities Not Subject to Section 106 of the National Historic Preservation Act. Where alterations are undertaken to a qualified historic building or facility that is not subject to section 106 of the National Historic Preservation Act, if the entity undertaking the alterations believes that compliance with the requirements for accessible routes (exterior and interior), ramps, entrances, or toilets would threaten or destroy the historic significance of the building or facility and that the alternative requirements in 4.1.7(3) should be used for the feature, the entity should consult with the State Historic Preservation Officer. If the State Historic Preservation Officer agrees that compliance with the accessibility requirements for accessible routes (exterior and interior), ramps, entrances or toilets would threaten or destroy the historical significance of the building or facility, the alternative requirements in 4.1.7(3) may be used.

(c) Consultation With Interested Persons. Interested persons should be invited to participate in the consultation process, including State or local accessibility officials, individuals with disabilities, and organizations representing individuals with disabilities.

(d) Certified Local Government Historic Preservation Programs. Where the State Historic Preservation Officer has delegated the consultation responsibility for purposes of this section to a local government historic preservation program that has been certified in accordance with section 101(c) of the National Historic Preservation Act of 1966 (16 U.S.C. 470a (c)) and implementing regulations (36 CFR 61.5), the responsibility may be carried out by the appropriate local government body or official.

(3) Historic Preservation: Minimum Requirements:

(a) At least one accessible route complying with 4.3 from a site access point to an accessible entrance shall be provided.

EXCEPTION: A ramp with a slope no greater than 1:6 for a run not to exceed 2 ft (610 mm) may be used as part of an accessible route to an entrance.

(b) At least one accessible entrance complying with 4.14 which is used by the public shall be provided.

EXCEPTION: If it is determined that no entrance used by the public can comply with 4.14, then access at any entrance not used by the general public but open (unlocked) with directional signage at the primary entrance may be used. The accessible entrance shall also have a notification system. Where security is a problem, remote monitoring may be used.

(c) If toilets are provided, then at least one toilet facility complying with 4.22 and 4.1.6 shall be provided along an accessible route that complies with 4.3. Such toilet facility may be unisex in design.

(d) Accessible routes from an accessible entrance to all publicly used spaces on at least the level of the accessible entrance shall be provided. Access shall be provided to all levels of a building or facility in compliance with 4.1 whenever practical.

(e) Displays and written information, documents, etc., should be located where they can be seen by a seated person. Exhibits and signage displayed horizontally (e.g., open books), should be no higher than 44 in (1120 mm) above the floor surface.

NOTE: The technical provisions of sections 4.2 through 4.35 are the same as those of the American National Standard Institute's document A117.1-1980, except as noted in the text.

4.2 Space Allowance and Reach Ranges.

4.2.1* Wheelchair Passage Width. The minimum clear width for single wheelchair passage shall be 32 in (815 mm) at a point and 36 in (915 mm) continuously (see Fig. 1 and 24(e)).

4.2.2 Width for Wheelchair Passing. The minimum width for two wheelchairs to pass is 60 in (1525 mm) (see Fig. 2).

4.2.3* Wheelchair Turning Space. The space required for a wheelchair to make a 180-degree turn is a clear space of 60 in (1525 mm)

Federal Register / Vol. 56, No. 144 / Friday, July 26, 1991 / Rules and Regulations

35621

4.2.4* Clear Floor or Ground Space for Wheelchairs

diameter (see Fig. 3(a)) or a T-shaped space (see Fig. 3(b)).

4.2.4* Clear Floor or Ground Space for Wheelchairs.

4.2.4.1 Size and Approach. The minimum clear floor or ground space required to accommodate a single, stationary wheelchair and occupant is 30 in by 48 in (760 mm by 1220 mm) (see Fig. 4(a)). The minimum clear floor or ground space for wheelchairs may be positioned for forward or parallel approach to an object (see Fig. 4(b) and (c)). Clear floor or ground space for wheelchairs may be part of the knee space required under some objects.

4.2.4.2 Relationship of Maneuvering Clearance to Wheelchair Spaces. One full unobstructed side of the clear floor or ground space for a wheelchair shall adjoin or overlap an accessible route or adjoin another wheelchair clear floor space. If a clear floor space is located in an alcove or otherwise confined on all or part of three sides, additional maneuvering clearances shall be provided as shown in Fig. 4(d) and (e).

4.2.4.3 Surfaces for Wheelchair Spaces. Clear floor or ground spaces for wheelchairs shall comply with 4.5.

4.2.5* Forward Reach. If the clear floor space only allows forward approach to an object, the maximum high forward reach allowed shall be 48 in (1220 mm) (see Fig. 5(a)). *The minimum low forward reach is 15 in (380 mm).* If the high forward reach is over an obstruction, reach and clearances shall be as shown in Fig. 5(b).

4.2.6* Side Reach. If the clear floor space allows parallel approach by a person in a wheelchair, the maximum high side reach allowed shall be 54 in (1370 mm) and the low side reach shall be no less than 9 in (230 mm) above the floor (Fig. 6(a) and (b)). If the side reach is over an obstruction, the reach and clearances shall be as shown in Fig 6(c).

4.3 Accessible Route.

4.3.1* General. All walks, halls, corridors, aisles, *skywalks, tunnels,* and other spaces

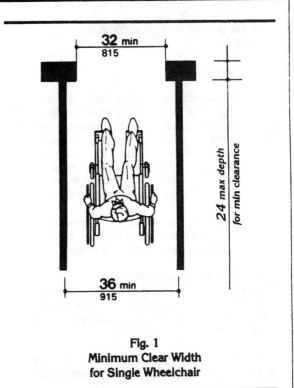

Fig. 1
Minimum Clear Width
for Single Wheelchair

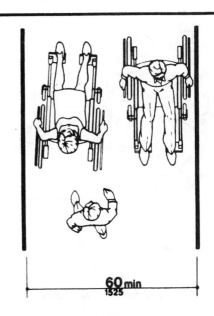

Fig. 2
Minimum Clear Width
for Two Wheelchairs

35622   Federal Register / Vol. 56, No. 144 / Friday, July 26, 1991 / Rules and Regulations

4.3 Accessible Route

that are part of an accessible route shall comply with 4.3.

4.3.2 Location.

(1) At least one accessible route *within the boundary of the site* shall be provided from public transportation stops, accessible parking, and accessible passenger loading zones, and public streets or sidewalks to the accessible building entrance they serve. *The accessible route shall, to the maximum extent feasible, coincide with the route for the general public.*

(2) At least one accessible route shall connect accessible buildings, facilities, elements, and spaces that are on the same site.

(3) At least one accessible route shall connect accessible building or facility entrances with all accessible spaces and elements and with all accessible dwelling units within the building or facility.

(4) An accessible route shall connect at least one accessible entrance of each accessible

dwelling unit with those exterior and interior spaces and facilities that serve the accessible dwelling unit.

4.3.3 Width.
The minimum clear width of an accessible route shall be 36 in (915 mm) except at doors (see 4.13.5 and 4.13.6). If a person in a wheelchair must make a turn around an obstruction, the minimum clear width of the accessible route shall be as shown in Fig. 7(a) and (b).

4.3.4 Passing Space.
If an accessible route has less than 60 in (1525 mm) clear width, then passing spaces at least 60 in by 60 in (1525 mm by 1525 mm) shall be located at reasonable intervals not to exceed 200 ft (61 m). A T-intersection of two corridors or walks is an acceptable passing place.

4.3.5 Head Room.
Accessible routes shall comply with 4.4.2.

4.3.6 Surface Textures.
The surface of an accessible route shall comply with 4.5.

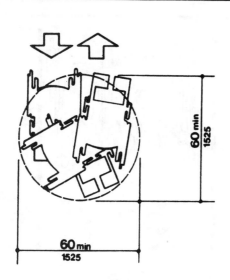

(a)
60-in (1525-mm)-Diameter Space

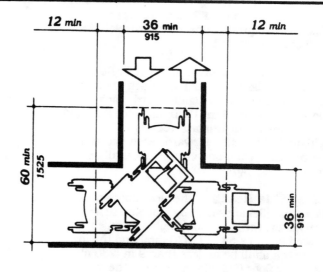

(b)
T-Shaped Space for 180° Turns

Fig. 3
Wheelchair Turning Space

Federal Register / Vol. 56, No. 144 / Friday, July 26, 1991 / Rules and Regulations 35623

4.3 Accessible Route

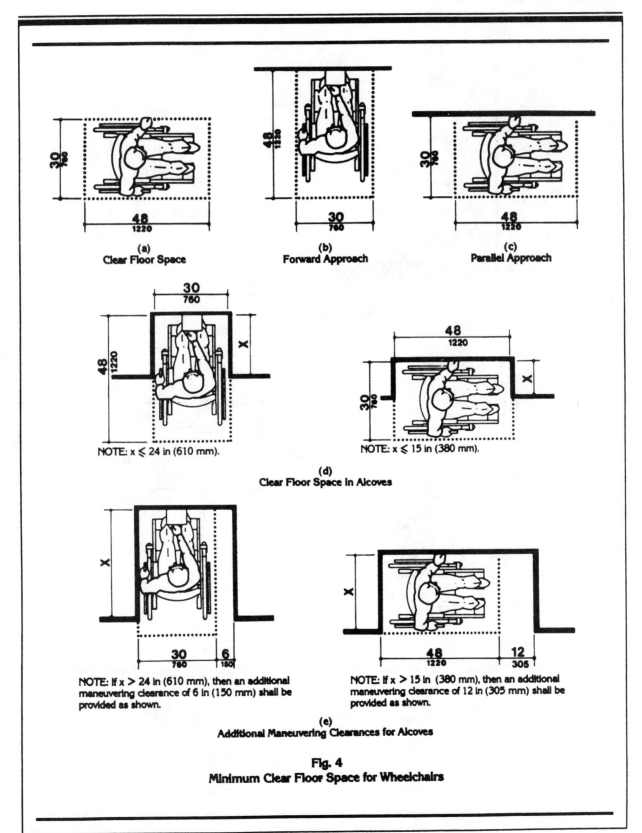

(a)
Clear Floor Space

(b)
Forward Approach

(c)
Parallel Approach

NOTE: x ≤ 24 in (610 mm).

NOTE: x ≤ 15 in (380 mm).

(d)
Clear Floor Space in Alcoves

NOTE: If x > 24 in (610 mm), then an additional maneuvering clearance of 6 in (150 mm) shall be provided as shown.

NOTE: If x > 15 in (380 mm), then an additional maneuvering clearance of 12 in (305 mm) shall be provided as shown.

(e)
Additional Maneuvering Clearances for Alcoves

Fig. 4
Minimum Clear Floor Space for Wheelchairs

35624   Federal Register / Vol. 56, No. 144 / Friday, July 26, 1991 / Rules and Regulations

4.3 Accessible Route

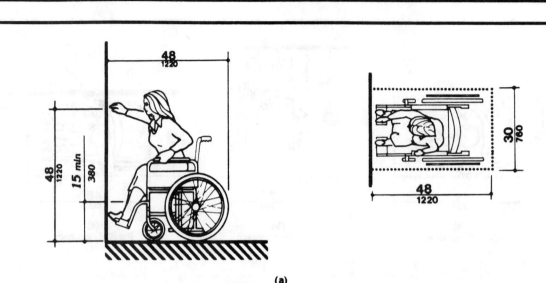

(a)
High Forward Reach Limit

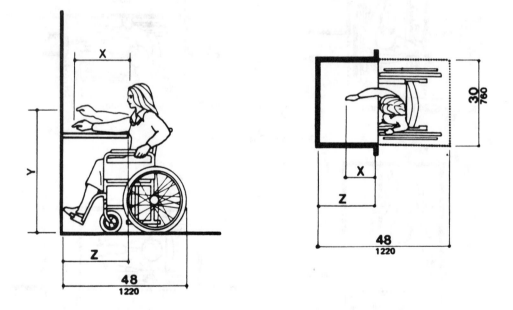

NOTE: x shall be ≤ 25 in (635 mm); z shall be ≥ x. When x < 20 in (510 mm), then y shall be 48 in (1220 mm) maximum.
When x is 20 to 25 in (510 to 635 mm), then y shall be 44 in (1120 mm) maximum.

(b)
Maximum Forward Reach over an Obstruction

Fig. 5
Forward Reach

Federal Register / Vol. 56, No. 144 / Friday, July 26, 1991 / Rules and Regulations   **35625**

4.3.7 Slope

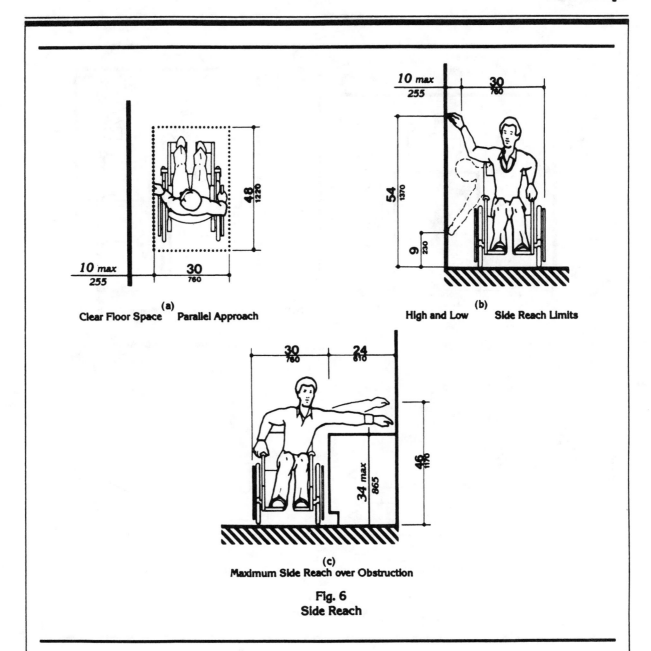

(a)
Clear Floor Space   Parallel Approach

(b)
High and Low   Side Reach Limits

(c)
Maximum Side Reach over Obstruction

Fig. 6
Side Reach

4.3.7 Slope. An accessible route with a running slope greater than 1:20 is a ramp and shall comply with 4.8. Nowhere shall the cross slope of an accessible route exceed 1:50.

4.3.8 Changes in Levels. Changes in levels along an accessible route shall comply with 4.5.2. If an accessible route has changes in level greater than 1/2 in (13 mm), then a curb

ramp, ramp, elevator, or platform lift *(as permitted in 4.1.3 and 4.1.6)* shall be provided that complies with 4.7, 4.8, 4.10, or 4.11, respectively. An accessible route does not include stairs, steps, or escalators. See definition of "egress, means of" in 3.5.

4.3.9 Doors. Doors along an accessible route shall comply with 4.13.

35626   Federal Register / Vol. 56, No. 144 / Friday, July 26, 1991 / Rules and Regulations

4.3.10* Egress

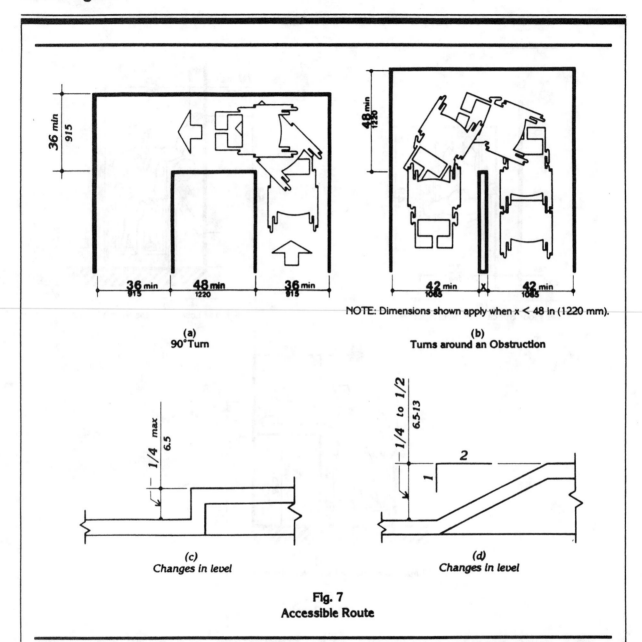

NOTE: Dimensions shown apply when x < 48 in (1220 mm).

(a)
90° Turn

(b)
Turns around an Obstruction

(c)
Changes in level

(d)
Changes in level

Fig. 7
Accessible Route

4.3.10* Egress. Accessible routes serving any accessible space or element shall also serve as a means of egress for emergencies or connect to an accessible area of *rescue assistance*.

4.3.11 Areas of Rescue Assistance.

4.3.11.1 Location and Construction. An area of rescue assistance shall be one of the following:

(1) A portion of a stairway landing within a smokeproof enclosure (complying with local requirements).

(2) A portion of an exterior exit balcony located immediately adjacent to an exit stairway when the balcony complies with local requirements for exterior exit balconies. Openings to the interior of the building located within 20 feet (6 m) of the

Federal Register / Vol. 56, No. 144 / Friday, July 26, 1991 / Rules and Regulations   35627

4.4 Protruding Objects

area of rescue assistance shall be protected with fire assemblies having a three-fourths hour fire protection rating.

(3) A portion of a one-hour fire-resistive corridor (complying with local requirements for fire-resistive construction and for openings) located immediately adjacent to an exit enclosure.

(4) A vestibule located immediately adjacent to an exit enclosure and constructed to the same fire-resistive standards as required for corridors and openings.

(5) A portion of a stairway landing within an exit enclosure which is vented to the exterior and is separated from the interior of the building with not less than one-hour fire-resistive doors.

(6) When approved by the appropriate local authority, an area or a room which is separated from other portions of the building by a smoke barrier. Smoke barriers shall have a fire-resistive rating of not less than one hour and shall completely enclose the area or room. Doors in the smoke barrier shall be tight-fitting smoke- and draft-control assemblies having a fire-protection rating of not less than 20 minutes and shall be self-closing or automatic closing. The area or room shall be provided with an exit directly to an exit enclosure. Where the room or area exits into an exit enclosure which is required to be of more than one-hour fire-resistive construction, the room or area shall have the same fire-resistive construction, including the same opening protection, as required for the adjacent exit enclosure.

(7) An elevator lobby when elevator shafts and adjacent lobbies are pressurized as required for smokeproof enclosures by local regulations and when complying with requirements herein for size, communication, and signage. Such pressurization system shall be activated by smoke detectors on each floor located in a manner approved by the appropriate local authority. Pressurization equipment and its duct work within the building shall be separated from other portions of the building by a minimum two-hour fire-resistive construction.

4.3.11.2 Size. Each area of rescue assistance shall provide at least two accessible areas each being not less than 30 inches by 48 inches (760 mm by 1220 mm). The area of rescue

assistance shall not encroach on any required exit width. The total number of such 30-inch by 48-inch (760 mm by 1220 mm) areas per story shall be not less than one for every 200 persons of calculated occupant load served by the area of rescue assistance.

EXCEPTION: The appropriate local authority may reduce the minimum number of 30-inch by 48-inch (760 mm by 1220 mm) areas to one for each area of rescue assistance on floors where the occupant load is less than 200.

4.3.11.3* Stairway Width. Each stairway adjacent to an area of rescue assistance shall have a minimum clear width of 48 inches between handrails.

4.3.11.4* Two-way Communication. A method of two-way communication, with both visible and audible signals, shall be provided between each area of rescue assistance and the primary entry. The fire department or appropriate local authority may approve a location other than the primary entry.

4.3.11.5 Identification. Each area of rescue assistance shall be identified by a sign which states "AREA OF RESCUE ASSISTANCE" and displays the international symbol of accessibility. The sign shall be illuminated when exit sign illumination is required. Signage shall also be installed at all inaccessible exits and where otherwise necessary to clearly indicate the direction to areas of rescue assistance. In each area of rescue assistance, instructions on the use of the area under emergency conditions shall be posted adjoining the two-way communication system.

4.4 Protruding Objects.

4.4.1* General. Objects projecting from walls (for example, telephones) with their leading edges between 27 in and 80 in (685 mm and 2030 mm) above the finished floor shall protrude no more than 4 in (100 mm) into walks, halls, corridors, passageways, or aisles (see Fig. 8(a)). Objects mounted with their leading edges at or below 27 in (685 mm) above the finished floor may protrude any amount (see Fig. 8(a) and (b)). Free-standing objects mounted on posts or pylons may overhang 12 in (305 mm) maximum from 27 in to 80 in (685 mm to 2030 mm) above the ground or

35628   Federal Register / Vol. 56, No. 144 / Friday, July 26, 1991 / Rules and Regulations

4.4 Protruding Objects

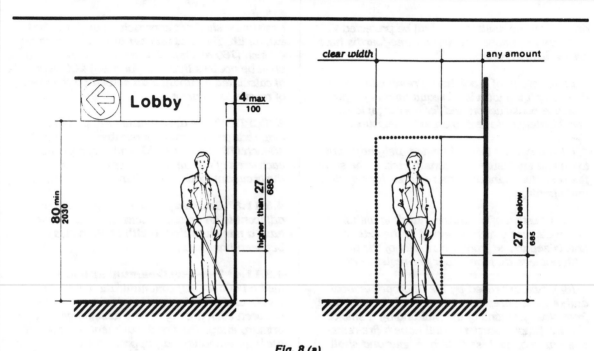

Fig. 8 (a)
Walking Parallel to a Wall

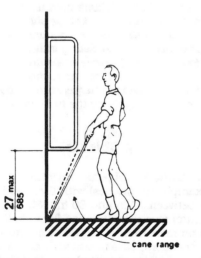

Fig. 8 (b)
Walking Perpendicular to a Wall

Fig. 8
Protruding Objects

finished floor (see Fig. 8(c) and (d)). Protruding objects shall not reduce the clear width of an accessible route or maneuvering space (see Fig. 8(e)).

4.4.2 Head Room. Walks, halls, corridors, passageways, aisles, or other circulation spaces shall have 80 in (2030 mm) minimum clear head room (see Fig. 8(a)). *If vertical clearance of an area adjoining an accessible route is reduced to less than 80 in (nominal dimension), a barrier to warn blind or visually-impaired persons shall be provided (see Fig. 8(c-1)).*

4.5 Ground and Floor Surfaces.

4.5.1* General. Ground and floor surfaces along accessible routes and in accessible rooms and spaces including floors, walks, ramps, stairs, and curb ramps, shall be stable, firm, slip-resistant, and shall comply with 4.5.

4.5.2 Changes in Level. Changes in level up to 1/4 in (6 mm) may be vertical and without edge treatment *(see Fig. 7(c)).* Changes in level between 1/4 in and 1/2 in (6 mm and 13 mm)

Federal Register / Vol. 56, No. 144 / Friday, July 26, 1991 / Rules and Regulations   **35629**

4.4 Protruding Objects

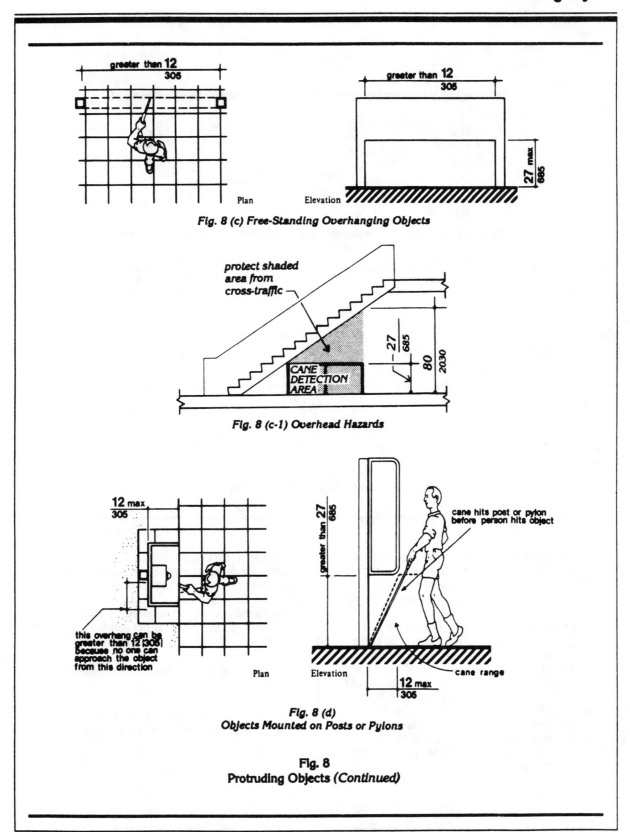

Fig. 8 (c) Free-Standing Overhanging Objects

Fig. 8 (c-1) Overhead Hazards

Fig. 8 (d)
Objects Mounted on Posts or Pylons

Fig. 8
Protruding Objects (Continued)

35630   Federal Register / Vol. 56, No. 144 / Friday, July 26, 1991 / Rules and Regulations

4.5 Ground and Floor Surfaces

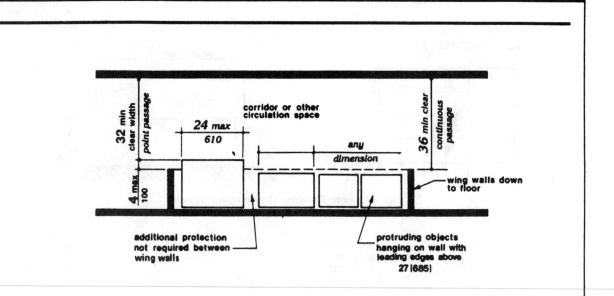

Fig. 8 (e)
Example of Protection around Wall-Mounted Objects and Measurements of Clear Widths

Fig. 8
Protruding Objects *(Continued)*

shall be beveled with a slope no greater than 1:2 *(see Fig. 7(d))*. Changes in level greater than 1/2 in (13 mm) shall be accomplished by means of a ramp that complies with 4.7 or 4.8.

4.5.3* Carpet. If carpet or carpet tile is used on a ground or floor surface, then it shall be securely attached; have a firm cushion, pad, or backing, or no cushion or pad; and have a level loop, textured loop, level cut pile, or level cut/uncut pile texture. The maximum pile *thickness* shall be 1/2 in (13 mm) (see Fig. 8(f)). Exposed edges of carpet shall be fastened to floor surfaces and have trim along the entire length of the exposed edge. Carpet edge trim shall comply with 4.5.2.

4.5.4 Gratings. If gratings are located in walking surfaces, then they shall have spaces no greater than 1/2 in (13 mm) wide in one direction *(see Fig. 8(g))*. If gratings have elongated openings, then they shall be placed so that the long dimension is perpendicular to the dominant direction of travel *(see Fig. 8(h))*.

4.6 Parking and Passenger Loading Zones.

4.6.1 Minimum Number. *Parking spaces required to be accessible by 4.1 shall comply with 4.6.2 through 4.6.5. Passenger loading zones required to be accessible by 4.1 shall comply with 4.6.5 and 4.6.6.*

Federal Register / Vol. 56, No. 144 / Friday, July 26, 1991 / Rules and Regulations   **35631**

4.6 Parking and Passenger Loading Zones

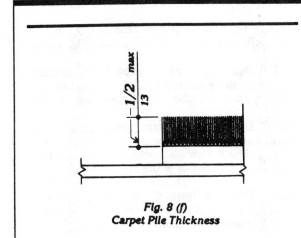

Fig. 8 (f)
Carpet Pile Thickness

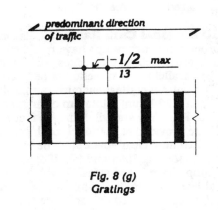

Fig. 8 (g)
Gratings

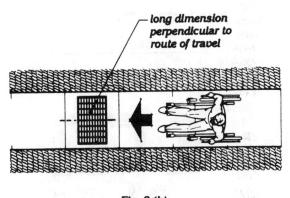

Fig. 8 (h)
Grating Orientation

4.6.2 Location. *Accessible parking spaces serving* a particular building shall be located on the shortest accessible route of travel *from adjacent parking* to an accessible entrance. *In parking facilities* that do not serve a particular building, *accessible parking* shall be located on the shortest accessible route *of travel* to an accessible pedestrian entrance of the parking facility. *In buildings with multiple accessible entrances with adjacent parking, accessible parking spaces shall be dispersed and located closest to the accessible entrances.*

4.6.3* Parking Spaces. *Accessible* parking spaces shall be at least 96 in (2440 mm) wide. Parking access aisles shall be part of an accessible route to the building or facility entrance and shall comply with 4.3. Two accessible parking spaces may share a common access aisle (see Fig. 9). Parked vehicle overhangs shall not reduce the clear width of an accessible route. *Parking spaces and access aisles shall be level with surface slopes not exceeding 1:50 (2%) in all directions.*

4.6.4* Signage. Accessible parking spaces shall be designated as reserved by a sign showing the symbol of accessibility (see 4.30.7). *Spaces complying with 4.1.2(5)(b) shall have an additional sign "Van-Accessible" mounted below the symbol of accessibility.* Such signs shall be located so they cannot be obscured by a vehicle parked in the space.

4.6.5* Vertical Clearance. *Provide minimum vertical clearance of 114 in (2895 mm) at accessible passenger loading zones and along at least one vehicle access route to such areas from site entrance(s) and exit(s). At parking spaces complying with 4.1.2(5)(b), provide minimum vertical clearance of 98 in (2490 mm) at the parking space and along at least one vehicle access route to such spaces from site entrance(s) and exit(s).*

4.6.6 Passenger Loading Zones. Passenger loading zones shall provide an access aisle at least 60 in (1525 mm) wide and 20 ft (240 in) (6100 mm) long adjacent and parallel to the vehicle pull-up space (see Fig. 10). If there are curbs between the access aisle and the vehicle pull-up space, then a curb ramp complying with 4.7 shall be provided. *Vehicle standing spaces and access aisles shall be level with*

35632   Federal Register / Vol. 56, No. 144 / Friday, July 26, 1991 / Rules and Regulations

4.7 Curb Ramps

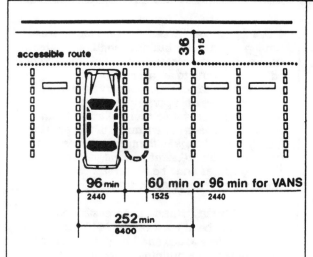

Fig. 9
Dimensions of Parking Spaces

surface slopes not exceeding 1:50 (2%) in all directions.

4.7 Curb Ramps.

4.7.1 Location. Curb ramps complying with 4.7 shall be provided wherever an accessible route crosses a curb.

4.7.2 Slope. Slopes of curb ramps shall comply with 4.8.2. The slope shall be measured as shown in Fig. 11. *Transitions from ramps to walks, gutters, or streets shall be flush and free of abrupt changes. Maximum slopes of adjoining gutters, road surface immediately adjacent to the curb ramp, or accessible route shall not exceed 1:20.*

4.7.3 Width. The minimum width of a curb ramp shall be 36 in (915 mm), exclusive of flared sides.

4.7.4 Surface. Surfaces of curb ramps shall comply with 4.5.

4.7.5 Sides of Curb Ramps. If a curb ramp is located where pedestrians must walk across the ramp, *or where it is not protected by hand-rails or guardrails,* it shall have flared sides; the maximum slope of the flare shall be 1:10 (see Fig. 12(a)). Curb ramps with returned curbs

may be used where pedestrians would not normally walk across the ramp (see Fig. 12(b)).

4.7.6 Built-up Curb Ramps. Built-up curb ramps shall be located so that they do not project into vehicular traffic lanes (see Fig. 13).

4.7.7 *Detectable Warnings.* A curb ramp shall have a *detectable* warning complying with 4.29.2. *The detectable warning shall extend* the full width and depth of the curb ramp.

4.7.8 Obstructions. Curb ramps shall be located or protected to prevent their obstruction by parked vehicles.

4.7.9 Location at Marked Crossings. Curb ramps at marked crossings shall be wholly contained within the markings, excluding any flared sides (see Fig. 15).

4.7.10 Diagonal Curb Ramps. If diagonal (or corner type) curb ramps have returned curbs or other well-defined edges, such edges shall be parallel to the direction of pedestrian flow. The bottom of diagonal curb ramps shall have 48 in (1220 mm) minimum clear space as shown in Fig. 15(c) and (d). If diagonal curb ramps are provided at marked crossings, the 48 in (1220 mm) clear space shall be within the markings (see Fig. 15(c) and (d)). If diagonal curb ramps have flared sides, they shall also have at least a 24 in (610 mm) long segment of straight curb located on each side of the curb ramp and within the marked crossing (see Fig. 15(c)).

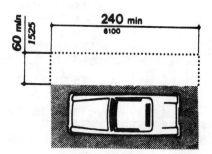

Fig. 10
Access Aisle at Passenger Loading Zones

Federal Register / Vol. 56, No. 144 / Friday, July 26, 1991 / Rules and Regulations   35633

4.8 Ramps

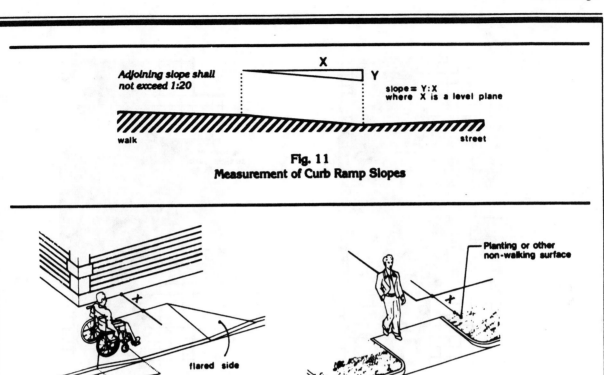

Fig. 11
Measurement of Curb Ramp Slopes

(a)
Flared Sides

*If X is less than 48 in,
then the slope of the flared side
shall not exceed 1:12.*

(b)
Returned Curb

Fig. 12
Sides of Curb Ramps

4.7.11 Islands. Any raised islands in crossings shall be cut through level with the street or have curb ramps at both sides and a level area at least 48 in (1220 mm) long between the curb ramps in the part of the island intersected by the crossings (see Fig. 15(a) and (b)).

4.8 Ramps.

4.8.1* General. Any part of an accessible route with a slope greater than 1:20 shall be considered a ramp and shall comply with 4.8.

4.8.2* Slope and Rise. The least possible slope shall be used for any ramp. The maximum slope of a ramp in new construction shall be 1:12. The maximum rise for any run shall be 30 in (760 mm) (see Fig. 16). Curb ramps

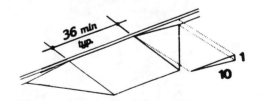

Fig. 13
Built-Up Curb Ramp

and ramps to be constructed on existing sites or in existing buildings or facilities may have slopes and rises as *allowed in 4.1.6(3)(a)* if space limitations prohibit the use of a 1:12 slope or less.

35634   Federal Register / Vol. 56, No. 144 / Friday, July 26, 1991 / Rules and Regulations

4.8 Ramps

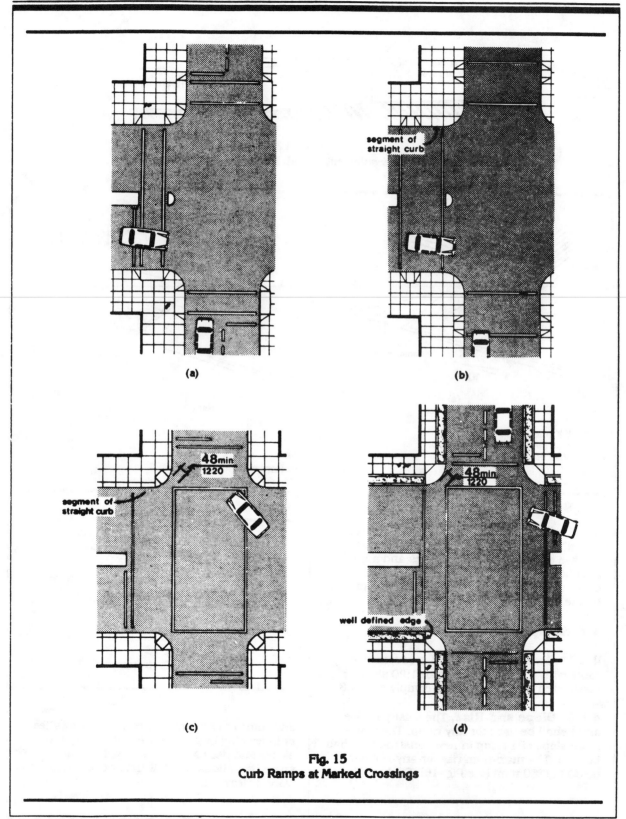

Fig. 15
Curb Ramps at Marked Crossings

Federal Register / Vol. 56, No. 144 / Friday, July 26, 1991 / Rules and Regulations   35487

4.8 Ramps

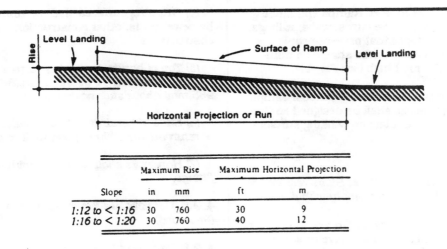

	Maximum Rise		Maximum Horizontal Projection	
Slope	in	mm	ft	m
1:12 to < 1:16	30	760	30	9
1:16 to < 1:20	30	760	40	12

Fig. 16
Components of a Single Ramp Run and Sample Ramp Dimensions

4.8.3 Clear Width. The minimum clear width of a ramp shall be 36 in (915 mm).

4.8.4* Landings. Ramps shall have level landings at bottom and top of *each ramp and each ramp* run. Landings shall have the following features:

(1) The landing shall be at least as wide as the ramp run leading to it.

(2) The landing length shall be a minimum of 60 in (1525 mm) clear.

(3) If ramps change direction at landings, the minimum landing size shall be 60 in by 60 in (1525 mm by 1525 mm).

(4) If a doorway is located at a landing, then the area in front of the doorway shall comply with 4.13.6.

4.8.5* Handrails. If a ramp run has a rise greater than 6 in (150 mm) or a horizontal projection greater than 72 in (1830 mm), then it shall have handrails on both sides. Handrails are not required on curb ramps *or adjacent to seating in assembly areas.* Handrails shall comply with 4.26 and shall have the following features:

(1) Handrails shall be provided along both sides of ramp segments. The inside handrail on switchback or dogleg ramps shall always be continuous.

(2) If handrails are not continuous, they shall extend at least 12 in (305 mm) beyond the top and bottom of the ramp segment and shall be parallel with the floor or ground surface (see Fig. 17).

(3) The clear space between the handrail and the wall shall be 1 - 1/2 in (38 mm).

(4) Gripping surfaces shall be continuous.

(5) *Top of handrail gripping surfaces shall be mounted between 34 in and 38 in (865 mm and 965 mm) above ramp surfaces.*

(6) *Ends of handrails shall be either rounded or returned smoothly to floor, wall, or post.*

(7) *Handrails shall not rotate within their fittings.*

4.8.6 Cross Slope and Surfaces. The cross slope of ramp surfaces shall be no greater than 1:50. Ramp surfaces shall comply with 4.5.

35636   Federal Register / Vol. 56, No. 144 / Friday, July 26, 1991 / Rules and Regulations

4.9 Stairs

4.8.7 Edge Protection. Ramps and landings with drop-offs shall have curbs, walls, railings, or projecting surfaces that prevent people from slipping off the ramp. Curbs shall be a minimum of 2 in (50 mm) high (see Fig. 17).

4.8.8 Outdoor Conditions. Outdoor ramps and their approaches shall be designed so that water will not accumulate on walking surfaces.

4.9 Stairs.

4.9.1* Minimum Number. *Stairs required to be accessible by 4.1 shall comply with 4.9.*

4.9.2 Treads and Risers. On any given flight of stairs, all steps shall have uniform riser heights and uniform tread widths. Stair treads shall be no less than 11 in (280 mm) wide, measured from riser to riser (see Fig. 18(a)). *Open risers are not permitted.*

4.9.3 Nosings. The undersides of nosings shall not be abrupt. The radius of curvature at the leading edge of the tread shall be no greater than 1/2 in (13 mm). Risers shall be sloped or the underside of the nosing shall have an angle not less than 60 degrees from the horizontal. Nosings shall project no more than 1-1/2 in (38 mm) (see Fig. 18).

4.9.4 Handrails. Stairways shall have handrails at both sides of all stairs. Handrails shall comply with 4.26 and shall have the following features:

(1) Handrails shall be continuous along both sides of stairs. The inside handrail on switchback or dogleg stairs shall always be continuous (see Fig. 19(a) and (b)).

(2) If handrails are not continuous, they shall extend at least 12 in (305 mm) beyond the top riser and at least 12 in (305 mm) plus the width of one tread beyond the bottom riser. At the top, the extension shall be parallel with the floor or ground surface. At the bottom, the handrail shall continue to slope for a distance of the width of one tread from the bottom riser; the remainder of the extension shall be horizontal (see Fig. 19(c) and (d)). Handrail extensions shall comply with 4.4.

(3) The clear space between handrails and wall shall be 1-1/2 in (38 mm).

(4) Gripping surfaces shall be uninterrupted by newel posts, other construction elements, or obstructions.

(5) *Top of handrail gripping surface shall be mounted between 34 in and 38 in (865 mm and 965 mm) above stair nosings.*

(6) *Ends of handrails shall be either rounded or returned smoothly to floor, wall or post.*

(7) *Handrails shall not rotate within their fittings.*

4.9.5 Detectable Warnings at Stairs. *(Reserved).*

4.9.6 Outdoor Conditions. Outdoor stairs and their approaches shall be designed so that water will not accumulate on walking surfaces.

4.10 Elevators.

4.10.1 General. *Accessible* elevators shall be on an accessible route and shall comply with 4.10 and with the *ASME A17.1-1990,* Safety Code for Elevators and Escalators. *Freight elevators shall not be considered as meeting the requirements of this section unless the only elevators provided are used as combination passenger and freight elevators for the public and employees.*

4.10.2 Automatic Operation. Elevator operation shall be automatic. Each car shall be equipped with a self-leveling feature that will automatically bring the car to floor landings within a tolerance of 1/2 in (13 mm) under rated loading to zero loading conditions. This self-leveling feature shall be automatic and independent of the operating device and shall correct the overtravel or undertravel.

4.10.3 Hall Call Buttons. Call buttons in elevator lobbies and halls shall be centered at 42 in (1065 mm) above the floor. Such call buttons shall have visual signals to indicate when each call is registered and when each call is answered. Call buttons shall be a minimum of 3/4 in (19 mm) in the smallest dimension. The button designating the up direction shall be on top. (See Fig. 20.) *Buttons shall be raised or flush. Objects mounted beneath hall call buttons shall not project into the elevator lobby more than 4 in (100 mm).*

Federal Register / Vol. 56, No. 144 / Friday, July 26, 1991 / Rules and Regulations   **35637**

4.10 Elevators

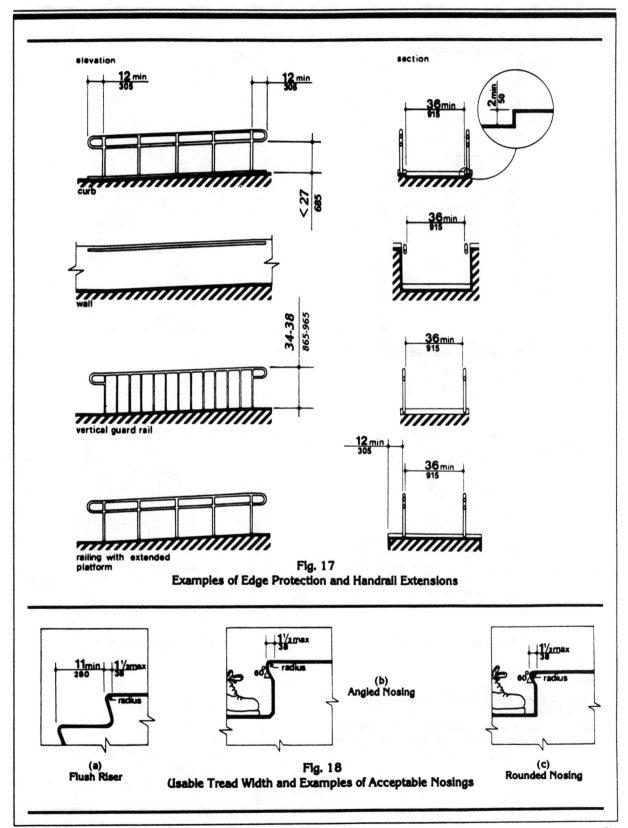

Fig. 17
Examples of Edge Protection and Handrail Extensions

Fig. 18
Usable Tread Width and Examples of Acceptable Nosings

35638 Federal Register / Vol. 56, No. 144 / Friday, July 26, 1991 / Rules and Regulations

4.10 Elevators

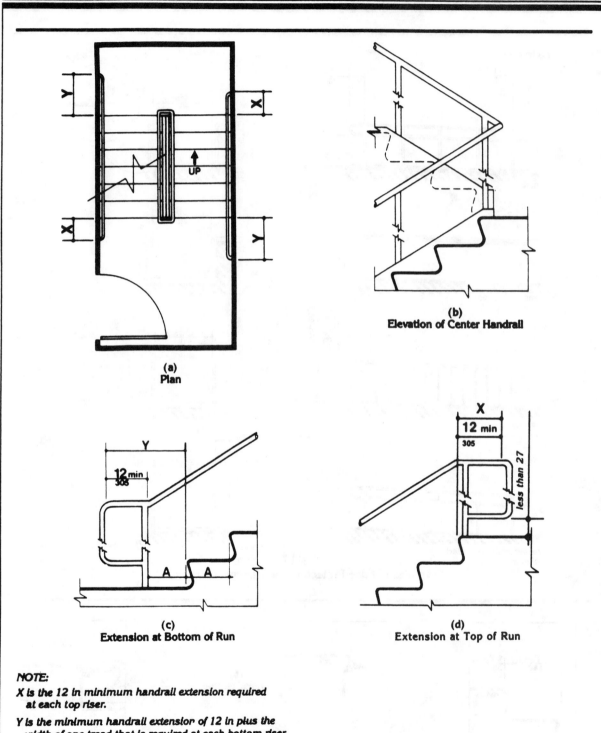

(a)
Plan

(b)
Elevation of Center Handrail

(c)
Extension at Bottom of Run

(d)
Extension at Top of Run

NOTE:

X is the 12 in minimum handrail extension required at each top riser.

Y is the minimum handrail extension of 12 in plus the width of one tread that is required at each bottom riser.

Fig. 19
Stair Handrails

Federal Register / Vol. 56, No. 144 / Friday, July 26, 1991 / Rules and Regulations   35639

4.10 Elevators

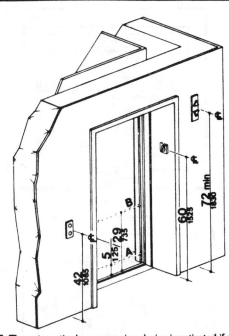

NOTE: The automatic door reopening device is activated if an object passes through either line A or line B. Line A and line B represent the vertical locations of the door reopening device not requiring contact.

Fig. 20
Hoistway and Elevator Entrances

4.10.4 Hall Lanterns. A visible and audible signal shall be provided at each hoistway entrance to indicate which car is answering a call. Audible signals shall sound once for the up direction and twice for the down direction or shall have verbal annunciators that say "up" or "down." Visible signals shall have the following features:

(1) Hall lantern fixtures shall be mounted so that their centerline is at least 72 in (1830 mm) above the lobby floor. (See Fig. 20.)

(2) Visual elements shall be at least 2-1/2 in (64 mm) in the smallest dimension.

(3) Signals shall be visible from the vicinity of the hall call button (see Fig. 20). In-car lanterns located in cars, visible from the vicinity of hall call buttons, and conforming to the above requirements, shall be acceptable.

4.10.5 Raised and Braille Characters on Hoistway Entrances. All elevator hoistway entrances shall have *raised and Braille* floor designations provided on both jambs. The centerline of the characters shall be 60 in (1525 mm) *above finish* floor. Such characters shall be 2 in (50 mm) high and shall comply with 4.30.4. Permanently applied plates are acceptable if they are permanently fixed to the jambs. (See Fig. 20).

4.10.6* Door Protective and Reopening Device. Elevator doors shall open and close automatically. They shall be provided with a reopening device that will stop and reopen a car door and hoistway door automatically if the door becomes obstructed by an object or person. The device shall be capable of completing these operations without requiring contact for an obstruction passing through the opening at heights of 5 in and 29 in (125 mm and 735 mm) above finish floor (see Fig. 20). Door reopening devices shall remain effective for at least 20 seconds. After such an interval, doors may close in accordance with the requirements of *ASME A17.1-1990.*

4.10.7* Door and Signal Timing for Hall Calls. The minimum acceptable time from notification that a car is answering a call until the doors of that car start to close shall be calculated from the following equation:

$$T = D/(1.5 \text{ ft/s}) \text{ or } T = D/(445 \text{ mm/s})$$

where T total time in seconds and D distance (in feet or millimeters) from a point in the lobby or corridor 60 in (1525 mm) directly in front of the farthest call button controlling that car to the centerline of its hoistway door (see Fig. 21). For cars with in-car lanterns, T begins when the lantern is visible from the vicinity of hall call buttons and an audible signal is sounded. *The minimum acceptable notification time shall be 5 seconds.*

4.10.8 Door Delay for Car Calls. The minimum time for elevator doors to remain fully open in response to a car call shall be 3 seconds.

4.10.9 Floor Plan of Elevator Cars. The floor area of elevator cars shall provide space for wheelchair users to enter the car, maneuver

35640   Federal Register / Vol. 56, No. 144 / Friday, July 26, 1991 / Rules and Regulations

4.10.12 Car Controls

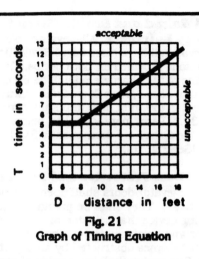

Fig. 21
Graph of Timing Equation

within reach of controls, and exit from the car. Acceptable door opening and inside dimensions shall be as shown in Fig. 22. The clearance between the car platform sill and the edge of any hoistway landing shall be no greater than 1-1/4 in (32 mm).

4.10.10 Floor Surfaces. Floor surfaces shall comply with 4.5.

4.10.11 Illumination Levels. The level of illumination at the car controls, platform, and car threshold and landing sill shall be at least 5 footcandles (53.8 lux).

4.10.12* Car Controls. Elevator control panels shall have the following features:

(1) Buttons. All control buttons shall be at least 3/4 in (19 mm) in their smallest dimension. They *shall* be *raised* or flush.

(2) Tactile, *Braille,* and Visual Control Indicators. All control buttons shall be designated by *Braille and by raised* standard alphabet characters for letters, arabic characters for numerals, or standard symbols as shown in Fig. 23(a), and as required in *ASME A17.1-1990. Raised and Braille* characters and symbols shall comply with 4.30. The call button for the main entry floor shall be designated by a *raised* star at the left of the floor designation (see Fig. 23(a)). All raised designations for control buttons shall be placed immediately to the left of the button to which they apply. Applied plates,

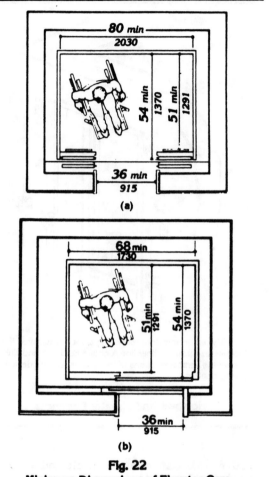

Fig. 22
Minimum Dimensions of Elevator Cars

permanently attached, are an acceptable means to provide raised control designations. Floor buttons shall be provided with visual indicators to show when each call is registered. The visual indicators shall be extinguished when each call is answered.

(3) Height. All floor buttons shall be no higher than 54 in (1370 mm) above the *finish* floor *for side approach and 48 in (1220 mm) for front approach.* Emergency controls, including the emergency alarm and emergency stop, shall be grouped at the bottom of the panel and shall have their centerlines no less than 35 in (890 mm) above the finish floor (see Fig. 23(a) and (b)).

4.10.13* Car Position Indicators

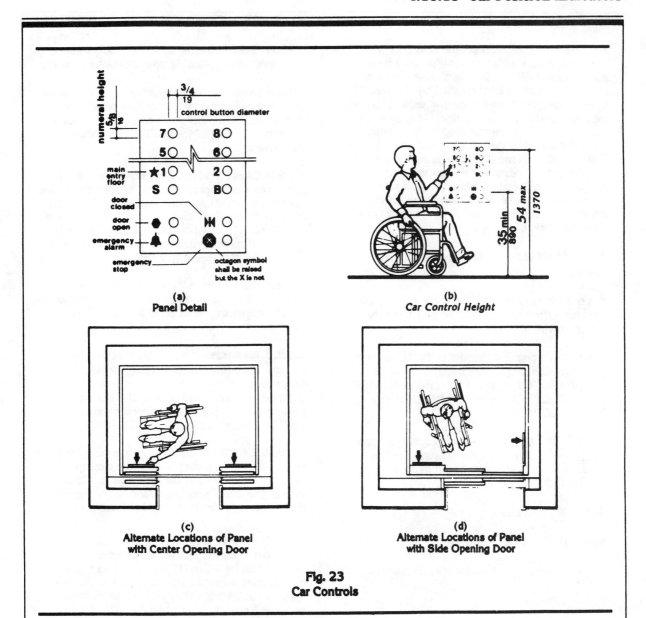

(a)
Panel Detail

(b)
Car Control Height

(c)
**Alternate Locations of Panel
with Center Opening Door**

(d)
**Alternate Locations of Panel
with Side Opening Door**

**Fig. 23
Car Controls**

(4) Location. Controls shall be located on a front wall if cars have center opening doors, and at the side wall or at the front wall next to the door if cars have side opening doors (see Fig. 23(c) and (d)).

4.10.13* Car Position Indicators. In elevator cars, a visual car position indicator shall be provided above the car control panel or over the door to show the position of the elevator in the hoistway. As the car passes or stops at a floor served by the elevators, the corresponding numerals shall illuminate,

and an audible signal shall sound. Numerals shall be a minimum of 1/2 in (13 mm) high. The audible signal shall be no less than 20 decibels with a frequency no higher than 1500 Hz. An automatic verbal announcement of the floor number at which a car stops or which a car passes may be substituted for the audible signal.

4.10.14* Emergency Communications. If provided, emergency two-way communication systems between the elevator and a point outside the hoistway shall comply with *ASME*

4.11 Platform Lifts (Wheelchair Lifts)

A17.1-1990. The highest operable part of a two-way communication system shall be a maximum of *48 in (1220 mm)* from the floor of the car. It shall be identified by a raised symbol and lettering complying with 4.30 and located adjacent to the device. If the system uses a handset then the length of the cord from the panel to the handset shall be at least 29 in (735 mm). *If the system is located in a closed compartment the compartment door hardware shall conform to 4.27, Controls and Operating Mechanisms. The emergency intercommunication system shall not require voice communication.*

4.11 Platform Lifts (Wheelchair Lifts).

4.11.1 Location. *Platform lifts (wheelchair lifts) permitted by 4.1 shall comply with the requirements of 4.11.*

4.11.2* Other Requirements. If platform lifts (wheelchair lifts) are used, they shall comply with 4.2.4, 4.5, 4.27, and *ASME A17.1 Safety Code for Elevators and Escalators, Section XX, 1990.*

4.11.3 Entrance. *If platform lifts are used then they shall facilitate unassisted entry, operation, and exit from the lift in compliance with 4.11.2.*

4.12 Windows.

4.12.1* General. *(Reserved).*

4.12.2* Window Hardware. *(Reserved).*

4.13 Doors.

4.13.1 General. *Doors required to be accessible by 4.1 shall comply with the requirements of 4.13.*

4.13.2 Revolving Doors and Turnstiles. Revolving doors or turnstiles shall not be the only means of passage at an accessible entrance or along an accessible route. *An accessible gate or door shall be provided adjacent to the turnstile or revolving door and shall be so designed as to facilitate the same use pattern.*

4.13.3 Gates. Gates, including ticket gates, shall meet all applicable specifications of 4.13.

4.13.4 Double-Leaf Doorways. If doorways have two *independently operated* door leaves, then at least one leaf shall meet the specifications in 4.13.5 and 4.13.6. That leaf shall be an active leaf.

4.13.5 Clear Width. Doorways shall have a minimum clear opening of 32 in (815 mm) with the door open 90 degrees, measured between the face of the door and the *opposite* stop (see Fig. 24(a), (b), (c), and (d)). Openings more than 24 in (610 mm) in depth shall comply with 4.2.1 and 4.3.3 (see Fig. 24(e)).

EXCEPTION: Doors not requiring full user passage, such as shallow closets, may have the clear opening reduced to 20 in (510 mm) minimum.

4.13.6 Maneuvering Clearances at Doors. Minimum maneuvering clearances at doors that are not automatic or power-assisted shall be as shown in Fig. 25. The floor or ground area within the required clearances shall be level and clear.

EXCEPTION: Entry doors to acute care hospital bedrooms for in-patients shall be exempted from the requirement for space at the latch side of the door (see dimension "x" in Fig. 25) if the door is at least 44 in (1120 mm) wide.

4.13.7 Two Doors in Series. The minimum space between two hinged or pivoted doors in series shall be 48 in (1220 mm) plus the width of any door swinging into the space. Doors in series shall swing either in the same direction or away from the space between the doors (see Fig. 26).

4.13.8* Thresholds at Doorways. Thresholds at doorways shall not exceed 3/4 in (19 mm) in height for exterior sliding doors or 1/2 in (13 mm) for other types of doors. Raised thresholds and floor level changes at accessible doorways shall be beveled with a slope no greater than 1:2 (see 4.5.2).

4.13.9* Door Hardware. Handles, pulls, latches, locks, and other operating devices on accessible doors shall have a shape that is easy

Federal Register / Vol. 56, No. 144 / Friday, July 26, 1991 / Rules and Regulations 35643

4.13 Doors

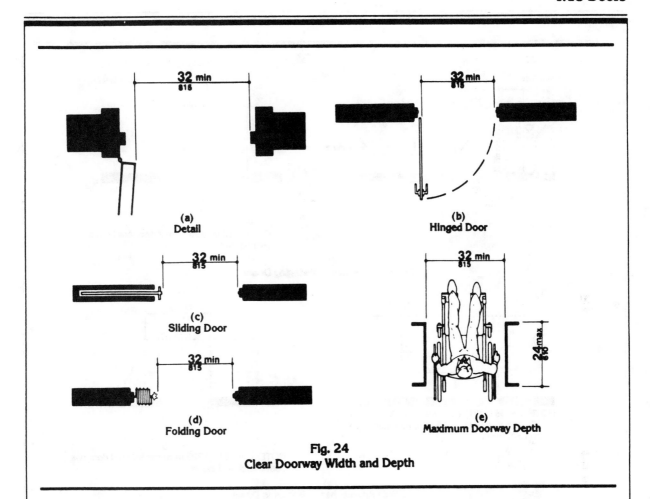

(a)
Detail

(b)
Hinged Door

(c)
Sliding Door

(d)
Folding Door

(e)
Maximum Doorway Depth

Fig. 24
Clear Doorway Width and Depth

to grasp with one hand and does not require tight grasping, tight pinching, or twisting of the wrist to operate. Lever-operated mechanisms, push-type mechanisms, and U-shaped handles are acceptable designs. When sliding doors are fully open, operating hardware shall be exposed and usable from both sides. *Hardware required for accessible door passage shall be mounted no higher than 48 in (1220 mm) above finished floor.*

4.13.10* Door Closers. If a door has a closer, then the sweep period of the closer shall be adjusted so that from an open position of 70 degrees, the door will take at least 3 seconds to move to a point 3 in (75 mm) from the latch, measured to the leading edge of the door.

4.13.11* Door Opening Force. The maximum force for pushing or pulling open a door shall be as follows:

(1) Fire doors shall have the minimum opening force allowable by the appropriate administrative authority.

(2) Other doors.

(a) exterior hinged doors: *(Reserved)*.

(b) interior hinged doors: 5 lbf (22.2N)

(c) sliding or folding doors: 5 lbf (22.2N)

These forces do not apply to the force required to retract latch bolts or disengage other devices that may hold the door in a closed position.

35644   Federal Register / Vol. 56, No. 144 / Friday, July 26, 1991 / Rules and Regulations

4.13 Doors

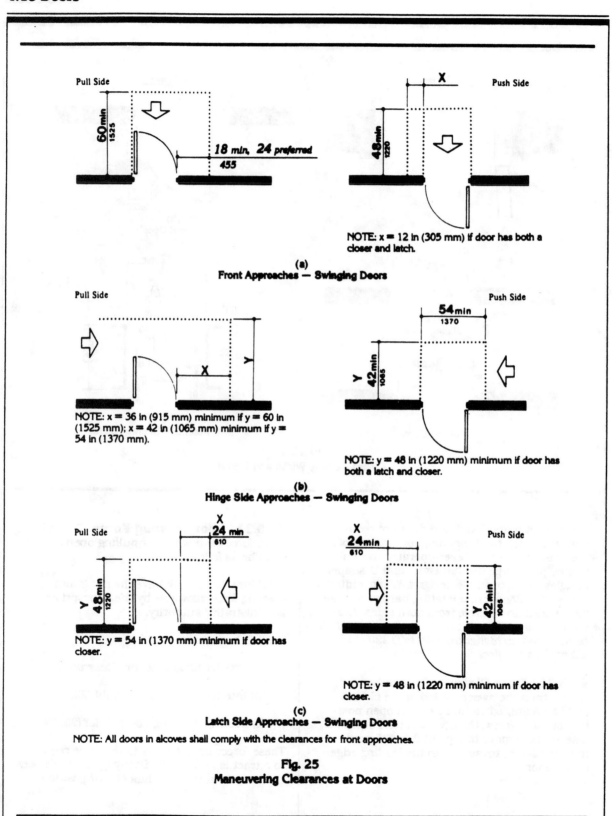

(a)
Front Approaches — Swinging Doors

NOTE: x = 12 in (305 mm) if door has both a closer and latch.

NOTE: x = 36 in (915 mm) minimum if y = 60 in (1525 mm); x = 42 in (1065 mm) minimum if y = 54 in (1370 mm).

NOTE: y = 48 in (1220 mm) minimum if door has both a latch and closer.

(b)
Hinge Side Approaches — Swinging Doors

NOTE: y = 54 in (1370 mm) minimum if door has closer.

NOTE: y = 48 in (1220 mm) minimum if door has closer.

(c)
Latch Side Approaches — Swinging Doors

NOTE: All doors in alcoves shall comply with the clearances for front approaches.

Fig. 25
Maneuvering Clearances at Doors

Federal Register / Vol. 56, No. 144 / Friday, July 26, 1991 / Rules and Regulations 35645

4.13 Doors

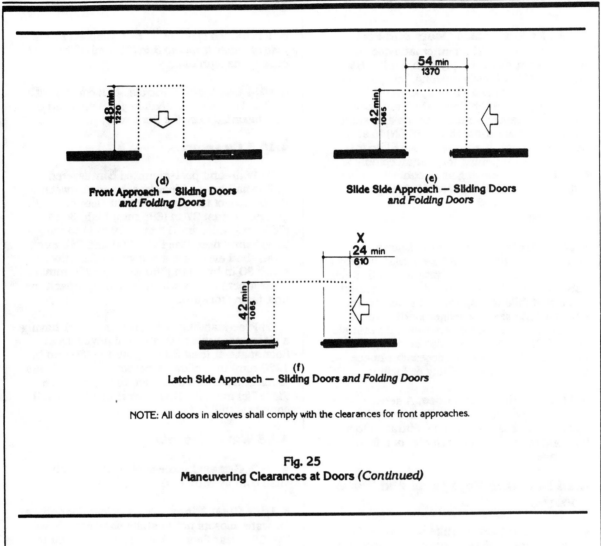

(d)
Front Approach — Sliding Doors
and *Folding Doors*

(e)
Slide Side Approach — Sliding Doors
and *Folding Doors*

(f)
Latch Side Approach — Sliding Doors *and Folding Doors*

NOTE: All doors in alcoves shall comply with the clearances for front approaches.

Fig. 25
Maneuvering Clearances at Doors *(Continued)*

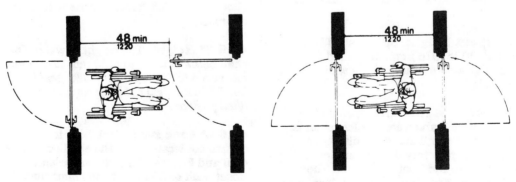

Fig. 26
Two Hinged Doors in Series

35646   Federal Register / Vol. 56, No. 144 / Friday, July 26, 1991 / Rules and Regulations

4.14 Entrances

4.13.12* Automatic Doors and Power-Assisted Doors.

If an automatic door is used, then it shall comply with *ANSI/BHMA A156.10-1985*. Slowly opening, low-powered, automatic doors shall *comply with ANSI A156.19-1984*. Such doors shall not open to back check faster than 3 seconds and shall require no more than 15 lbf (66.6N) to stop door movement. If a power-assisted door is used, its door-opening force shall comply with 4.13.11 and its closing shall conform to the requirements in *ANSI A156.19-1984*.

4.14 Entrances.

4.14.1 Minimum Number. *Entrances required to be accessible by 4.1* shall be part of an accessible route complying with 4.3. Such entrances shall be connected by an accessible route to public transportation stops, to accessible parking and passenger loading zones, and to public streets or sidewalks if available (see 4.3.2(1)). They shall also be connected by an accessible route to all accessible spaces or elements within the building or facility.

4.14.2 Service Entrances. A service entrance shall not be the sole accessible entrance unless it is the only entrance to a building or facility (for example, in a factory or garage).

4.15 Drinking Fountains and Water Coolers.

4.15.1 Minimum Number. *Drinking fountains or water coolers required to be accessible by 4.1* shall comply with 4.15.

4.15.2* Spout Height. Spouts shall be no higher than 36 in (915 mm), measured from the floor or ground surfaces to the spout outlet (see Fig. 27(a)).

4.15.3 Spout Location. The spouts of drinking fountains and water coolers shall be at the front of the unit and shall direct the water flow in a trajectory that is parallel or nearly parallel to the front of the unit. The spout shall provide a flow of water at least 4 in (100 mm) high so as to allow the insertion of a cup or glass under the flow of water. *On an accessible drinking fountain with a round or*

oval bowl, the spout must be positioned so the flow of water is within 3 in (75 mm) of the front edge of the fountain.

4.15.4 Controls. Controls shall comply with 4.27.4. *Unit controls shall be front mounted or side mounted near the front edge.*

4.15.5 Clearances.

(1) Wall- and post-mounted cantilevered units shall have a clear knee space between the bottom of the apron and the floor or ground at least 27 in (685 mm) high, 30 in (760 mm) wide, and 17 in to 19 in (430 mm to 485 mm) deep (see Fig. 27(a) and (b)). Such units shall also have a minimum clear floor space 30 in by 48 in (760 mm by 1220 mm) to allow a person in a wheelchair to approach the unit facing forward.

(2) Free-standing or built-in units not having a clear space under them shall have a clear floor space at least 30 in by 48 in (760 mm by 1220 mm) that allows a person in a wheelchair to make a parallel approach to the unit (see Fig. 27(c) and (d)). This clear floor space shall comply with 4.2.4.

4.16 Water Closets.

4.16.1 General. Accessible water closets shall comply with 4.16.

4.16.2 Clear Floor Space. Clear floor space for water closets not in stalls shall comply with Fig. 28. Clear floor space may be arranged to allow either a left-handed or right-handed approach.

4.16.3* Height. The height of water closets shall be 17 in to 19 in (430 mm to 485 mm), measured to the top of the toilet seat (see Fig. 29(b)). *Seats shall not be sprung to return to a lifted position.*

4.16.4* Grab Bars. Grab bars for water closets not located in stalls shall comply with 4.26 and Fig. 29. *The grab bar behind the water closet shall be 36 in (915 mm) minimum.*

4.16.5* Flush Controls. Flush controls shall be hand operated *or automatic* and shall comply with 4.27.4. Controls for flush valves

Federal Register / Vol. 56, No. 144 / Friday, July 26, 1991 / Rules and Regulations 35647

4.17 Toilet Stalls

shall be mounted on the wide side of toilet areas no more than 44 in (1120 mm) above the floor.

4.16.6 Dispensers. Toilet paper dispensers shall be installed within reach, as shown in Fig. 29(b). *Dispensers that control delivery, or that do not permit continuous paper flow, shall not be used.*

4.17 Toilet Stalls.

4.17.1 Location. Accessible toilet stalls shall be on an accessible route and shall meet the requirements of 4.17.

4.17.2 Water Closets. Water closets in accessible stalls shall comply with 4.16.

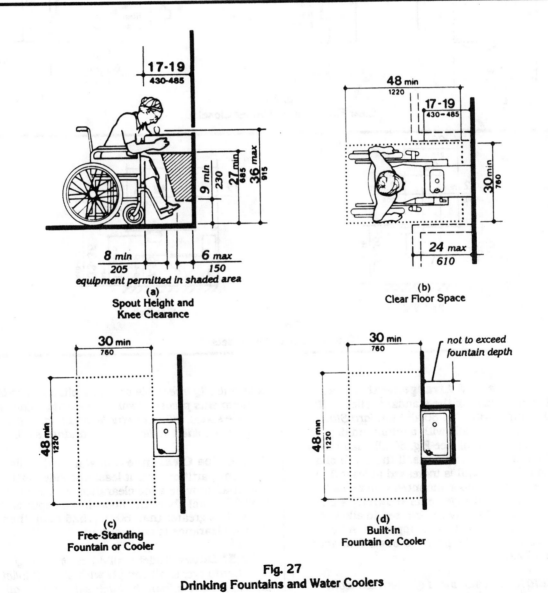

(a)
Spout Height and
Knee Clearance

(b)
Clear Floor Space

(c)
Free-Standing
Fountain or Cooler

(d)
Built-In
Fountain or Cooler

Fig. 27
Drinking Fountains and Water Coolers

35648   Federal Register / Vol. 56, No. 144 / Friday, July 26, 1991 / Rules and Regulations

4.17 Toilet Stalls

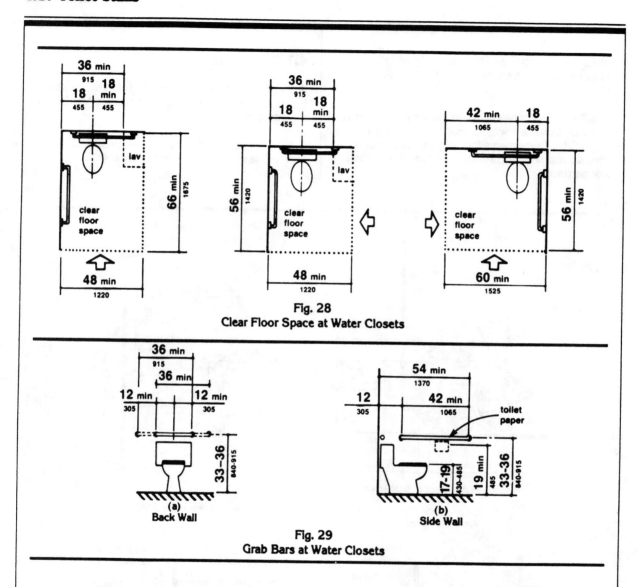

Fig. 28
Clear Floor Space at Water Closets

Fig. 29
Grab Bars at Water Closets

4.17.3* Size and Arrangement. The size and arrangement of the standard toilet stall shall comply with Fig. 30(a), *Standard Stall.* Standard toilet stalls with a minimum depth of 56 in (1420 mm) (see Fig. 30(a)) shall have wall-mounted water closets. If the depth of a standard toilet stall is increased at least 3 in (75 mm), then a floor-mounted water closet may be used. Arrangements shown for standard toilet stalls may be reversed to allow either a left- or right-hand approach. Additional stalls shall be provided in conformance with 4.22.4.

EXCEPTION: In instances of alteration work where provision of a standard stall (Fig. 30(a))

is technically infeasible or where plumbing code requirements prevent combining existing stalls to provide space, either alternate stall (Fig. 30(b)) may be provided in lieu of the standard stall.

4.17.4 Toe Clearances. In standard stalls, the front partition and at least one side partition shall provide a toe clearance of at least 9 in (230 mm) above the floor. If the depth of the stall is greater than 60 in (1525 mm), then the toe clearance is not required.

4.17.5* Doors. Toilet stall doors, *including door hardware,* shall comply with 4.13. *If toilet stall approach is from the latch side of the stall door, clearance between the door side of the*

Federal Register / Vol. 56, No. 144 / Friday, July 26, 1991 / Rules and Regulations   35649

4.17 Toilet Stalls

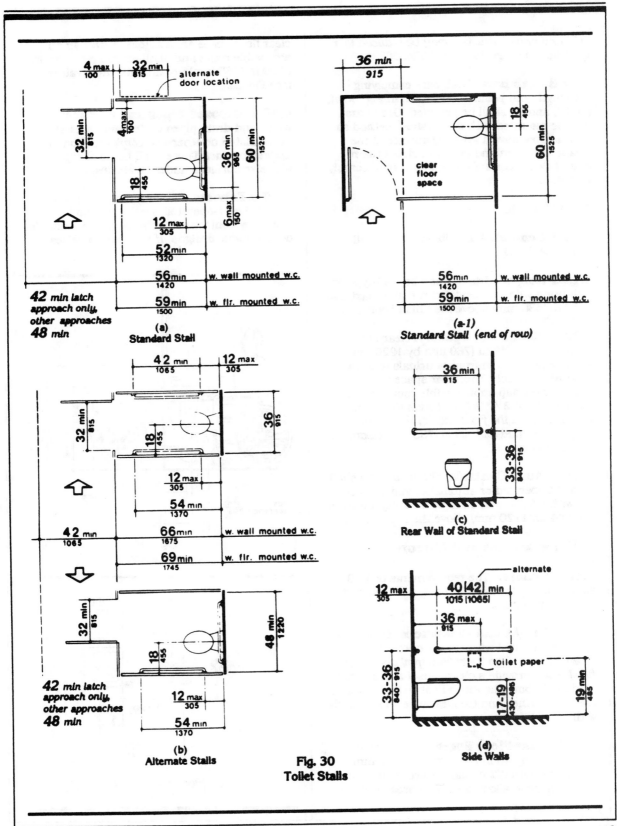

Fig. 30
Toilet Stalls

(a) Standard Stall

(a-1) Standard Stall (end of row)

(b) Alternate Stalls

(c) Rear Wall of Standard Stall

(d) Side Walls

35650   Federal Register / Vol. 56, No. 144 / Friday, July 26, 1991 / Rules and Regulations

4.19 Lavatories and Mirrors

stall and any obstruction may be reduced to a minimum of 42 in (1065 mm) (Fig. 30).

4.17.6 Grab Bars. Grab bars complying with the length and positioning shown in Fig. 30(a), (b), (c), and (d) shall be provided. Grab bars may be mounted with any desired method as long as they have a gripping surface at the locations shown and do not obstruct the required clear floor area. Grab bars shall comply with 4.26.

4.18 Urinals.

4.18.1 General. Accessible urinals shall comply with 4.18.

4.18.2 Height. Urinals shall be stall-type or wall-hung with an elongated rim at a maximum of 17 in (430 mm) above the finish floor.

4.18.3 Clear Floor Space. A clear floor space 30 in by 48 in (760 mm by 1220 mm) shall be provided in front of urinals to allow forward approach. This clear space shall adjoin or overlap an accessible route and shall comply with 4.2.4. *Urinal shields that do not extend beyond the front edge of the urinal rim may be provided with 29 in (735 mm) clearance between them.*

4.18.4 Flush Controls. Flush controls shall be hand operated or automatic, and shall comply with 4.27.4, and shall be mounted no more than 44 in (1120 mm) above the finish floor.

4.19 Lavatories and Mirrors.

4.19.1 General. The requirements of 4.19 shall apply to lavatory fixtures, vanities, and built-in lavatories.

4.19.2 Height and Clearances. Lavatories shall be mounted with *the rim or counter surface no higher than 34 in (865 mm) above the finish floor.* Provide a clearance of at least 29 in (735 mm) above the finish floor to the bottom of the apron. Knee and toe clearance shall comply with Fig. 31.

4.19.3 Clear Floor Space. A clear floor space 30 in by 48 in (760 mm by 1220 mm) complying with 4.2.4 shall be provided in front of a lavatory to allow forward approach. Such

clear floor space shall adjoin or overlap an accessible route and shall extend a maximum of 19 in (485 mm) underneath the lavatory (see Fig. 32).

4.19.4 Exposed Pipes and Surfaces. Hot water and drain pipes under lavatories shall be insulated or otherwise *configured to protect against contact.* There shall be no sharp or abrasive surfaces under lavatories.

4.19.5 Faucets. Faucets shall comply with 4.27.4. Lever-operated, push-type, and electronically controlled mechanisms are examples of acceptable designs. *If self-closing valves are*

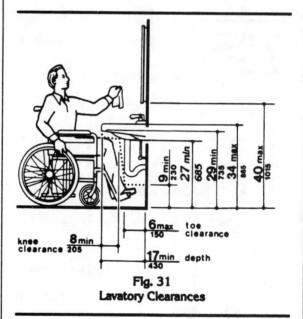

Fig. 31
Lavatory Clearances

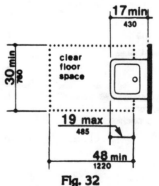

Fig. 32
Clear Floor Space at Lavatories

Federal Register / Vol. 56, No. 144 / Friday, July 26, 1991 / Rules and Regulations   **35651**

4.20 Bathtubs

used the faucet *shall remain* open for at least 10 seconds.

4.19.6* Mirrors. Mirrors shall be mounted with the bottom edge *of the reflecting surface* no higher than 40 in (1015 mm) *above the finish* floor (see Fig. 31).

4.20 Bathtubs.

4.20.1 General. Accessible bathtubs shall comply with 4.20.

4.20.2 Floor Space. Clear floor space in front of bathtubs shall be as shown in Fig. 33.

4.20.3 Seat. An in-tub seat or a seat at the head end of the tub shall be provided as shown in Fig. 33 and 34. The structural strength of seats and their attachments shall comply with 4.26.3. Seats shall be mounted securely and shall not slip during use.

4.20.4 Grab Bars. Grab bars complying with 4.26 shall be provided as shown in Fig. 33 and 34.

4.20.5 Controls. Faucets and other controls complying with 4.27.4 shall be located as shown in Fig. 34.

4.20.6 Shower Unit. A shower spray unit with a hose at least 60 in (1525 mm) long that can be used *both* as a fixed shower head *and* as a hand-held shower shall be provided.

4.20.7 Bathtub Enclosures. If provided, enclosures for bathtubs shall not obstruct controls or transfer from wheelchairs onto bathtub seats or into tubs. Enclosures on bathtubs shall not have tracks mounted on their rims.

4.21 Shower Stalls.

4.21.1* General. Accessible shower stalls shall comply with 4.21.

4.21.2 Size and Clearances. Except as specified in 9.1.2, shower stall size and clear floor space shall comply with Fig. 35(a) or (b). The shower stall in Fig. 35(a) shall be 36 in by 36 in (915 mm by 915 mm). Shower stalls required by 9.1.2 shall comply with Fig. 57(a) or (b). The shower stall in Fig. 35(b) will fit into the space required for a bathtub.

4.21.3 Seat. A seat shall be provided in shower stalls 36 in by 36 in (915 mm by 915 mm) and shall be as shown in Fig. 36. The seat shall be mounted 17 in to 19 in (430 mm to 485 mm) from the bathroom floor and shall extend the full depth of the stall. In a 36 in by 36 in (915 mm by 915 mm) shower stall, the seat shall be on the wall opposite the controls. *Where a fixed seat is provided in a 30 in by 60 in minimum (760 mm by 1525 mm) shower stall, it shall be a folding type and shall be mounted on the wall adjacent to the controls as shown in Fig. 57.* The structural strength of seats and their attachments shall comply with 4.26.3.

4.21.4 Grab Bars. Grab bars complying with 4.26 shall be provided as shown in Fig. 37.

4.21.5 Controls. Faucets and other controls complying with 4.27.4 shall be located as shown in Fig. 37. In shower stalls 36 in by 36 in (915 mm by 915 mm), all controls, faucets, and the shower unit shall be mounted on the side wall opposite the seat.

4.21.6 Shower Unit. A shower spray unit with a hose at least 60 in (1525 mm) long that can be used *both* as a fixed shower head *and* as a hand-held shower shall be provided.

EXCEPTION: In unmonitored facilities where vandalism is a consideration, a fixed shower head mounted at 48 in (1220 mm) above the shower floor may be used in lieu of a hand-held shower head.

4.21.7 Curbs. If provided, curbs in shower stalls 36 in by 36 in (915 mm by 915 mm) shall be no higher than *1/2 in (13 mm).* Shower stalls that are 30 in by 60 in (760 mm by 1525 mm) minimum shall not have curbs.

4.21.8 Shower Enclosures. If provided, enclosures for shower stalls shall not obstruct controls or obstruct transfer from wheelchairs onto shower seats.

4.22 Toilet Rooms.

4.22.1 Minimum Number. *Toilet facilities required to be accessible by 4.1 shall comply*

4.21 Shower Stalls

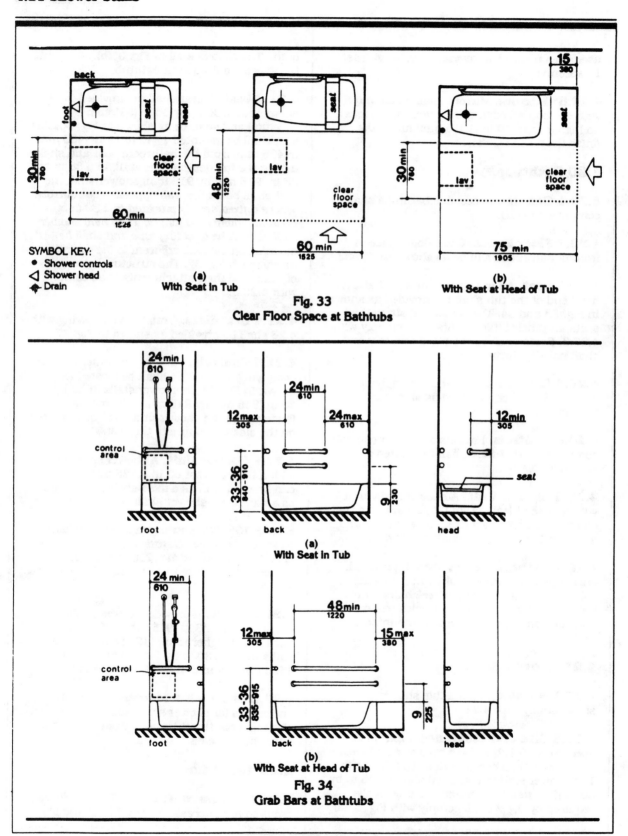

SYMBOL KEY:
- ● Shower controls
- ◁ Shower head
- ✦ Drain

(a)
With Seat in Tub

(b)
With Seat at Head of Tub

Fig. 33
Clear Floor Space at Bathtubs

(a)
With Seat in Tub

(b)
With Seat at Head of Tub

Fig. 34
Grab Bars at Bathtubs

Federal Register / Vol. 56, No. 144 / Friday, July 26, 1991 / Rules and Regulations

35653

4.22 Toilet Rooms

with 4.22. Accessible toilet rooms shall be on an accessible route.

4.22.2 Doors. All doors to accessible toilet rooms shall comply with 4.13. Doors shall not swing into the clear floor space required for any fixture.

4.22.3* Clear Floor Space. The accessible fixtures and controls required in 4.22.4, 4.22.5, 4.22.6, and 4.22.7 shall be on an accessible route. An unobstructed turning space complying with 4.2.3 shall be provided within an accessible toilet room. The clear floor space at fixtures and controls, the accessible route, and the turning space may overlap.

4.22.4 Water Closets. If toilet stalls are provided, then at least one shall be a standard toilet stall complying with 4.17; *where 6 or more stalls are provided, in addition to the stall complying with 4.17.3, at least one stall 36 in (915 mm) wide with an outward swinging, self-closing door and parallel grab bars complying with Fig. 30(d) and 4.26 shall be provided.* Water closets in such stalls shall comply with 4.16. If water closets are not in stalls, then at least one shall comply with 4.16.

4.22.5 Urinals. If urinals are provided, *then* at least one shall comply with 4.18.

4.22.6 Lavatories and Mirrors. If lavatories and mirrors are provided, *then* at least one of each shall comply with 4.19.

4.22.7 Controls and Dispensers. If controls, dispensers, receptacles, or other

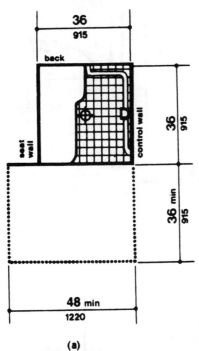

(a)
36-in by 36-in
(915-mm by 915-mm) Stall

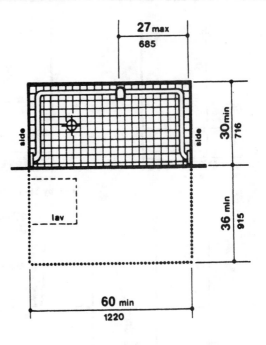

(b)
30-in by 60-in
(760-mm by 1525-mm) Stall

Fig. 35
Shower Size and Clearances

4.23 Bathrooms, Bathing Facilities, and Shower Rooms

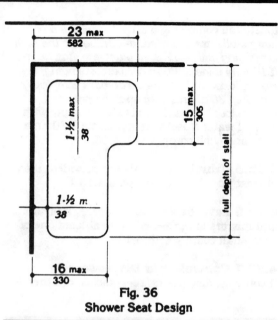

Fig. 36
Shower Seat Design

equipment are provided, *then* at least one of each shall be on an accessible route and shall comply with 4.27.

4.23 Bathrooms, Bathing Facilities, and Shower Rooms.

4.23.1 Minimum Number. Bathrooms, bathing facilities, or shower rooms *required to be accessible by 4.1* shall comply with 4.23 and shall be on an accessible route.

4.23.2 Doors. Doors to accessible bathrooms shall comply with 4.13. Doors shall not swing into the floor space required for any fixture.

4.23.3* Clear Floor Space. The accessible fixtures and controls required in 4.23.4, 4.23.5, 4.23.6, 4.23.7, 4.23.8, and 4.23.9 shall be on an accessible route. An unobstructed turning

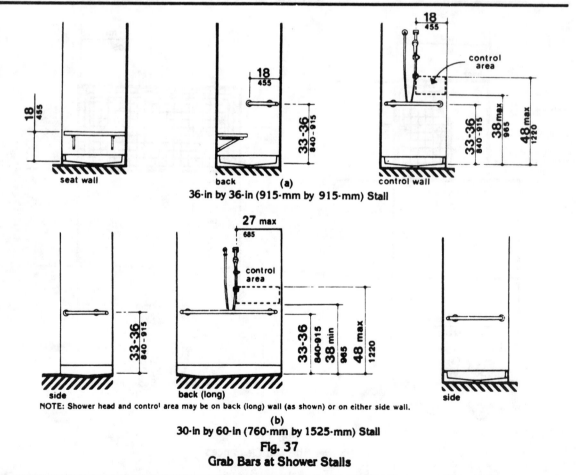

36-in by 36-in (915-mm by 915-mm) Stall (a)

NOTE: Shower head and control area may be on back (long) wall (as shown) or on either side wall.

(b)
30-in by 60-in (760-mm by 1525-mm) Stall
Fig. 37
Grab Bars at Shower Stalls

Federal Register / Vol. 56, No. 144 / Friday, July 26, 1991 / Rules and Regulations **35655**

4.24 Sinks

space complying with 4.2.3 shall be provided within an accessible bathroom. The clear floor spaces at fixtures and controls, the accessible route, and the turning space may overlap.

4.23.4 Water Closets. If toilet stalls are provided, then at least one shall be a standard toilet stall complying with 4.17; *where 6 or more stalls are provided, in addition to the stall complying with 4.17.3, at least one stall 36 in (915 mm) wide with an outward swinging, self-closing door and parallel grab bars complying with Fig. 30(d) and 4.26 shall be provided. Water closets in such stalls* shall comply with 4.16. If water closets are not in stalls, then at least one shall comply with 4.16.

4.23.5 Urinals. If urinals are provided, then at least one shall comply with 4.18.

4.23.6 Lavatories and Mirrors. If lavatories and mirrors are provided, then at least one of each shall comply with 4.19.

4.23.7 Controls and Dispensers. If controls, dispensers, receptacles, or other equipment *are* provided, *then* at least one of each shall be on an accessible route and shall comply with 4.27.

4.23.8 Bathing and Shower Facilities. If tubs or showers are provided, then at least one accessible tub that complies with 4.20 or at least one accessible shower that complies with 4.21 shall be provided.

4.23.9* Medicine Cabinets. If medicine cabinets are provided, at least one shall be located with a usable shelf no higher than 44 in (1120 mm) above the floor space. The floor space shall comply with 4.2.4.

4.24 Sinks.

4.24.1 General. Sinks *required to be accessible by 4.1* shall comply with 4.24.

4.24.2 Height. Sinks shall be mounted with the counter or rim no higher than 34 in (865 mm) *above the finish* floor.

4.24.3 Knee Clearance. Knee clearance that is at least 27 in (685 mm) high, 30 in (760 mm) wide, and 19 in (485 mm) deep shall be pro-

vided underneath sinks.

4.24.4 Depth. Each sink shall be a maximum of 6-1/2 in (165 mm) deep.

4.24.5 Clear Floor Space. A clear floor space at least 30 in by 48 in (760 mm by 1220 mm) complying with 4.2.4 shall be provided in front of a sink to allow forward approach. The clear floor space shall be on an accessible route and shall extend a maximum of 19 in (485 mm) underneath the sink (see Fig. 32).

4.24.6 Exposed Pipes and Surfaces. Hot water and drain pipes exposed under sinks shall be insulated or otherwise *configured so as to protect against contact.* There shall be no sharp or abrasive surfaces under sinks.

4.24.7 Faucets. Faucets shall comply with 4.27.4. Lever-operated, push-type, touch-type, or electronically controlled mechanisms are acceptable designs.

4.25 Storage.

4.25.1 General. *Fixed* storage facilities such as cabinets, shelves, closets, and drawers *required to be accessible by 4.1* shall comply with 4.25.

4.25.2 Clear Floor Space. A clear floor space at least 30 in by 48 in (760 mm by 1220 mm) complying with 4.2.4 that allows either a forward or parallel approach by a person using a wheelchair shall be provided at accessible storage facilities.

4.25.3 Height. Accessible storage spaces shall be within at least one of the reach ranges specified in 4.2.5 and 4.2.6 *(see Fig. 5 and Fig. 6).* Clothes rods or shelves shall be a maximum of 54 in (1370 mm) *above the finish* floor *for a side approach. Where the distance from the wheelchair to the clothes rod or shelf exceeds 10 in (255 mm) (as in closets without accessible doors) the height and depth to the rod or shelf shall comply with Fig. 38(a) and Fig. 38(b).*

4.25.4 Hardware. Hardware for accessible storage facilities shall comply with 4.27.4. Touch latches and U-shaped pulls are acceptable.

35656   Federal Register / Vol. 56, No. 144 / Friday, July 26, 1991 / Rules and Regulations

4.26 Handrails, Grab Bars, and Tub and Shower Seats

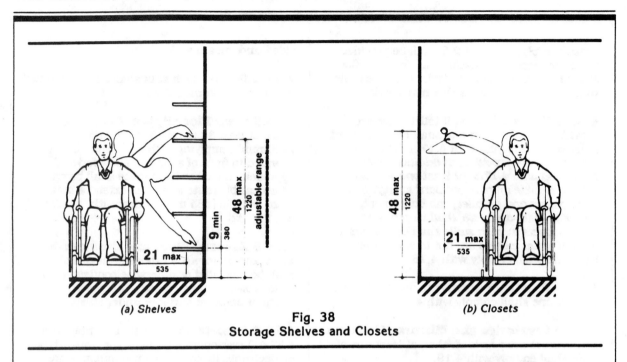

(a) Shelves

(b) Closets

Fig. 38
Storage Shelves and Closets

4.26 Handrails, Grab Bars, and Tub and Shower Seats.

4.26.1* General. All handrails, grab bars, and tub and shower seats *required to be accessible by 4.1, 4.8, 4.9, 4.16, 4.17, 4.20 or 4.21* shall comply with 4.26.

4.26.2* Size and Spacing of Grab Bars and Handrails. The diameter or width of the gripping surfaces of a handrail or grab bar shall be 1-1/4 in to 1-1/2 in (32 mm to 38 mm), or the shape shall provide an equivalent gripping surface. If handrails or grab bars are mounted adjacent to a wall, the space between the wall and the grab bar shall be 1-1/2 in (38 mm) (see Fig. 39(a), (b), (c), and (e)). Handrails may be located in a recess if the recess is a maximum of 3 in (75 mm) deep and extends at least 18 in (455 mm) above the top of the rail (see Fig. 39(d)).

4.26.3 Structural Strength. The structural strength of grab bars, tub and shower seats, fasteners, and mounting devices shall meet the following specification:

(1) Bending stress in a grab bar or seat induced by the maximum bending moment from the application of 250 lbf (1112N) shall be less than the allowable stress for the material of the grab bar or seat.

(2) Shear stress induced in a grab bar or seat by the application of 250 lbf (1112N) shall be less than the allowable shear stress for the material of the grab bar or seat. If the connection between the grab bar or seat and its mounting bracket or other support is considered to be fully restrained, then direct and torsional shear stresses shall be totaled for the combined shear stress, which shall not exceed the allowable shear stress.

(3) Shear force induced in a fastener or mounting device from the application of 250 lbf (1112N) shall be less than the allowable lateral load of either the fastener or mounting device or the supporting structure, whichever is the smaller allowable load.

(4) Tensile force induced in a fastener by a direct tension force of 250 lbf (1112N) plus the maximum moment from the application of 250 lbf (1112N) shall be less than the allowable withdrawal load between the fastener and the supporting structure.

(5) Grab bars shall not rotate within their fittings.

Federal Register / Vol. 56, No. 144 / Friday, July 26, 1991 / Rules and Regulations   **35657**

4.26 Handrails, Grab Bars, and Tub and Shower Seats

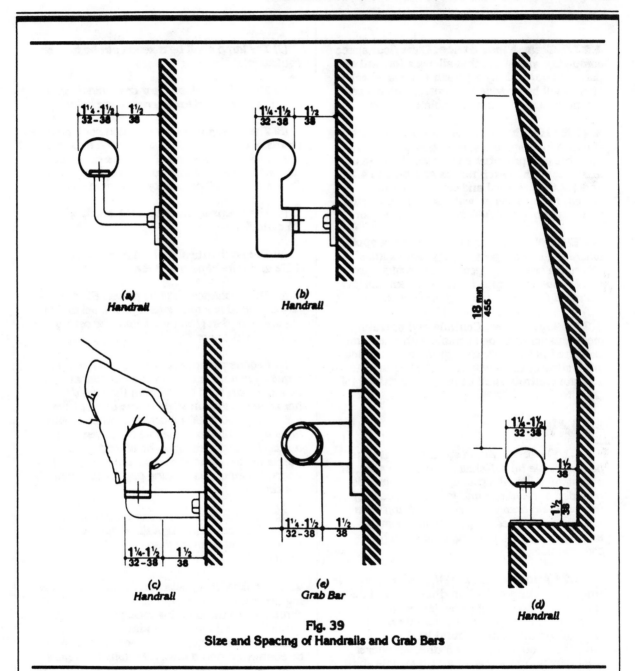

Fig. 39
Size and Spacing of Handrails and Grab Bars

4.26.4 Eliminating Hazards. A handrail or grab bar and any wall or other surface adjacent to it shall be free of any sharp or abrasive elements. Edges shall have a minimum radius of 1/8 in (3.2 mm).

4.27 Controls and Operating Mechanisms.

4.27.1 General. Controls and operating mechanisms *required to be accessible by 4.1* shall comply with 4.27.

35658 Federal Register / Vol. 56, No. 144 / Friday, July 26, 1991 / Rules and Regulations

4.28 Alarms

4.27.2 Clear Floor Space. Clear floor space complying with 4.2.4 that allows a forward or a parallel approach by a person using a wheelchair shall be provided at controls, dispensers, receptacles, and other operable equipment.

4.27.3* Height. The highest operable part of controls, dispensers, receptacles, and other operable equipment shall be placed within at least one of the reach ranges specified in 4.2.5 and 4.2.6. Electrical and communications system receptacles on walls shall be mounted no less than 15 in (380 mm) above the floor.

EXCEPTION: These requirements do not apply where the use of special equipment dictates otherwise or where electrical and communications systems receptacles are not normally intended for use by building occupants.

4.27.4 Operation. Controls and operating mechanisms shall be operable with one hand and shall not require tight grasping, pinching, or twisting of the wrist. The force required to activate controls shall be no greater than 5 lbf (22.2 N).

4.28 Alarms.

4.28.1 General. *Alarm systems required to be accessible by 4.1 shall comply with 4.28. At a minimum, visual signal appliances shall be provided in buildings and facilities in each of the following areas: restrooms and any other general usage areas (e.g., meeting rooms), hallways, lobbies, and any other area for common use.*

4.28.2* Audible Alarms. If provided, audible emergency alarms shall produce a sound that exceeds the prevailing equivalent sound level in the room or space by at least 15 dbA or exceeds any maximum sound level with a duration of 60 seconds by 5 dbA, whichever is louder. Sound levels for alarm signals shall not exceed 120 dbA.

4.28.3* Visual Alarms. *Visual alarm signal appliances shall be integrated into the building or facility alarm system. If single station audible alarms are provided then single station visual alarm signals shall be provided. Visual alarm signals shall have the following minimum photometric and location features:*

(1) The lamp shall be a xenon strobe type or equivalent.

(2) The color shall be clear or nominal white (i.e., unfiltered or clear filtered white light).

(3) The maximum pulse duration shall be two-tenths of one second (0.2 sec) with a maximum duty cycle of 40 percent. The pulse duration is defined as the time interval between initial and final points of 10 percent of maximum signal.

(4) The intensity shall be a minimum of 75 candela.

(5) The flash rate shall be a minimum of 1 Hz and a maximum of 3 Hz.

(6) The appliance shall be placed 80 in (2030 mm) above the highest floor level within the space or 6 in (152 mm) below the ceiling, whichever is lower.

(7) In general, no place in any room or space required to have a visual signal appliance shall be more than 50 ft (15 m) from the signal (in the horizontal plane). In large rooms and spaces exceeding 100 ft (30 m) across, without obstructions 6 ft (2 m) above the finish floor, such as auditoriums, devices may be placed around the perimeter, spaced a maximum 100 ft (30 m) apart, in lieu of suspending appliances from the ceiling.

(8) No place in common corridors or hallways in which visual alarm signalling appliances are required shall be more than 50 ft (15 m) from the signal.

4.28.4* Auxiliary Alarms. *Units and sleeping accommodations shall have a visual alarm connected to the building emergency alarm system or shall have a standard 110-volt electrical receptacle into which such an alarm can be connected and a means by which a signal from the building emergency alarm system can trigger such an auxiliary alarm. When visual alarms are in place the signal shall be visible in all areas of the unit or room. Instructions for use of the auxiliary alarm or receptacle shall be provided.*

Federal Register / Vol. 56, No. 144 / Friday, July 26, 1991 / Rules and Regulations   35659

4.29 Detectable Warnings.

4.29.1 General. *Detectable warnings required by 4.1 and 4.7 shall comply with 4.29.*

4.29.2* Detectable Warnings on Walking Surfaces. *Detectable warnings shall consist of raised truncated domes with a diameter of nominal 0.9 in (23 mm), a height of nominal 0.2 in (5 mm) and a center-to-center spacing of nominal 2.35 in (60 mm) and shall contrast visually with adjoining surfaces, either light-on-dark, or dark-on-light.*

The material used to provide contrast shall be an integral part of the walking surface. Detectable warnings used on interior surfaces shall differ from adjoining walking surfaces in resiliency or sound-on-cane contact.

4.29.3 Detectable Warnings on Doors To Hazardous Areas. *(Reserved).*

4.29.4 Detectable Warnings at Stairs. *(Reserved).*

4.29.5 Detectable Warnings at Hazardous Vehicular Areas. If a walk crosses or adjoins a vehicular way, *and the walking surfaces are not separated by* curbs, railings, or other elements *between the pedestrian areas and vehicular areas,* the boundary between the areas shall be defined by a continuous *detectable warning which is 36 in (915 mm) wide,* complying with 4.29.2.

4.29.6 Detectable Warnings at Reflecting Pools. The edges of reflecting pools shall be protected by railings, walls, curbs, or *detectable warnings* complying with 4.29.2.

4.29.7 Standardization. *(Reserved).*

4.30 Signage.

4.30.1* General. *Signage required to be accessible by 4.1 shall comply with the applicable provisions of 4.30.*

4.30.2* Character Proportion. Letters and numbers on signs shall have a width-to-height ratio between 3:5 and 1:1 and a stroke-width-to-height ratio between 1:5 and 1:10.

4.30.3 Character Height. *Characters and numbers on signs shall be sized according to the viewing distance from which they are to be read. The minimum height is measured using an upper case X. Lower case characters are permitted.*

Height Above Finished Floor	Minimum Character Height
Suspended or Projected Overhead in compliance with 4.4.2	3 in. (75 mm) minimum

4.30.4* Raised and Brailled Characters and Pictorial Symbol Signs (Pictograms). Letters and numerals shall be raised 1/32 in, upper case, sans serif or simple serif type and shall be accompanied with Grade 2 Braille. Raised characters shall be at least 5/8 in (16 mm) high, but no higher than 2 in (50 mm). *Pictograms shall be accompanied by the equivalent verbal description placed directly below the pictogram. The border dimension of the pictogram shall be 6 in (152 mm) minimum in height.*

4.30.5* Finish and Contrast. *The characters and background of signs shall be eggshell, matte, or other non-glare finish.* Characters and symbols shall contrast with their background — either light characters on a dark background or dark characters on a light background.

4.30.6 Mounting Location and Height. *Where permanent identification is provided for rooms and spaces, signs shall be installed on the wall adjacent to the latch side of the door. Where there is no wall space to the latch side of the door, including at double leaf doors, signs shall be placed on the nearest adjacent wall. Mounting height shall be 60 in (1525 mm) above the finish floor to the centerline of the sign. Mounting location for such signage shall be so that a person may approach within 3 in (76 mm) of signage without encountering protruding objects or standing within the swing of a door.*

4.30.7* Symbols of Accessibility.

(1) Facilities and elements required to be identified as accessible by 4.1 shall use the international symbol of accessibility. The

35660   Federal Register / Vol. 56, No. 144 / Friday, July 26, 1991 / Rules and Regulations

4.30 Signage

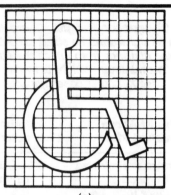

(a)
Proportions
International Symbol of Accessibility

(b)
Display Conditions
International Symbol of Accessibility

(c)
International TDD Symbol

(d)
International Symbol of Access for Hearing Loss

Fig. 43
International Symbols

symbol shall be displayed as shown in Fig. 43(a) and (b).

(2) Volume Control Telephones. Telephones required to have a volume control by 4.1.3(17)(b) shall be identified by a sign containing a depiction of a telephone handset with radiating sound waves.

(3) Text Telephones. Text telephones required by 4.1.3 (17)(c) shall be identified by the international TDD symbol (Fig 43(c)). In addition, if a facility has a public text telephone, directional signage indicating the location of the nearest text telephone shall be placed adjacent to all banks of telephones which do not contain a text telephone. Such directional signage shall include the international TDD symbol. If a facility has no banks of telephones, the directional signage shall be provided at the entrance (e.g., in a building directory).

(4) Assistive Listening Systems. In assembly areas where permanently installed assistive listening systems are required by 4.1.3(19)(b) the availability of such systems shall be identified with signage that includes the international symbol of access for hearing loss (Fig 43(d)).

4.30.8* Illumination Levels. *(Reserved).*

4.31 Telephones.

4.31.1 General. Public telephones *required to be accessible by 4.1* shall comply with 4.31.

4.31.2 Clear Floor or Ground Space. A clear floor or ground space at least 30 in by 48 in (760 mm by 1220 mm) that allows either a forward or parallel approach by a person using a wheelchair shall be provided at telephones (see Fig. 44). The clear floor or ground space shall comply with 4.2.4. Bases, enclosures, and fixed seats shall not impede approaches to telephones by people who use wheelchairs.

4.31.3* Mounting Height. The highest operable part of the telephone shall be within the reach ranges specified in 4.2.5 or 4.2.6.

4.31.4 Protruding Objects. *Telephones shall comply with 4.4.*

Federal Register / Vol. 56, No. 144 / Friday, July 26, 1991 / Rules and Regulations   35661

4.31 Telephones

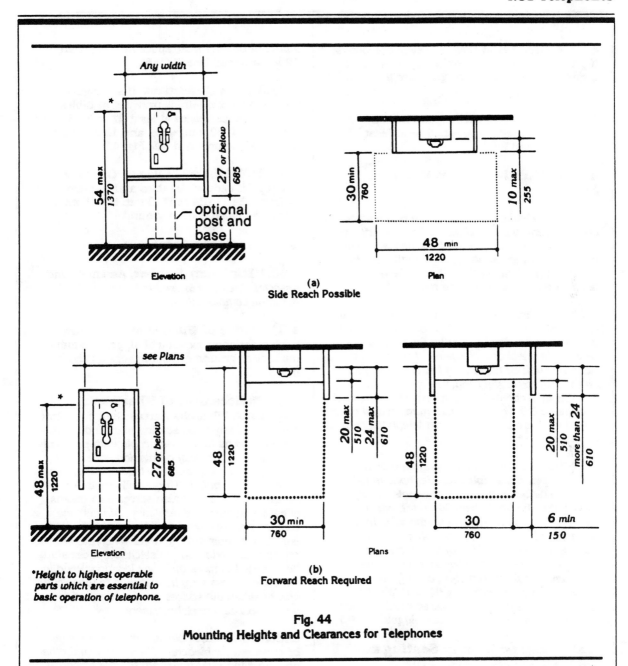

Fig. 44
Mounting Heights and Clearances for Telephones

4.31.5 Hearing Aid Compatible and Volume Control Telephones Required by 4.1.

(1) Telephones shall be hearing aid compatible.

(2) Volume controls, *capable of a minimum of 12 dbA and a maximum of 18 dbA above*

normal, shall be provided in accordance with 4.1.3. If an automatic reset is provided then 18 dbA may be exceeded.

4.31.6 Controls. Telephones shall have pushbutton controls where service for such equipment is available.

35662   Federal Register / Vol. 56, No. 144 / Friday, July 26, 1991 / Rules and Regulations

4.32 *Fixed or Built-in Seating and Tables*

4.31.7 Telephone Books. Telephone books, if provided, shall be located *in a position that complies with the reach ranges specified in 4.2.5 and 4.2.6.*

4.31.8 Cord Length. The cord from the telephone to the handset shall be at least 29 in (735 mm) long.

4.31.9* Text Telephones Required by 4.1.

(1) *Text telephones used with a pay telephone shall be permanently affixed within, or adjacent to, the telephone enclosure. If an acoustic coupler is used, the telephone cord shall be sufficiently long to allow connection of the text telephone and the telephone receiver.*

(2) *Pay telephones designed to accommodate a portable text telephone shall be equipped with a shelf and an electrical outlet within or adjacent to the telephone enclosure. The telephone handset shall be capable of being placed flush on the surface of the shelf. The shelf shall be capable of accommodating a text telephone and shall have 6 in (152 mm) minimum vertical clearance in the area where the text telephone is to be placed.*

(3) *Equivalent facilitation may be provided. For example, a portable text telephone may be made available in a hotel at the registration desk if it is available on a 24-hour basis for use with nearby public pay telephones. In this instance, at least one pay telephone shall comply with paragraph 2 of this section. In addition, if an acoustic coupler is used, the telephone handset cord shall be sufficiently long so as to allow connection of the text telephone and the telephone receiver. Directional signage shall be provided and shall comply with 4.30.7.*

4.32 Fixed or Built-in Seating and Tables.

4.32.1 Minimum Number. Fixed or built-in seating or tables *required to be accessible by 4.1* shall comply with 4.32.

4.32.2 Seating. If seating spaces for people in wheelchairs are provided at *fixed* tables or counters, clear floor space complying with 4.2.4 shall be provided. Such clear floor space

shall not overlap knee space by more than 19 in (485 mm) (see Fig. 45).

4.32.3 Knee Clearances. If seating for people in wheelchairs is provided at tables *or* counters, knee spaces at least 27 in (685 mm) high, 30 in (760 mm) wide, and 19 in (485 mm) deep shall be provided (see Fig. 45).

4.32.4* Height of Tables or Counters. *The tops of accessible tables and counters shall be from 28 in to 34 in (710 mm to 865 mm) above the finish floor or ground.*

4.33 Assembly Areas.

4.33.1 Minimum Number. Assembly *and associated areas required to be accessible by 4.1 shall comply with 4.33.*

4.33.2* Size of Wheelchair Locations. Each wheelchair location shall provide minimum clear ground or floor spaces as shown in Fig. 46.

4.33.3* Placement of Wheelchair Locations. Wheelchair areas shall be an integral part of any fixed seating plan and shall be *provided so as to provide people with physical disabilities a choice of admission prices and lines of sight comparable to those for members of the general public.* They shall adjoin an accessible route that also serves as a means of egress in case of emergency. *At least one companion fixed seat shall be provided next to each wheelchair seating area. When the seating capacity exceeds 300, wheelchair spaces shall be provided in more than one location. Readily removable seats may be installed in wheelchair spaces when the spaces are not required to accommodate wheelchair users.*

EXCEPTION: *Accessible viewing positions may be clustered for bleachers, balconies, and other areas having sight lines that require slopes of greater than 5 percent. Equivalent accessible viewing positions may be located on levels having accessible egress.*

4.33.4 Surfaces. The ground or floor at wheelchair locations shall be level and shall comply with 4.5.

4.33 Assembly Areas

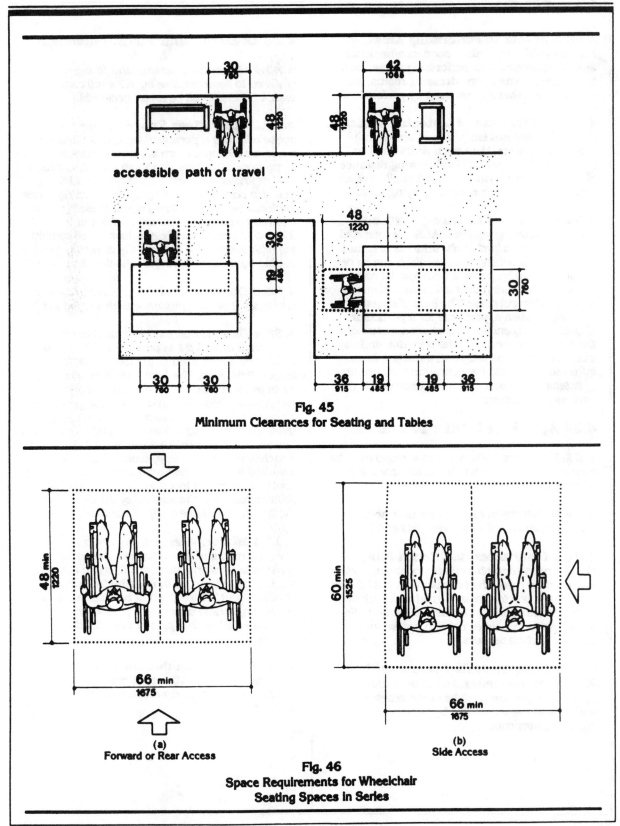

accessible path of travel

Fig. 45
Minimum Clearances for Seating and Tables

(a)
Forward or Rear Access

(b)
Side Access

Fig. 46
Space Requirements for Wheelchair
Seating Spaces in Series

35664   Federal Register / Vol. 56, No. 144 / Friday, July 26, 1991 / Rules and Regulations

4.34 Automated Teller Machines

4.33.5 Access to Performing Areas.
An accessible route shall connect wheelchair seating locations with performing areas, including stages, arena floors, dressing rooms, locker rooms, and other spaces used by performers.

4.33.6* Placement of Listening Systems.
If the listening system provided serves individual fixed seats, then such seats shall be located within a 50 ft (15 m) viewing distance of the stage or playing area and shall have a complete view of the stage or playing area.

4.33.7* Types of Listening Systems.
Assistive listening systems (ALS) are intended to augment standard public address and audio systems by providing signals which can be received directly by persons with special receivers or their own hearing aids and which eliminate or filter background noise. The type of assistive listening system appropriate for a particular application depends on the characteristics of the setting, the nature of the program, and the intended audience. Magnetic induction loops, infra-red and radio frequency systems are types of listening systems which are appropriate for various applications.

4.34 Automated Teller Machines.

4.34.1 General. *Each machine required to be accessible by 4.1.3 shall be on an accessible route and shall comply with 4.34.*

4.34.2 Controls. *Controls for user activation shall comply with the requirements of 4.27.*

4.34.3 Clearances and Reach Range.
Free standing or built-in units not having a clear space under them shall comply with 4.27.2 and 4.27.3 and provide for a parallel approach and both a forward and side reach to the unit allowing a person in a wheelchair to access the controls and dispensers.

4.34.4 Equipment for Persons with Vision Impairments. *Instructions and all information for use shall be made accessible to and independently usable by persons with vision impairments.*

4.35 Dressing and Fitting Rooms.

4.35.1 General. *Dressing and fitting rooms required to be accessible by 4.1 shall comply with 4.35 and shall be on an accessible route.*

4.35.2 Clear Floor Space. *A clear floor space allowing a person using a wheelchair to make a 180-degree turn shall be provided in every accessible dressing room entered through a swinging or sliding door. No door shall swing into any part of the turning space. Turning space shall not be required in a private dressing room entered through a curtained opening at least 32 in (815 mm) wide if clear floor space complying with section 4.2 renders the dressing room usable by a person using a wheelchair.*

4.35.3 Doors. *All doors to accessible dressing rooms shall be in compliance with section 4.13.*

4.35.4 Bench. *Every accessible dressing room shall have a 24 in by 48 in (610 mm by 1220 mm) bench fixed to the wall along the longer dimension. The bench shall be mounted 17 in to 19 in (430 mm to 485 mm) above the finish floor. Clear floor space shall be provided alongside the bench to allow a person using a wheelchair to make a parallel transfer onto the bench. The structural strength of the bench and attachments shall comply with 4.26.3. Where installed in conjunction with showers, swimming pools, or other wet locations, water shall not accumulate upon the surface of the bench and the bench shall have a slip-resistant surface.*

4.35.5 Mirror. *Where mirrors are provided in dressing rooms of the same use, then in an accessible dressing room, a full-length mirror, measuring at least 18 in wide by 54 in high (460 mm by 1370 mm), shall be mounted in a position affording a view to a person on the bench as well as to a person in a standing position.*

NOTE: Sections 4.1.1 through 4.1.7 and sections 5 through 10 are different from ANSI A117.1 in their entirety and are printed in standard type.

Federal Register / Vol. 56, No. 144 / Friday, July 26, 1991 / Rules and Regulations

35665

5.0 Restaurants and Cafeterias

5. RESTAURANTS AND CAFETERIAS.

5.1* General. Except as specified or modified in this section, restaurants and cafeterias shall comply with the requirements of 4.1 to 4.35. Where fixed tables (or dining counters where food is consumed but there is no service) are provided, at least 5 percent, but not less than one, of the fixed tables (or a portion of the dining counter) shall be accessible and shall comply with 4.32 as required in 4.1.3(18). In establishments where separate areas are designated for smoking and non-smoking patrons, the required number of accessible fixed tables (or counters) shall be proportionally distributed between the smoking and non-smoking areas. In new construction, and where practicable in alterations, accessible fixed tables (or counters) shall be distributed throughout the space or facility.

5.2 Counters and Bars. Where food or drink is served at counters exceeding 34 in (865 mm) in height for consumption by customers seated on stools or standing at the counter, a portion of the main counter which is 60 in (1525 mm) in length minimum shall be provided in compliance with 4.32 or service shall be available at accessible tables within the same area.

5.3 Access Aisles. All accessible fixed tables shall be accessible by means of an access aisle at least 36 in (915 mm) clear between parallel edges of tables or between a wall and the table edges.

5.4 Dining Areas. In new construction, all dining areas, including raised or sunken dining areas, loggias, and outdoor seating areas, shall be accessible. In non-elevator buildings, an accessible means of vertical access to the mezzanine is not required under the following conditions: 1) the area of mezzanine seating measures no more than 33 percent of the area of the total accessible seating area; 2) the same services and decor are provided in an accessible space usable by the general public; and, 3) the accessible areas are not restricted to use by people with disabilities. In alterations, accessibility to raised or sunken dining areas, or to all parts of outdoor seating areas is not required provided that the same services and decor are provided in an accessible space usable by the general public and are not restricted to use by people with disabilities.

5.5 Food Service Lines. Food service lines shall have a minimum clear width of 36 in (915 mm), with a preferred clear width of 42 in (1065 mm) to allow passage around a person using a wheelchair. Tray slides shall be mounted no higher than 34 in (865 mm) above the floor (see Fig. 53). If self-service shelves

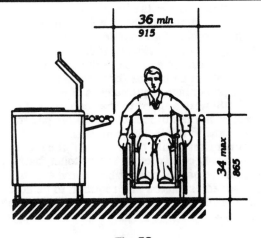

Fig. 53
Food Service Lines

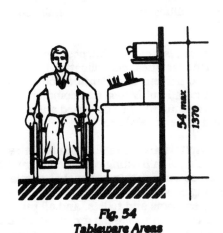

Fig. 54
Tableware Areas

35666   Federal Register / Vol. 56, No. 144 / Friday, July 26, 1991 / Rules and Regulations

6.0 Medical Care Facilities

are provided, at least 50 percent of each type must be within reach ranges specified in 4.2.5 and 4.2.6.

5.6 Tableware and Condiment Areas.
Self-service shelves and dispensing devices for tableware, dishware, condiments, food and beverages shall be installed to comply with 4.2 (see Fig. 54).

5.7 Raised Platforms.
In banquet rooms or spaces where a head table or speaker's lectern is located on a raised platform, the platform shall be accessible in compliance with 4.8 or 4.11. Open edges of a raised platform shall be protected by placement of tables or by a curb.

5.8 Vending Machines and Other Equipment.
Spaces for vending machines and other equipment shall comply with 4.2 and shall be located on an accessible route.

5.9 Quiet Areas. (Reserved).

6. MEDICAL CARE FACILITIES.

6.1 General.
Medical care facilities included in this section are those in which people receive physical or medical treatment or care and where persons may need assistance in responding to an emergency and where the period of stay may exceed twenty-four hours. In addition to the requirements of 4.1 through 4.35, medical care facilities and buildings shall comply with 6.

(1) Hospitals - general purpose hospitals, psychiatric facilities, detoxification facilities — At least 10 percent of patient bedrooms and toilets, and all public use and common use areas are required to be designed and constructed to be accessible.

(2) Hospitals and rehabilitation facilities that specialize in treating conditions that affect mobility, or units within either that specialize in treating conditions that affect mobility — All patient bedrooms and toilets, and all public use and common use areas are required to be designed and constructed to be accessible.

(3) Long term care facilities, nursing homes — At least 50 percent of patient bedrooms and toilets, and all public use and common use areas are required to be designed and constructed to be accessible.

(4) Alterations to patient bedrooms.

(a) When patient bedrooms are being added or altered as part of a planned renovation of an entire wing, a department, or other discrete area of an existing medical facility, a percentage of the patient bedrooms that are being added or altered shall comply with 6.3. The percentage of accessible rooms provided shall be consistent with the percentage of rooms required to be accessible by the applicable requirements of 6.1(1), 6.1(2), or 6.1(3), until the number of accessible patient bedrooms in the facility equals the overall number that would be required if the facility were newly constructed. (For example, if 20 patient bedrooms are being altered in the obstetrics department of a hospital, 2 of the altered rooms must be made accessible. If, within the same hospital, 20 patient bedrooms are being altered in a unit that specializes in treating mobility impairments, all of the altered rooms must be made accessible.) Where toilet/bath rooms are part of patient bedrooms which are added or altered and required to be accessible, each such patient toilet/bathroom shall comply with 6.4.

(b) When patient bedrooms are being added or altered individually, and not as part of an alteration of the entire area, the altered patient bedrooms shall comply with 6.3, unless either: a) the number of accessible rooms provided in the department or area containing the altered patient bedroom equals the number of accessible patient bedrooms that would be required if the percentage requirements of 6.1(1), 6.1(2), or 6.1(3) were applied to that department or area; or b) the number of accessible patient bedrooms in the facility equals the overall number that would be required if the facility were newly constructed. Where toilet/bathrooms are part of patient bedrooms which are added or altered and required to be accessible, each such toilet/bathroom shall comply with 6.4.

Federal Register / Vol. 56, No. 144 / Friday, July 26, 1991 / Rules and Regulations   **35667**

7.0 Business and Mercantile

6.2 Entrances. At least one accessible entrance that complies with 4.14 shall be protected from the weather by canopy or roof overhang. Such entrances shall incorporate a passenger loading zone that complies with 4.6.6.

6.3 Patient Bedrooms. Provide accessible patient bedrooms in compliance with 4.1 through 4.35. Accessible patient bedrooms shall comply with the following:

(1) Each bedroom shall have a door that complies with 4.13.

EXCEPTION: Entry doors to acute care hospital bedrooms for in-patients shall be exempted from the requirement in 4.13.6 for maneuvering space at the latch side of the door if the door is at least 44 in (1120 mm) wide.

(2) Each bedroom shall have adequate space to provide a maneuvering space that complies with 4.2.3. In rooms with 2 beds, it is preferable that this space be located between beds.

(3) Each bedroom shall have adequate space to provide a minimum clear floor space of 36 in (915 mm) along each side of the bed and to provide an accessible route complying with 4.3.3 to each side of each bed.

6.4 Patient Toilet Rooms. Where toilet/bath rooms are provided as a part of a patient bedroom, each patient bedroom that is required to be accessible shall have an accessible toilet/bath room that complies with 4.22 or 4.23 and shall be on an accessible route.

7. BUSINESS AND MERCANTILE.

7.1 General. In addition to the requirements of 4.1 to 4.35, the design of all areas used for business transactions with the public shall comply with 7.

7.2 Sales and Service Counters, Teller Windows, Information Counters.

(1) In department stores and miscellaneous retail stores where counters have cash registers and are provided for sales or distribution of goods or services to the public, at least one of each type shall have a portion of the counter which is at least 36 in (915 mm) in length with a maximum height of 36 in (915 mm) above the finish floor. It shall be on an accessible route complying with 4.3. The accessible counters must be dispersed throughout the building or facility. In alterations where it is technically infeasible to provide an accessible counter, an auxiliary counter meeting these requirements may be provided.

(2) At ticketing counters, teller stations in a bank, registration counters in hotels and motels, box office ticket counters, and other counters that may not have a cash register but at which goods or services are sold or distributed, either:

(i) a portion of the main counter which is a minimum of 36 in (915 mm) in length shall be provided with a maximum height of 36 in (915 mm); or

(ii) an auxiliary counter with a maximum height of 36 in (915 mm) in close proximity to the main counter shall be provided; or

(iii) equivalent facilitation shall be provided (e.g., at a hotel registration counter, equivalent facilitation might consist of: (1) provision of a folding shelf attached to the main counter on which an individual with disabilities can write, and (2) use of the space on the side of the counter or at the concierge desk, for handing materials back and forth).

All accessible sales and service counters shall be on an accessible route complying with 4.3.

(3)* Assistive Listening Devices. (Reserved)

35668   Federal Register / Vol. 56, No. 144 / Friday, July 26, 1991 / Rules and Regulations

8.0 Libraries

7.3* Check-out Aisles.

(1) In new construction, accessible check-out aisles shall be provided in conformance with the table below:

Total Check-out Aisles of Each Design	Minimum Number of Accessible Check-out Aisles (of each design)
1 – 4	1
5 – 8	2
8 – 15	3
over 15	3, plus 20% of additional aisles

EXCEPTION: In new construction, where the selling space is under 5000 square feet, only one check-out aisle is required to be accessible.

EXCEPTION: In alterations, at least one check-out aisle shall be accessible in facilities under 5000 square feet of selling space. In facilities of 5000 or more square feet of selling space, at least one of each design of check-out aisle shall be made accessible when altered until the number of accessible check-out aisles of each design equals the number required in new construction.

Examples of check-out aisles of different "design" include those which are specifically designed to serve different functions. Different "design" includes but is not limited to the following features - length of belt or no belt; or permanent signage designating the aisle as an express lane.

(2) Clear aisle width for accessible check-out aisles shall comply with 4.2.1 and maximum adjoining counter height shall not exceed 38 in (965 mm) above the finish floor. The top of the lip shall not exceed 40 in (1015 mm) above the finish floor.

(3) Signage identifying accessible check-out aisles shall comply with 4.30.7 and shall be mounted above the check-out aisle in the same location where the check-out number or type of check-out is displayed.

7.4 Security Bollards.
Any device used to prevent the removal of shopping carts from store premises shall not prevent access or egress to people in wheelchairs. An alternate entry that is equally convenient to that provided for the ambulatory population is acceptable.

8. | LIBRARIES.

8.1 General. In addition to the requirements of 4.1 to 4.35, the design of all public areas of a library shall comply with 8, including reading and study areas, stacks, reference rooms, reserve areas, and special facilities or collections.

8.2 Reading and Study Areas. At least 5 percent or a minimum of one of each element of fixed seating, tables, or study carrels shall comply with 4.2 and 4.32. Clearances between fixed accessible tables and between study carrels shall comply with 4.3.

8.3 Check-Out Areas. At least one lane at each check-out area shall comply with 7.2(1). Any traffic control or book security gates or turnstiles shall comply with 4.13.

8.4 Card Catalogs and Magazine Displays. Minimum clear aisle space at card catalogs and magazine displays shall comply with Fig. 55. Maximum reach height shall comply with 4.2, with a height of 48 in (1220 mm) preferred irrespective of approach allowed.

8.5 Stacks. Minimum clear aisle width between stacks shall comply with 4.3, with a minimum clear aisle width of 42 in (1065 mm) preferred where possible. Shelf height in stack areas is unrestricted (see Fig. 56).

Federal Register / Vol. 56, No. 144 / Friday, July 26, 1991 / Rules and Regulations   35669

9.0 Accessible Transient Lodging

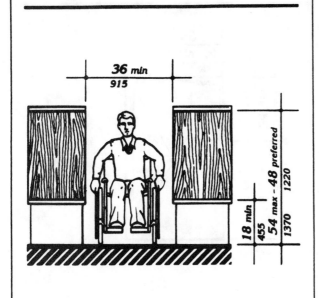

Fig. 55
Card Catalog

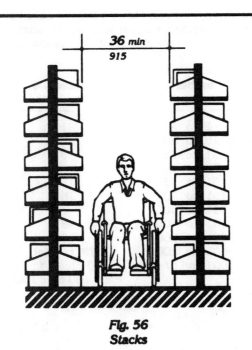

Fig. 56
Stacks

9. ACCESSIBLE TRANSIENT LODGING.

(1) Except as specified in the special technical provisions of this section, accessible transient lodging shall comply with the applicable requirements of 4.1 through 4.35. Transient lodging includes facilities or portions thereof used for sleeping accommodations, when not classed as a medical care facility.

9.1 Hotels, Motels, Inns, Boarding Houses, Dormitories, Resorts and Other Similar Places of Transient Lodging.

9.1.1 General. All public use and common use areas are required to be designed and constructed to comply with section 4 (Accessible Elements and Spaces: Scope and Technical Requirements).

EXCEPTION: Sections 9.1 through 9.4 do not apply to an establishment located within a building that contains not more than five rooms for rent or hire and that is actually occupied by the proprietor of such establishment as the residence of such proprietor.

9.1.2 Accessible Units, Sleeping Rooms, and Suites. Accessible sleeping rooms or suites that comply with the requirements of 9.2 (Requirements for Accessible Units, Sleeping Rooms, and Suites) shall be provided in conformance with the table below. In addition, in hotels, of 50 or more sleeping rooms or suites, additional accessible sleeping rooms or suites that include a roll-in shower shall also be provided in conformance with the table below. Such accommodations shall comply with the requirements of 9.2, 4.21, and Figure 57(a) or (b).

35670   Federal Register / Vol. 56, No. 144 / Friday, July 26, 1991 / Rules and Regulations

9.1.3 Sleeping Accommodations for Persons with Hearing Impairments

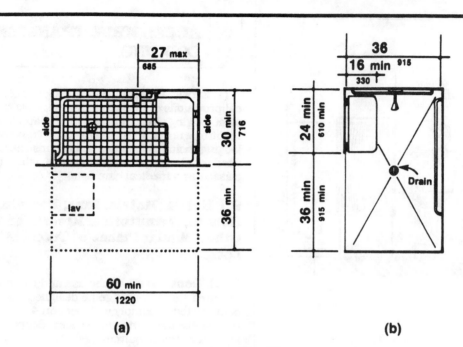

Fig. 57
Roll-in Shower with Folding Seat

Number of Rooms	Accessible Rooms	Rooms with Roll-in Showers
1 to 25	1	
26 to 50	2	
51 to 75	3	1
76 to 100	4	1
101 to 150	5	2
151 to 200	6	2
201 to 300	7	3
301 to 400	8	4
401 to 500	9	4 plus one for each additional 100 over 400
501 to 1000	2% of total	
1001 and over	20 plus 1 for each 100 over 1000	

and suites that comply with 9.3 (Visual Alarms, Notification Devices, and Telephones) shall be provided in conformance with the following table:

Number of Elements	Accessible Elements
1 to 25	1
26 to 50	2
51 to 75	3
76 to 100	4
101 to 150	5
151 to 200	6
201 to 300	7
301 to 400	8
401 to 500	9
501 to 1000	2% of total
1001 and over	20 plus 1 for each 100 over 1000

9.1.3 Sleeping Accommodations for Persons with Hearing Impairments.

In addition to those accessible sleeping rooms and suites required by 9.1.2, sleeping rooms

Federal Register / Vol. 56, No. 144 / Friday, July 26, 1991 / Rules and Regulations   **35671**

9.2 Requirements for Accessible Units, Sleeping Rooms and Suites

9.1.4 Classes of Sleeping Accommodations.

(1) In order to provide persons with disabilities a range of options equivalent to those available to other persons served by the facility, sleeping rooms and suites required to be accessible by 9.1.2 shall be dispersed among the various classes of sleeping accommodations available to patrons of the place of transient lodging. Factors to be considered include room size, cost, amenities provided, and the number of beds provided.

(2) Equivalent Facilitation. For purposes of this section, it shall be deemed equivalent facilitation if the operator of a facility elects to limit construction of accessible rooms to those intended for multiple occupancy, provided that such rooms are made available at the cost of a single-occupancy room to an individual with disabilities who requests a single-occupancy room.

9.1.5. Alterations to Accessible Units, Sleeping Rooms, and Suites. When sleeping rooms are being altered in an existing facility, or portion thereof, subject to the requirements of this section, at least one sleeping room or suite that complies with the requirements of 9.2 (Requirements for Accessible Units, Sleeping Rooms, and Suites) shall be provided for each 25 sleeping rooms, or fraction thereof, of rooms being altered until the number of such rooms provided equals the number required to be accessible with 9.1.2. In addition, at least one sleeping room or suite that complies with the requirements of 9.3 (Visual Alarms, Notification Devices, and Telephones) shall be provided for each 25 sleeping rooms, or fraction thereof, of rooms being altered until the number of such rooms equals the number required to be accessible by 9.1.3.

9.2 Requirements for Accessible Units, Sleeping Rooms and Suites.

9.2.1 General. Units, sleeping rooms, and suites required to be accessible by 9.1 shall comply with 9.2.

9.2.2 Minimum Requirements. An accessible unit, sleeping room or suite shall be on an accessible route complying with 4.3 and have the following accessible elements and spaces.

(1) Accessible sleeping rooms shall have a 36 in (915 mm) clear width maneuvering space located along both sides of a bed, except that where two beds are provided, this requirement can be met by providing a 36 in (915 mm) wide maneuvering space located between the two beds.

(2) An accessible route complying with 4.3 shall connect all accessible spaces and elements, including telephones, within the unit, sleeping room, or suite. This is not intended to require an elevator in multi-story units as long as the spaces identified in 9.2.2(6) and (7) are on accessible levels and the accessible sleeping area is suitable for dual occupancy.

(3) Doors and doorways designed to allow passage into and within all sleeping rooms, suites or other covered units shall comply with 4.13.

(4) If fixed or built-in storage facilities such as cabinets, shelves, closets, and drawers are provided in accessible spaces, at least one of each type provided shall contain storage space complying with 4.25. Additional storage may be provided outside of the dimensions required by 4.25.

(5) All controls in accessible units, sleeping rooms, and suites shall comply with 4.27.

(6) Where provided as part of an accessible unit, sleeping room, or suite, the following spaces shall be accessible and shall be on an accessible route:

(a) the living area.

(b) the dining area.

(c) at least one sleeping area.

(d) patios, terraces, or balconies.

EXCEPTION: The requirements of 4.13.8 and 4.3.8 do not apply where it is necessary to utilize a higher door threshold or a change in level to protect the integrity of the unit from wind/water damage. Where this exception results in patios, terraces or balconies that are not at an accessible level, equivalent facilitation

35672   Federal Register / Vol. 56, No. 144 / Friday, July 26, 1991 / Rules and Regulations

9.3 Visual Alarms, Notification Devices and Telephones

shall be provided. (E.g., equivalent facilitation at a hotel patio or balcony might consist of providing raised decking or a ramp to provide accessibility.)

(e) at least one full bathroom (i.e., one with a water closet, a lavatory, and a bathtub or shower).

(f) if only half baths are provided, at least one half bath.

(g) carports, garages or parking spaces.

(7) Kitchens, Kitchenettes, or Wet Bars. When provided as accessory to a sleeping room or suite, kitchens, kitchenettes, wet bars, or similar amenities shall be accessible. Clear floor space for a front or parallel approach to cabinets, counters, sinks, and appliances shall be provided to comply with 4.2.4. Countertops and sinks shall be mounted at a maximum height of 34 in (865 mm) above the floor. At least fifty percent of shelf space in cabinets or refrigerator/freezers shall be within the reach ranges of 4.2.5 or 4.2.6 and space shall be designed to allow for the operation of cabinet and/or appliance doors so that all cabinets and appliances are accessible and usable. Controls and operating mechanisms shall comply with 4.27.

(8) Sleeping room accommodations for persons with hearing impairments required by 9.1 and complying with 9.3 shall be provided in the accessible sleeping room or suite.

9.3 Visual Alarms, Notification Devices and Telephones.

9.3.1 General. In sleeping rooms required to comply with this section, auxiliary visual alarms shall be provided and shall comply with 4.28.4. Visual notification devices shall also be provided in units, sleeping rooms and suites to alert room occupants of incoming telephone calls and a door knock or bell. Notification devices shall **not** be connected to auxiliary visual alarm signal appliances. Permanently installed telephones shall have volume controls complying with 4.31.5; an accessible electrical outlet within 4 ft (1220 mm) of a telephone connection shall be provided to facilitate the use of a text telephone.

9.3.2 Equivalent Facilitation. For purposes of this section, equivalent facilitation shall include the installation of electrical outlets (including outlets connected to a facility's central alarm system) and telephone wiring in sleeping rooms and suites to enable persons with hearing impairments to utilize portable visual alarms and communication devices provided by the operator of the facility.

9.4 Other Sleeping Rooms and Suites.
Doors and doorways designed to allow passage into and within all sleeping units or other covered units shall comply with 4.13.5.

9.5 Transient Lodging in Homeless Shelters, Halfway Houses, Transient Group Homes, and Other Social Service Establishments.

9.5.1 New Construction. In new construction all public use and common use areas are required to be designed and constructed to comply with section 4. At least one of each type of amenity (such as washers, dryers and similar equipment installed for the use of occupants) in each common area shall be accessible and shall be located on an accessible route to any accessible unit or sleeping accommodation.

EXCEPTION: Where elevators are not provided as allowed in 4.1.3(5), accessible amenities are not required on inaccessible floors as long as one of each type is provided in common areas on accessible floors.

9.5.2 Alterations.

(1) Social service establishments which are not homeless shelters:

(a) The provisions of 9.5.3 and 9.1.5 shall apply to sleeping rooms and beds.

(b) Alteration of other areas shall be consistent with the new construction provisions of 9.5.1.

(2) Homeless shelters. If the following elements are altered, the following requirements apply:

Federal Register / Vol. 56, No. 144 / Friday, July 26, 1991 / Rules and Regulations 35673

10.0 Transportation Facilities

(a) at least one public entrance shall allow a person with mobility impairments to approach, enter and exit including a minimum clear door width of 32 in (815 mm).

(b) sleeping space for homeless persons as provided in the scoping provisions of 9.1.2 shall include doors to the sleeping area with a minimum clear width of 32 in (815 mm) and maneuvering space around the beds for persons with mobility impairments complying with 9.2.2(1).

(c) at least one toilet room for each gender or one unisex toilet room shall have a minimum clear door width of 32 in (815 mm), minimum turning space complying with 4.2.3, one water closet complying with 4.16, one lavatory complying with 4.19 and the door shall have a privacy latch; and, if provided, at least one tub or shower shall comply with 4.20 or 4.21, respectively.

(d) at least one common area which a person with mobility impairments can approach, enter and exit including a minimum clear door width of 32 in (815 mm).

(e) at least one route connecting elements (a), (b), (c) and (d) which a person with mobility impairments can use including minimum clear width of 36 in (915 mm), passing space complying with 4.3.4, turning space complying with 4.2.3 and changes in levels complying with 4.3.8.

(f) homeless shelters can comply with the provisions of (a)-(e) by providing the above elements on one accessible floor.

9.5.3. Accessible Sleeping Accommodations in New Construction.
Accessible sleeping rooms shall be provided in conformance with the table in 9.1.2 and shall comply with 9.2 Accessible Units, Sleeping Rooms and Suites (where the items are provided). Additional sleeping rooms that comply with 9.3 Sleeping Accommodations for Persons with Hearing Impairments shall be provided in conformance with the table provided in 9.1.3.

In facilities with multi-bed rooms or spaces, a percentage of the beds equal to the table provided in 9.1.2 shall comply with 9.2.2(1).

10. TRANSPORTATION FACILITIES. (Reserved).

35674   Federal Register / Vol. 56, No. 144 / Friday, July 26, 1991 / Rules and Regulations

APPENDIX

This appendix contains *materials of an advisory nature* and provides additional information that should help the reader to understand the minimum requirements of the *guidelines* or to design buildings or facilities for greater accessibility. The paragraph numbers correspond to the sections or paragraphs of the *guideline* to which the material relates and are therefore not consecutive (for example, A4.2.1 contains additional information relevant to 4.2.1). *Sections of the guidelines* for which additional material appears in this appendix have been indicated by an asterisk. *Nothing in this appendix shall in any way obviate any obligation to comply with the requirements of the guidelines itself.*

A2.2 Equivalent Facilitation. *Specific examples of equivalent facilitation are found in the following sections:*

4.1.6(3)(c)	*Elevators in Alterations*
4.31.9	*Text Telephones*
7.2	*Sales and Service Counters, Teller Windows, Information Counters*
9.1.4	*Classes of Sleeping Accommodations*
9.2.2(6)(d)	*Requirements for Accessible Units, Sleeping Rooms, and Suites*

A4.1.1 Application.

A4.1.1(3) Areas Used Only by Employees as Work Areas. *Where there are a series of individual work stations of the same type (e.g., laboratories, service counters, ticket booths), 5%, but not less than one, of each type of work station should be constructed so that an individual with disabilities can maneuver within the work stations. Rooms housing individual offices in a typical office building must meet the requirements of the guidelines concerning doors, accessible routes, etc. but do not need to allow for maneuvering space around individual desks. Modifications required to permit maneuvering within the work area may be accomplished as a reasonable accommodation to individual employees with disabilities under Title I of the ADA. Consideration should also be given to placing shelves in employee work areas at a* convenient height for accessibility or installing commercially available shelving that is adjustable so that reasonable accommodations can be made in the future.

If work stations are made accessible they should comply with the applicable provisions of 4.2 through 4.35.

A4.1.2 Accessible Sites and Exterior Facilities: New Construction.

A4.1.2(5)(e) Valet Parking. *Valet parking is not always usable by individuals with disabilities. For instance, an individual may use a type of vehicle controls that render the regular controls inoperable or the driver's seat in a van may be removed. In these situations, another person cannot park the vehicle. It is recommended that some self-parking spaces be provided at valet parking facilities for individuals whose vehicles cannot be parked by another person and that such spaces be located on an accessible route to the entrance of the facility.*

A4.1.3 Accessible Buildings: New Construction.

A4.1.3(5) *Only full passenger elevators are covered by the accessibility provisions of 4.10. Materials and equipment hoists, freight elevators not intended for passenger use, dumbwaiters, and construction elevators are not covered by these guidelines. If a building is exempt from the elevator requirement, it is not necessary to provide a platform lift or other means of vertical access in lieu of an elevator.*

Under Exception 4, platform lifts are allowed where existing conditions make it impractical to install a ramp or elevator. Such conditions generally occur where it is essential to provide access to small raised or lowered areas where space may not be available for a ramp. Examples include, but are not limited to, raised pharmacy platforms, commercial offices raised above a sales floor, or radio and news booths.

A4.1.3(9) *Supervised automatic sprinkler systems have built in signals for monitoring features of the system such as the opening and closing of water control valves, the power supplies for needed pumps, water tank levels, and for indicating conditions that will impair the satisfactory operation of the sprinkler system.*

Federal Register / Vol. 56, No. 144 / Friday, July 26, 1991 / Rules and Regulations   **35675**

A4.2 Space Allowances and Reach Ranges

Because of these monitoring features, supervised automatic sprinkler systems have a high level of satisfactory performance and response to fire conditions.

A4.1.3(10) *If an odd number of drinking fountains is provided on a floor, the requirement in 4.1.3(10)(b) may be met by rounding down the odd number to an even number and calculating 50% of the even number. When more than one drinking fountain on a floor is required to comply with 4.15, those fountains should be dispersed to allow wheelchair users convenient access. For example, in a large facility such as a convention center that has water fountains at several locations on a floor, the accessible water fountains should be located so that wheelchair users do not have to travel a greater distance than other people to use a drinking fountain.*

A4.1.3(17)(b) *In addition to the requirements of section 4.1.3(17)(b), the installation of additional volume controls is encouraged. Volume controls may be installed on any telephone.*

A4.1.3(19)(a) *Readily removable or folding seating units may be installed in lieu of providing an open space for wheelchair users. Folding seating units are usually two fixed seats that can be easily folded into a fixed center bar to allow for one or two open spaces for wheelchair users when necessary. These units are more easily adapted than removable seats which generally require the seat to be removed in advance by the facility management.*

Either a sign or a marker placed on seating with removable or folding arm rests is required by this section. Consideration should be given for ensuring identification of such seats in a darkened theater. For example, a marker which contrasts (light on dark or dark on light) and which also reflects light could be placed on the side of such seating so as to be visible in a lighted auditorium and also to reflect light from a flashlight.

A4.1.6 Accessible Buildings: Alterations.

A4.1.6(1)(h) *When an entrance is being altered, it is preferable that those entrances being altered be made accessible to the extent feasible.*

A4.2 Space Allowances and Reach Ranges.

A4.2.1 Wheelchair Passage Width.

(1) Space Requirements for Wheelchairs. Many persons who use wheelchairs need a 30 in (760 mm) clear opening width for doorways, gates, and the like, when the latter are entered head-on. If the *person* is unfamiliar with a building, if competing traffic is heavy, if sudden or frequent movements are needed, or if the wheelchair must be turned at an opening, then greater clear widths are needed. For most situations, the addition of an inch of leeway on either side is sufficient. Thus, a minimum clear width of 32 in (815 mm) will provide adequate clearance. However, when an opening or a restriction in a passageway is more than 24 in (610 mm) long, it is essentially a passageway and must be at least 36 in (915 mm) wide.

(2) Space Requirements for Use of Walking Aids. Although people who use walking aids can maneuver through clear width openings of 32 in (815 mm), they need 36 in (915 mm) wide passageways and walks for comfortable gaits. Crutch tips, often extending down at a wide angle, are a hazard in narrow passageways where they might not be seen by other pedestrians. Thus, the 36 in (915 mm) width provides a safety allowance both for the person *with a disability* and for others.

(3) Space Requirements for Passing. Able-bodied *persons* in winter clothing, walking

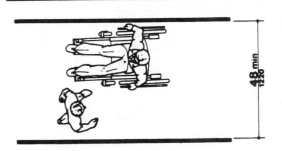

Fig. A1
**Minimum Passage Width for One Wheelchair
and One Ambulatory Person**

35676   Federal Register / Vol. 56, No. 144 / Friday, July 26, 1991 / Rules and Regulations

A4.2 Space Allowances and Reach Ranges

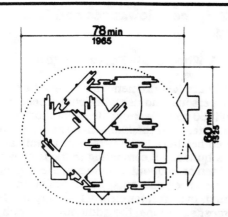

Fig. A2
Space Needed for Smooth U-Turn in a Wheelchair

straight ahead with arms swinging, need
32 in (815 mm) of width, which includes 2 in
(50 mm) on either side for sway, and another
1 in (25 mm) tolerance on either side for clear-
ing nearby objects or other pedestrians. Almost
all wheelchair users and those who use walking aids can also manage within this 32 in
(815 mm) width for short distances. Thus, two
streams of traffic can pass in 64 in (1625 mm)
in a comfortable flow. Sixty inches (1525 mm)
provides a minimum width for a somewhat
more restricted flow. If the clear width is less
than 60 in (1525 mm), two wheelchair users
will not be able to pass but will have to seek
a wider place for passing. Forty-eight inches
(1220 mm) is the minimum width needed for
an ambulatory person to pass a nonambu-
latory or semi-ambulatory person. Within
this 48 in (1220 mm) width, the ambulatory
person will have to twist to pass a wheelchair
user, a person with a *service animal*, or a

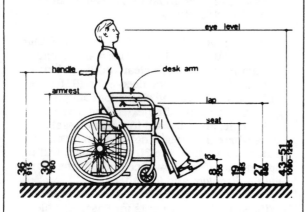

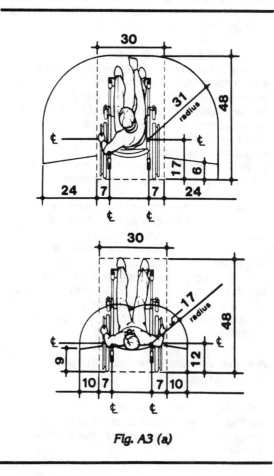

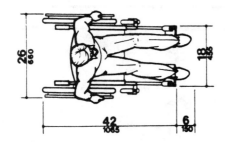

NOTE: Footrests may extend further for tall people

Fig. A3
Dimensions of Adult-Sized Wheelchairs

Fig. A3 (a)

Federal Register / Vol. 56, No. 144 / Friday, July 26, 1991 / Rules and Regulations   35677

A4.3 Accessible Route

semi-ambulatory person. There will be little leeway for swaying or missteps (see Fig. A1).

A4.2.3 Wheelchair Turning Space.
These guidelines specify a minimum space of 60 in (1525 mm) diameter *or a 60 in by 60 in (1525 mm by 1525 mm) T-shaped space* for a pivoting 180-degree turn of a wheelchair. This space is usually satisfactory for turning around, but many people will not be able to turn without repeated tries and bumping into surrounding objects. The space shown in Fig. A2 will allow most wheelchair users to complete U-turns without difficulty.

A4.2.4 Clear Floor or Ground Space for Wheelchairs. The wheelchair and user shown in Fig. A3 represent typical dimensions for a large adult male. The space requirements in this *guideline* are based upon maneuvering clearances that will accommodate most wheelchairs. Fig. A3 provides a uniform reference for design not covered by this *guideline*.

A4.2.5 & A4.2.6 Reach. *Reach ranges for persons seated in wheelchairs may be further clarified by Fig. A3(a). These drawings approximate in the plan view the information shown in Fig. 4, 5, and 6.*

A4.3 Accessible Route.

A4.3.1 General.

(1) Travel Distances. Many people with mobility impairments can move at only very slow speeds; for many, traveling 200 ft (61 m) could take about 2 minutes. This assumes a rate of about 1.5 ft/s (455 mm/s) on level ground. It also assumes that the traveler would move continuously. However, on trips over 100 ft (30 m), disabled people are apt to rest frequently, which substantially increases their trip times. Resting periods of 2 minutes for every 100 ft (30 m) can be used to estimate travel times for people with severely limited stamina. In inclement weather, slow progress and resting can greatly increase a disabled person's exposure to the elements.

(2) Sites. Level, indirect routes or those with running slopes lower than 1:20 can sometimes provide more convenience than direct routes with maximum allowable slopes or with ramps.

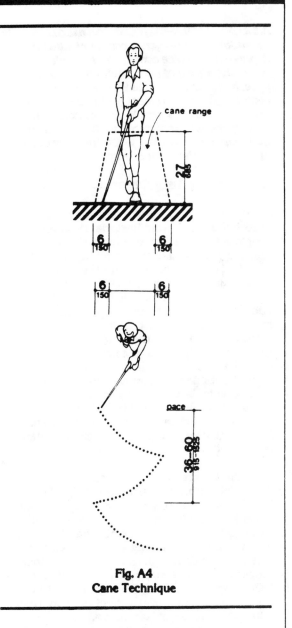

Fig. A4
Cane Technique

A4.3.10 Egress. Because people with disabilities may visit, be employed or be a resident in any building, emergency management plans with specific provisions to ensure their safe evacuation also play an essential role in fire safety and life safety.

A4.3.11.3 Stairway Width. *A 48 inch (1220 mm) wide exit stairway is needed to allow assisted evacuation (e.g., carrying a person in a wheelchair) without encroaching on the exit path for ambulatory persons.*

A4.3.11.4 Two-way Communication. *It is essential that emergency communication not be dependent on voice communications alone because the safety of people with hearing or speech impairments could be jeopardized. The visible signal requirement could be satisfied with something as simple as a button in the area of rescue assistance that lights, indicating that help is on the way, when the message is answered at the point of entry.*

A4.4 Protruding Objects.

A4.4.1 General. *Service animals* are trained to recognize and avoid hazards. However, most people with severe impairments of vision use the long cane as an aid to mobility. The two principal cane techniques are the touch technique, where the cane arcs from side to side and touches points outside both shoulders; and the diagonal technique, where the cane is held in a stationary position diagonally across the body with the cane tip touching or just above the ground at a point outside one shoulder and the handle or grip extending to a point outside the other shoulder. The touch technique is used primarily in uncontrolled areas, while the diagonal technique is used primarily in certain limited, controlled, and familiar environments. Cane users are often trained to use both techniques.

Potential hazardous objects are noticed only if they fall within the detection range of canes (see Fig. A4). Visually impaired people walking toward an object can detect an overhang if its lowest surface is not higher than 27 in (685 mm). When walking alongside *protruding* objects, they cannot detect overhangs. Since proper cane and *service animal* techniques keep people away from the edge of a path or from walls, a slight overhang of no more than 4 in (100 mm) is not hazardous.

A4.5 Ground and Floor Surfaces.

A4.5.1 General. *People who have difficulty walking* or maintaining balance *or who use crutches, canes, or walkers,* and those with restricted gaits are particularly sensitive to slipping and tripping hazards. For such people, a stable and regular surface is necessary for safe walking, particularly on stairs. Wheelchairs can be propelled most easily on surfaces that are hard, stable, and regular. Soft loose surfaces such as shag carpet, loose sand or gravel, wet clay, and irregular surfaces such as cobblestones can significantly impede wheelchair movement.

Slip resistance is based on the frictional force necessary to keep a shoe heel or crutch tip from slipping on a walking surface under conditions likely to be found on the surface. *While the dynamic coefficient of friction during walking varies in a complex and non-uniform way, the static coefficient of friction, which can be measured in several ways, provides a close approximation of the slip resistance of a surface. Contrary to popular belief, some slippage is necessary to walking, especially for persons with restricted gaits; a truly "non-slip" surface could not be negotiated.*

The Occupational Safety and Health Administration recommends that walking surfaces have a static coefficient of friction of 0.5. A research project sponsored by the Architectural and Transportation Barriers Compliance Board (Access Board) conducted tests with persons with disabilities and concluded that a higher coefficient of friction was needed by such persons. A static coefficient of friction of 0.6 is recommended for accessible routes and 0.8 for ramps.

It is recognized that the coefficient of friction varies considerably due to the presence of contaminants, water, floor finishes, and other factors not under the control of the designer or builder and not subject to design and construction guidelines and that compliance would be difficult to measure on the building site. Nevertheless, many common building materials suitable for flooring are now labeled with information on the static coefficient of friction. While it may not be possible to compare one product directly with another, or to guarantee a constant measure, builders and designers are encouraged to specify materials with appropriate values. As more products include information on slip resistance, improved uniformity in measurement and specification is likely. The Access Board's advisory guidelines on Slip Resistant Surfaces provides additional information on this subject.

Cross slopes on walks and ground or floor surfaces can cause considerable difficulty in propelling a wheelchair in a straight line.

Federal Register / Vol. 56, No. 144 / Friday, July 26, 1991 / Rules and Regulations   35679

A4.6 Parking and Passenger Loading Zones

A4.5.3 Carpet. Much more needs to be done in developing both quantitative and qualitative criteria for carpeting (*i.e., problems associated with texture and weave need to be studied*). However, certain functional characteristics are well established. When both carpet and padding are used, it is desirable to have minimum movement (preferably none) between the floor and the pad and the pad and the carpet which would allow the carpet to hump or warp. In heavily trafficked areas, a thick, soft (plush) pad or cushion, particularly in combination with long carpet pile, makes it difficult for individuals in wheelchairs and those with other ambulatory disabilities to get about. Firm carpeting can be achieved through proper selection and combination of pad and carpet, sometimes with the elimination of the pad or cushion, and with proper installation. *Carpeting designed with a weave that causes a zig-zag effect when wheeled across is strongly discouraged.*

A4.6 Parking and Passenger Loading Zones.

A4.6.3 Parking Spaces. *The increasing use of vans with side-mounted lifts or ramps by persons with disabilities has necessitated some revisions in specifications for parking spaces and adjacent access aisles. The typical accessible parking space is 96 in (2440 mm) wide with an adjacent 60 in (1525 mm) access aisle. However, this aisle does not permit lifts or ramps to be deployed and still leave room for a person using a wheelchair or other mobility aid to exit the lift platform or ramp. In tests conducted with actual lift/van/wheelchair combinations, (under a Board-sponsored Accessible Parking and Loading Zones Project) researchers found that a space and aisle totaling almost 204 in (5180 mm) wide was needed to deploy a lift and exit conveniently. The "van accessible" parking space required by these guidelines provides a 96 in (2440 mm) wide space with a 96 in (2440 mm) adjacent access aisle which is just wide enough to maneuver and exit from a side mounted lift. If a 96 in (2440 mm) access aisle is placed between two spaces, two "van accessible" spaces are created. Alternatively, if the wide access aisle is provided at the end of a row (an area often unused), it may be possible to provide the wide access aisle without additional space (see Fig. A5(a)).*

A sign is needed to alert van users to the presence of the wider aisle, but the space is not intended to be restricted only to vans.

"Universal" Parking Space Design. An alternative to the provision of a percentage of spaces with a wide aisle, and the associated need to include additional signage, is the use of what has been called the "universal" parking space design. Under this design, all accessible spaces are 132 in (3350 mm) wide with a 60 in (1525 mm) access aisle (see Fig. A5(b)). One

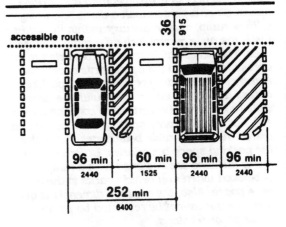

(a)
Van Accessible Space at End Row

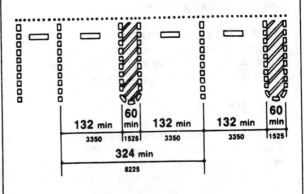

(b)
Universal Parking Space Design

Fig. A5
Parking Space Alternatives

35680   **Federal Register** / Vol. 56, No. 144 / Friday, July 26, 1991 / Rules and Regulations

advantage to this design is that no additional signage is needed because all spaces can accommodate a van with a side-mounted lift or ramp. Also, there is no competition between cars and vans for spaces since all spaces can accommodate either. Furthermore, the wider space permits vehicles to park to one side or the other within the 132 in (3350 mm) space to allow persons to exit and enter the vehicle on either the driver or passenger side, although, in some cases, this would require exiting or entering without a marked access aisle.

An essential consideration for any design is having the access aisle level with the parking space. Since a person with a disability, using a lift or ramp, must maneuver within the access aisle, the aisle cannot include a ramp or sloped area. The access aisle must be connected to an accessible route to the appropriate accessible entrance of a building or facility. The parking access aisle must either blend with the accessible route or have a curb ramp complying with 4.7. Such a curb ramp opening must be located within the access aisle boundaries, not within the parking space boundaries. Unfortunately, many facilities are designed with a ramp that is blocked when any vehicle parks in the accessible space. Also, the required dimensions of the access aisle cannot be restricted by planters, curbs or wheel stops.

A4.6.4 Signage. Signs designating parking places for disabled people can be seen from a driver's seat if the signs are mounted high enough above the ground and located at the front of a parking space.

A4.6.5 Vertical Clearance. High-top vans, which disabled people or transportation services often use, require higher clearances in parking garages than automobiles.

A4.8 Ramps.

A4.8.1 General. Ramps are essential for wheelchair users if elevators or lifts are not available to connect different levels. However, some people who use walking aids have difficulty with ramps and prefer stairs.

A4.8.2 Slope and Rise. *Ramp slopes between 1:16 and 1:20 are preferred.* The ability to manage an incline is related to both its slope and its length. Wheelchair users with

disabilities affecting *their* arms or with low stamina have serious difficulty using inclines. Most ambulatory people and most people who use wheelchairs can manage a slope of 1:16. Many people cannot manage a slope of 1:12 for 30 ft (9 m).

A4.8.4 Landings. *Level landings are essential toward maintaining an aggregate slope that complies with these guidelines. A ramp landing that is not level causes individuals using wheelchairs to tip backward or bottom out when the ramp is approached.*

A4.8.5 Handrails. The requirements for stair and ramp handrails in this *guideline* are for adults. When children are principal users in a building or facility, a second set of handrails at an appropriate height can assist them and aid in preventing accidents.

A4.9 Stairs.

A4.9.1 Minimum Number. *Only interior and exterior stairs connecting levels that are not connected by an elevator, ramp, or other accessible means of vertical access have to comply with 4.9.*

A4.10 Elevators.

A4.10.6 Door Protective and Reopening Device. The required door reopening device would hold the door open for 20 seconds if the doorway remains obstructed. After 20 seconds, the door may begin to close. However, if designed in accordance with *ASME A17.1-1990*, the door closing movement could still be stopped if a person or object exerts sufficient force at any point on the door edge.

A4.10.7 Door and Signal Timing for Hall Calls. This paragraph allows variation in the location of call buttons, advance time for warning signals, and the door-holding period used to meet the time requirement.

A4.10.12 Car Controls. Industry-wide standardization of elevator control panel design would make all elevators significantly more convenient for use by people with severe visual impairments. In many cases, it will be possible to locate the highest control on elevator panels within 48 in (1220 mm) from the floor.

A4.11 Platform Lifts (Wheelchair Lifts)

A4.10.13 Car Position Indicators. A special button may be provided that would activate the audible signal within the given elevator only for the desired trip, rather than maintaining the audible signal in constant operation.

A4.10.14 Emergency Communications. A device that requires no handset is easier to use by people who have difficulty reaching. *Also, small handles on handset compartment doors are not usable by people who have difficulty grasping.*

Ideally, emergency two-way communication systems should provide both voice and visual display intercommunication so that persons with hearing impairments and persons with vision impairments can receive information regarding the status of a rescue. A voice intercommunication system cannot be the only means of communication because it is not accessible to people with speech and hearing impairments. While a voice intercommunication system is not required, at a minimum, the system should provide both an audio and visual indication that a rescue is on the way.

A4.11 Platform Lifts (Wheelchair Lifts).

A4.11.2 Other Requirements. *Inclined stairway chairlifts, and inclined and vertical platform lifts (wheelchair lifts) are available for short-distance, vertical transportation of people with disabilities. Care should be taken in selecting lifts as some lifts are not equally suitable for use by both wheelchair users and semi-ambulatory individuals.*

A4.12 Windows.

A4.12.1 General. *Windows intended to be operated by occupants in accessible spaces should comply with 4.12.*

A4.12.2 Window Hardware. *Windows requiring pushing, pulling, or lifting to open (for example, double-hung, sliding, or casement and awning units without cranks) should require no more than 5 lbf (22.2 N) to open or close. Locks, cranks, and other window hardware should comply with 4.27.*

A4.13 Doors.

A4.13.8 Thresholds at Doorways. Thresholds and surface height changes in doorways are particularly inconvenient for wheelchair users who also have low stamina or restrictions in arm movement because complex maneuvering is required to get over the level change while operating the door.

A4.13.9 Door Hardware. Some disabled persons must push against a door with their chair or walker to open it. Applied kickplates on doors with closers can reduce required maintenance by withstanding abuse from wheelchairs and canes. To be effective, they should cover the door width, less approximately 2 in (51 mm), up to a height of 16 in (405 mm) from its bottom edge and be centered across the *width of the door.*

A4.13.10 Door Closers. Closers with delayed action features give a person more time to maneuver through doorways. They are particularly useful on frequently used interior doors such as entrances to toilet rooms.

A4.13.11 Door Opening Force. Although most people with disabilities can exert at least 5 lbf (22.2N), both pushing and pulling from a stationary position, a few people with severe disabilities cannot exert 3 lbf (13.13N). Although some people cannot manage the allowable forces in this guideline and many others have difficulty, door closers must have certain minimum closing forces to close doors satisfactorily. Forces for pushing or pulling doors open are measured with a push-pull scale under the following conditions:

(1) Hinged doors: Force applied perpendicular to the door at the door opener or 30 in (760 mm) from the hinged side, whichever is farther from the hinge.

(2) Sliding or folding doors: Force applied parallel to the door at the door pull or latch.

(3) Application of force: Apply force gradually so that the applied force does not exceed the resistance of the door. In high-rise buildings, air-pressure differentials may require a modification of this specification in order to meet the functional intent.

35682   Federal Register / Vol. 56, No. 144 / Friday, July 26, 1991 / Rules and Regulations

A4.15 Drinking Fountains and Water Coolers

A4.13.12 Automatic Doors and Power-Assisted Doors. Sliding automatic doors do not need guard rails and are more convenient for wheelchair users and visually impaired people to use. If slowly opening automatic doors can be reactivated before their closing cycle is completed, they will be more convenient in busy doorways.

A4.15 Drinking Fountains and Water Coolers.

A4.15.2 Spout Height. Two drinking fountains, mounted side by side or on a single post, are usable by people with disabilities and people who find it difficult to bend over.

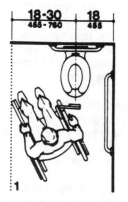

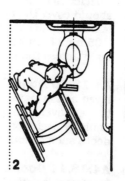

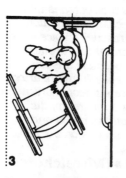

1 Takes transfer position, swings footrest out of the way, sets brakes.

2 Removes armrest, transfers.

3 Moves wheelchair out of the way, changes position (some people fold chair or pivot it 90° to the toilet).

4 Positions on toilet, releases brake.

(a)
Diagonal Approach

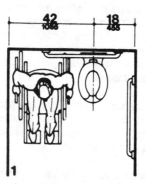

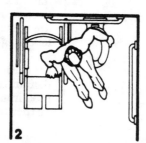

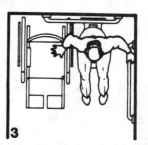

1 Takes transfer position, removes armrest, sets brakes.

2 Transfers.

3 Positions on toilet.

(b)
Side Approach

Fig. A6
Wheelchair Transfers

A4.16 Water Closets

A4.16 Water Closets.

A4.16.3 Height. Height preferences for toilet seats vary considerably among disabled people. Higher seat heights may be an advantage to some ambulatory disabled people, but are often a disadvantage for wheelchair users and others. Toilet seats 18 in (455 mm) high seem to be a reasonable compromise. Thick seats and filler rings are available to adapt standard fixtures to these requirements.

A4.16.4 Grab Bars. Fig. A6(a) and (b) show the diagonal and side approaches most commonly used to transfer from a wheelchair to a water closet. Some wheelchair users can transfer from the front of the toilet while others use a 90-degree approach. Most people who use the two additional approaches can also use either the diagonal approach or the side approach.

A4.16.5 Flush Controls. Flush valves and related plumbing can be located behind walls or to the side of the toilet, or a toilet seat lid can be provided if plumbing fittings are directly behind the toilet seat. Such designs reduce the chance of injury and imbalance caused by leaning back against the fittings. Flush controls for tank-type toilets have a standardized mounting location on the left side of the tank (facing the tank). Tanks can be obtained by special order with controls mounted on the right side. If administrative authorities require flush controls for flush valves to be located in a position that conflicts with the location of the rear grab bar, then that bar may be split or shifted toward the wide side of the toilet area.

A4.17 Toilet Stalls.

A4.17.3 Size and Arrangement. This section requires use of the 60 in (1525 mm) standard stall (Figure 30(a)) and permits the 36 in (915 mm) or 48 in (1220 mm) wide alternate stall (Figure 30(b)) only in alterations where provision of the standard stall is technically infeasible or where local plumbing codes prohibit reduction in the number of fixtures. A standard stall provides a clear space on one side of the water closet to enable persons who use wheelchairs to perform a side or diagonal transfer from the wheelchair to the water closet. However, some persons with disabilities who use mobility aids such as walkers, canes or crutches

are better able to use the two parallel grab bars in the 36 in (915 mm) wide alternate stall to achieve a standing position.

In large toilet rooms, where six or more toilet stalls are provided, it is therefore required that a 36 in (915 mm) wide stall with parallel grab bars be provided __in addition__ to the standard stall required in new construction. The 36 in (915 mm) width is necessary to achieve proper use of the grab bars; wider stalls would position the grab bars too far apart to be easily used and narrower stalls would position the grab bars too close to the water closet. Since the stall is primarily intended for use by persons using canes, crutches and walkers, rather than wheelchairs, the length of the stall could be conventional. The door, however, must swing outward to ensure a usable space for people who use crutches or walkers.

A4.17.5 Doors. To make it easier for wheelchair users to close toilet stall doors, doors can be provided with closers, spring hinges, or a pull bar mounted on the inside surface of the door near the hinge side.

A4.19 Lavatories and Mirrors.

A4.19.6 Mirrors. If mirrors are to be used by both ambulatory people and wheelchair users, then they must be at least 74 in (1880 mm) high at their topmost edge. A single full length mirror can accommodate all people, including children.

A4.21 Shower Stalls.

A4.21.1 General. Shower stalls that are 36 in by 36 in (915 mm by 915 mm) wide provide additional safety to people who have difficulty maintaining balance because all grab bars and walls are within easy reach. Seated people use the walls of 36 in by 36 in (915 mm by 915 mm) showers for back support. Shower stalls that are 60 in (1525 mm) wide and have no curb may increase usability of a bathroom by wheelchair users because the shower area provides additional maneuvering space.

A4.22 Toilet Rooms.

A4.22.3 Clear Floor Space. In many small facilities, single-user restrooms may be the only

A4.22 Toilet Rooms

facilities provided for all building users. In addition, the guidelines allow the use of "unisex" or "family" accessible toilet rooms in alterations when technical infeasibility can be demonstrated. Experience has shown that the provision of accessible "unisex" or single-user restrooms is a reasonable way to provide access for wheelchair users and any attendants, especially when attendants are of the opposite sex. Since these facilities have proven so useful, it is often considered advantageous to install a "unisex" toilet room in new facilities in addition to making the multi-stall restrooms accessible, especially in shopping malls, large auditoriums, and convention centers.

Figure 28 (section 4.16) provides minimum clear floor space dimensions for toilets in accessible "unisex" toilet rooms. The dotted lines designate the minimum clear floor space, depending on the direction of approach, required for wheelchair users to transfer onto the water closet. The dimensions of 48 in (1220 mm) and 60 in (1525 mm), respectively, correspond to the space required for the two common transfer approaches utilized by wheelchair users (see Fig. A6). It is important to keep in mind that the placement of the lavatory to the immediate side of the water closet will preclude the side approach transfer illustrated in Figure A6(b).

To accommodate the side transfer, the space adjacent to the water closet must remain clear of obstruction for 42 in (1065 mm) from the centerline of the toilet (Figure 28) and the lavatory must not be located within this clear space. A turning circle or T-turn, the clear floor space at the lavatory, and maneuvering space at the door must be considered when determining the possible wall locations. A privacy latch or other accessible means of ensuring privacy during use should be provided at the door.

RECOMMENDATIONS:

1. In new construction, accessible single-user restrooms may be desirable in some situations because they can accommodate a wide variety of building users. However, they cannot be used in lieu of making the multi-stall toilet rooms accessible as required.

2. Where strict compliance to the guidelines for accessible toilet facilities is technically infeasible in the alteration of existing facilities, accessible "unisex" toilets are a reasonable alternative.

3. In designing accessible single-user restrooms, the provisions of adequate space to allow a side transfer will provide accommodation to the largest number of wheelchair users.

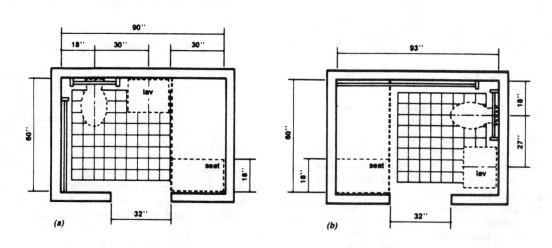

Fig. A7

Federal Register / Vol. 56, No. 144 / Friday, July 26, 1991 / Rules and Regulations **35685**

A4.23 Bathrooms, Bathing Facilities, and Shower Rooms

A4.23 Bathrooms, Bathing Facilities, and Shower Rooms.

A4.23.3 Clear Floor Space. *Figure A7 shows two possible configurations of a toilet room with a roll-in shower. The specific shower shown is designed to fit exactly within the dimensions of a standard bathtub. Since the shower does not have a lip, the floor space can be used for required maneuvering space. This would permit a toilet room to be smaller than would be permitted with a bathtub and still provide enough floor space to be considered accessible. This design can provide accessibility in facilities where space is at a premium (i.e., hotels and medical care facilities). The alternate roll-in shower (Fig. 57b) also provides sufficient room for the "T-turn" and does not require plumbing to be on more than one wall.*

A4.23.9 Medicine Cabinets. Other alternatives for storing medical and personal care items are very useful to disabled people. Shelves, drawers, and floor-mounted cabinets can be provided within the reach ranges of disabled people.

A4.26 Handrails, Grab Bars, and Tub and Shower Seats.

A4.26.1 General. Many disabled people rely heavily upon grab bars and handrails to maintain balance and prevent serious falls. Many people brace their forearms between supports and walls to give them more leverage and stability in maintaining balance or for lifting. The grab bar clearance of 1-1/2 in (38 mm) required in this guideline is a safety clearance to prevent injuries resulting from arms slipping through the openings. It also provides adequate gripping room.

A4.26.2 Size and Spacing of Grab Bars and Handrails. This specification allows for alternate shapes of handrails as long as they allow an opposing grip similar to that provided by a circular section of 1-1/4 in to 1-1/2 in (32 mm to 38 mm).

A4.27 Controls and Operating Mechanisms.

A4.27.3 Height. *Fig. A8 further illustrates*

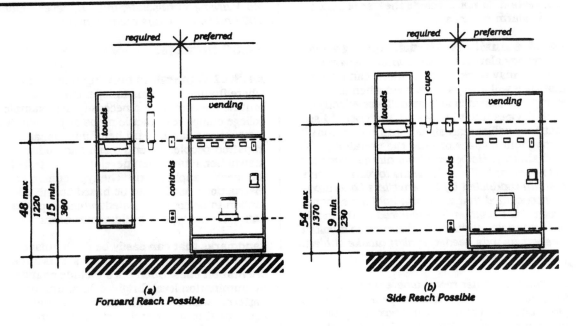

(a)
Forward Reach Possible

(b)
Side Reach Possible

Fig. A8
Control Reach Limitations

mandatory and advisory control mounting height provisions for typical equipment.

Electrical receptacles installed to serve individual appliances and not intended for regular or frequent use by building occupants are not required to be mounted within the specified reach ranges. Examples would be receptacles installed specifically for wall-mounted clocks, refrigerators, and microwave ovens.

A4.28 Alarms.

A4.28.2 Audible Alarms. Audible emergency signals must have an intensity and frequency that can attract the attention of individuals who have partial hearing loss. People over 60 years of age generally have difficulty perceiving frequencies higher than 10,000 Hz. An alarm signal which has a periodic element to its signal, such as single stroke bells (clang-pause-clang-pause), hi-low (up-down-up-down) and fast whoop (on-off-on-off) are best. Avoid continuous or reverberating tones. Select a signal which has a sound characterized by three or four clear tones without a great deal of "noise" in between.

A4.28.3 Visual Alarms. The specifications in this section do not preclude the use of zoned or coded alarm systems.

A4.28.4 Auxiliary Alarms. Locating visual emergency alarms in rooms where persons who are deaf may work or reside alone can ensure that they will always be warned when an emergency alarm is activated. To be effective, such devices must be located and oriented so that they will spread signals and reflections throughout a space or raise the overall light level sharply. *However, visual alarms alone are not necessarily the best means to alert sleepers. A study conducted by Underwriters Laboratory (UL) concluded that a flashing light more than seven times brighter was required (110 candela v. 15 candela, at the same distance) to awaken sleepers as was needed to alert awake subjects in a normal daytime illuminated room.*

For hotel and other rooms where people are likely to be asleep, a signal-activated vibrator placed between mattress and box spring or under a pillow was found by UL to be much more effective in alerting sleepers. Many readily available devices are sound-activated so that they could respond to an alarm clock, clock

radio, wake-up telephone call or room smoke detector. Activation by a building alarm system can either be accomplished by a separate circuit activating an auditory alarm which would, in turn, trigger the vibrator or by a signal transmitted through the ordinary 110-volt outlet. Transmission of signals through the power line is relatively simple and is the basis of common, inexpensive remote light control systems sold in many department and electronic stores for home use. So-called "wireless" intercoms operate on the same principal.

A4.29 Detectable Warnings.

A4.29.2 Detectable Warnings on Walking Surfaces. *The material used to provide contrast should contrast by at least 70%. Contrast in percent is determined by:*

$$Contrast = [(B_1 - B_2)/B_1] \times 100$$

*where B_1 = light reflectance value (LRV) of the lighter area
and B_2 = light reflectance value (LRV) of the darker area.*

Note that in any application both white and black are never absolute; thus, B_1 never equals 100 and B_2 is always greater than 0.

A4.30 Signage.

A4.30.1 General. In building complexes where finding locations independently on a routine basis may be a necessity (for example, college campuses), tactile maps or prerecorded instructions can be very helpful to visually impaired people. Several maps and auditory instructions have been developed and tested for specific applications. The type of map or instructions used must be based on the information to be communicated, which depends highly on the type of buildings or users.

Landmarks that can easily be distinguished by visually impaired individuals are useful as orientation cues. Such cues include changes in illumination level, bright colors, unique patterns, wall murals, location of special equipment or other architectural features.

Many people with disabilities have limitations in movement of their heads and reduced peripheral vision. Thus, signage positioned

Federal Register / Vol. 56, No. 144 / Friday, July 26, 1991 / Rules and Regulations

35687

A4.30 Signage

perpendicular to the path of travel is easiest for them to notice. People can generally distinguish signage within an angle of 30 degrees to either side of the centerlines of their faces without moving their heads.

A4.30.2 Character Proportion. The legibility of printed characters is a function of the viewing distance, character height, the ratio of the stroke width to the height of the character, the contrast of color between character and background, and print font. The size of characters must be based upon the intended viewing distance. A severely nearsighted person may have to be much closer to recognize a character of a given size than a person with normal visual acuity.

A4.30.4 Raised and Brailled Characters and Pictorial Symbol Signs (Pictograms). *The standard dimensions for literary Braille are as follows:*

Dot diameter	.059 in.
Inter-dot spacing	.090 in.
Horizontal separation between cells	.241 in.
Vertical separation between cells	.395 in.

Raised borders around signs containing raised characters may make them confusing to read unless the border is set far away from the characters. *Accessible signage with descriptive materials about public buildings, monuments, and objects of cultural interest may not provide sufficiently detailed and meaningful information. Interpretive guides, audio tape devices, or other methods may be more effective in presenting such information.*

A4.30.5 Finish and Contrast. *An eggshell finish (11 to 19 degree gloss on 60 degree glossimeter) is recommended. Research indicates that signs are more legible for persons with low vision when characters contrast with their background by at least 70 percent. Contrast in percent shall be determined by:*

$$Contrast = [(B_1 - B_2)/B_1] \times 100$$

where B_1 = light reflectance value (LRV) of the lighter area and B_2 = light reflectance value (LRV) of the darker area.

Note that in any application both white and black are never absolute; thus, B_1 never equals 100 and B_2 is always greater than 0.

The greatest readability is usually achieved through the use of light-colored characters or symbols on a dark background.

A4.30.7 Symbols of Accessibility for Different Types of Listening Systems. *Paragraph 4 of this section requires signage indicating the availability of an assistive listening system. An appropriate message should be displayed with the international symbol of access for hearing loss since this symbol conveys general accessibility for people with hearing loss. Some suggestions are:*

INFRARED
ASSISTIVE LISTENING SYSTEM
AVAILABLE
——PLEASE ASK——

AUDIO LOOP IN USE
TURN T-SWITCH FOR
BETTER HEARING
——OR ASK FOR HELP——

FM
ASSISTIVE LISTENING
SYSTEM AVAILABLE
——PLEASE ASK——

The symbol may be used to notify persons of the availability of other auxiliary aids and services such as: real time captioning, captioned note taking, sign language interpreters, and oral interpreters.

A4.30.8 Illumination Levels. *Illumination levels on the sign surface shall be in the 100 to 300 lux range (10 to 30 footcandles) and shall be uniform over the sign surface. Signs shall be located such that the illumination level on the surface of the sign is not significantly exceeded by the ambient light or visible bright lighting source behind or in front of the sign.*

A4.31 Telephones.

A4.31.3 Mounting Height. In localities where the dial-tone first system is in operation, calls can be placed at a coin telephone through the operator without inserting coins. The operator button is located at a height of 46 in (1170 mm) if the coin slot of the telephone is at 54 in (1370 mm). A generally available public telephone with a coin slot mounted lower on the equipment would allow universal installation of telephones at a height of 48 in (1220 mm) or less to all operable parts.

A4.31.9 Text Telephones. *A public text telephone may be an integrated text telephone pay phone unit or a conventional portable text telephone that is permanently affixed within, or adjacent to, the telephone enclosure. In order to be usable with a pay phone, a text telephone which is not a single integrated text telephone pay phone unit will require a shelf large enough (10 in (255mm) wide by 10 in (255 mm) deep with a 6 in (150 mm) vertical clearance minimum) to accommodate the device, an electrical outlet, and a power cord. Movable or portable text telephones may be used to provide equivalent facilitation. A text telephone should be readily available so that a person using it may access the text telephone easily and conveniently. As currently designed pocket-type text telephones for personal use do not accommodate a wide range of users. Such devices would not be considered substantially equivalent to conventional text telephones. However, in the future as technology develops this could change.*

A4.32 Fixed or Built-in Seating and Tables.

A4.32.4 Height of *Tables or Counters*. Different types of work require different *table or counter* heights for comfort and optimal performance. Light detailed work such as writing requires a *table or counter* close to elbow height for a standing person. Heavy manual work such as rolling dough requires a *counter or table* height about 10 in (255 mm) below elbow height for a standing person. This principle of *high/low table or counter heights* also applies for seated persons; however, the limiting condition for seated manual work is clearance under the *table or counter*.

Table A1 shows convenient *counter heights* for seated persons. The great variety of heights for comfort and optimal performance indicates a need for alternatives or a compromise in height if people who stand and people who sit will be using the same counter area.

Table A1
Convenient Heights of Tables and Counters for Seated People[1]

Conditions of Use	Short Women in	mm	Tall Men in	mm
Seated in a wheelchair:				
Manual work—				
Desk or removeable armrests	26	660	30	760
Fixed, full-size armrests[2]	32[3]	815	32[3]	815
Light detailed work:				
Desk or removable armrests	29	735	34	865
Fixed, full-size armrests[2]	32[3]	815	34	865
Seated in a 16-in. (405-mm)				
High chair:				
Manual work	26	660	27	685
Light detailed work	28	710	31	785

[1] All dimensions are based on a work-surface thickness of 1 1/2 in (38 mm) and a clearance of 1 1/2 in (38 mm) between legs and the underside of a work surface.

[2] This type of wheelchair arm does not interfere with the positioning of a wheelchair under a work surface.

[3] This dimension is limited by the height of the armrests: a lower height would be preferable. Some people in this group prefer lower work surfaces, which require positioning the wheelchair back from the edge of the counter.

A4.33 Assembly Areas.

A4.33.2 Size of Wheelchair Locations. Spaces large enough for two wheelchairs allow people who are coming to a performance together to sit together.

A4.33.3 Placement of Wheelchair Locations. The location of wheelchair areas can be planned so that a variety of positions

Federal Register / Vol. 56, No. 144 / Friday, July 26, 1991 / Rules and Regulations   35689

Table A2. Summary of Assistive Listening Devices

within the seating area are provided. This will allow choice in viewing and price categories.

Building/life safety codes set minimum distances between rows of fixed seats with consideration of the number of seats in a row, the exit aisle width and arrangement, and the location of exit doors. "Continental" seating, with a greater number of seats per row and a *commensurate increase in row spacing and exit doors, facilitates emergency egress for all people and increases ease of access to mid-row seats especially for people who walk with difficulty. Consideration of this positive attribute of "continental" seating should be included along with all other factors in the design of fixed seating areas.*

Table A2. Summary of Assistive Listening Devices

System	Advantages	Disadvantages	Typical Applications
Induction Loop Transmitter: Transducer wired to induction loop around listening area. Receiver: Self-contained induction receiver or personal hearing aid with telecoil.	Cost-Effective Low Maintenance Easy to use Unobtrusive May be possible to integrate into existing public address system. Some hearing aids can function as receivers.	Signal spills over to adjacent rooms. Susceptible to electrical interference. Limited portability Inconsistent signal strength. Head position affects signal strength. Lack of standards for induction coil performance.	Meeting areas Theaters Churches and Temples Conference rooms Classrooms TV viewing
FM Transmitter: Flashlight-sized worn by speaker. Receiver: With personal hearing aid via DAI or induction neck-loop and telecoil; or self-contained with earphone(s).	Highly portable Different channels allow use by different groups within the same room. High user mobility Variable for large range of hearing losses.	High cost of receivers Equipment fragile Equipment obtrusive High maintenance Expensive to maintain Custom fitting to individual user may be required	Classrooms Tour groups Meeting areas Outdoor events One-on-one
Infrared Transmitter: Emitter in line-of-sight with receiver. Receiver: Self-contained. Or with personal hearing aid via DAI or induction neckloop and telecoil.	Easy to use Insures privacy or confidentiality Moderate cost Can often be integrated into existing public address system.	Line-of-sight required between emitter and receiver. Ineffective outdoors Limited portability Requires installation	Theaters Churches and Temples Auditoriums Meetings requiring confidentiality TV viewing

Source: Rehab Brief, National Institute on Disability and Rehabilitation Research, Washington, DC, Vol. XII, No. 10, (1990).

A5.0 Restaurants and Cafeterias

A4.33.6 Placement of Listening Systems.

A distance of 50 ft (15 m) allows a person to distinguish performers' facial expressions.

A4.33.7 Types of Listening Systems.

An assistive listening system appropriate for an assembly area for a group of persons or where the specific individuals are not known in advance, such as a playhouse, lecture hall or movie theater, may be different from the system appropriate for a particular individual provided as an auxiliary aid or as part of a reasonable accommodation. The appropriate device for an individual is the type that individual can use, whereas the appropriate system for an assembly area will necessarily be geared toward the "average" or aggregate needs of various individuals. A listening system that can be used from any seat in a seating area is the most flexible way to meet this specification. Earphone jacks with variable volume controls can benefit only people who have slight hearing loss and do not help people who use hearing aids. At the present time, *magnetic induction* loops are the most feasible type of listening system for people who use hearing aids *equipped with "T-coils,"* but people without hearing aids or those with hearing aids not equipped with inductive pick-ups cannot use them *without special receivers.* Radio frequency systems can be extremely effective and inexpensive. People without hearing aids can use them, but people with hearing aids need a special receiver to use them as they are presently designed. If hearing aids had a jack to allow a by-pass of microphones, then radio frequency systems would be suitable for people with and without hearing aids. Some listening systems may be subject to interference from other equipment and feedback from hearing aids of people who are using the systems. Such interference can be controlled by careful engineering design that anticipates feedback sources in the surrounding area.

Table A2, reprinted from a National Institute of Disability and Rehabilitation Research "Rehab Brief," shows some of the advantages and disadvantages of different types of assistive listening systems. In addition, the Architectural and Transportation Barriers Compliance Board (Access Board) has published a pamphlet on Assistive Listening Systems which lists demonstration centers across the country where technical assistance can be obtained in selecting and installing appropriate systems. The state of New York has also adopted a detailed technical specification which may be useful.

A5.0 Restaurants and Cafeterias.

A5.1 General.

Dining counters (where there is no service) are typically found in small carry-out restaurants, bakeries, or coffee shops and may only be a narrow eating surface attached to a wall. This section requires that where such a dining counter is provided, a portion of the counter shall be at the required accessible height.

A7.0 Business and Mercantile.

A7.2(3) Assistive Listening Devices.

At all sales and service counters, teller windows, box offices, and information kiosks where a physical barrier separates service personnel and customers, it is recommended that at least one permanently installed assistive listening device complying with 4.33 be provided at each location or series. Where assistive listening devices are installed, signage should be provided identifying those stations which are so equipped.

A7.3 Check-out Aisles.

Section 7.2 refers to counters without aisles; section 7.3 concerns check-out aisles. A counter without an aisle (7.2) can be approached from more than one direction such as in a convenience store. In order to use a check-out aisle (7.3), customers must enter a defined area (an aisle) at a particular point, pay for goods, and exit at a particular point.

Index